Pubs & Inns
of Britain

- Including Family-friendly & Dog-friendly Pubs
- Accommodation, food and traditional good-cheer

winalot

Crown Country Inn, Munslow, Shropshire (page 85)

Foreword

Since early times there have been inns and taverns to cater for the traveller, and for the working man (and woman) needing refreshment after a hard and gruelling day. Some of these inns and taverns still exist today, along with numerous, more recently built pubs and small hotels, all of which offer the traveller, and the casual or regular visitor, the chance to rest, enjoy good food and drink, and exchange pleasantries with friends and new acquaintances.

In **Pubs & Inns of Britain** 2010 you will find a number of such establishments where you can stop for meal or a drink, or even for a longer stay. Refer to our Pet Friendly or Family Friendly Supplements starting on page 174 if you are travelling with children or pets, or use our Readers' Offer Vouchers on pages 183-204 to save money on family outings.

Anne Cuthbertson
Editor

© FHG Guides Ltd, 2010
ISBN 978-1-85055-421-9

Maps: ©MAPS IN MINUTES™ / Collins Bartholomew (2009)

Typeset by FHG Guides Ltd, Paisley.
Printed and bound in China by Imago.

Distribution. Book Trade: ORCA Book Services, Stanley House,
3 Fleets Lane, Poole, Dorset BH15 3AJ
(Tel: 01202 665432; Fax: 01202 666219)
e-mail: mail@orcabookservices.co.uk
Published by FHG Guides Ltd., Abbey Mill Business Centre,
Seedhill, Paisley PA1 ITJ (Tel: 0141-887 0428 Fax: 0141-889 7204).
e-mail: admin@fhguides.co.uk

Recommended Inns & Pubs of Britain is published by FHG Guides Ltd,
part of Kuperard Group.

Cover design: FHG Guides
Cover Picture:
White Buck Inn, Burley, Hampshire, courtesy of Fullers Inns. (full details on Outside Back Cover)

Contents

Foreword	2
Pet Friendly Pubs	174
Family Friendly Pubs	179
Readers' Offer Vouchers	183
Index	221

SOUTH WEST ENGLAND — 7
Cornwall, Devon, Dorset, Gloucestershire, Somerset, Wiltshire

LONDON & SOUTH EAST ENGLAND — 37
London (Central & Greater), Berkshire, Buckinghamshire, Hampshire, Isle of Wight, Kent, Oxfordshire, Surrey, East Sussex, West Sussex

EAST OF ENGLAND — 59
Bedfordshire, Cambridgeshire, Essex, Hertfordshire, Norfolk, Suffolk

MIDLANDS — 74
Derbyshire, Herefordshire, Leicestershire & Rutland, Lincolnshire, Northamptonshire, Nottinghamshire, Shropshire, Staffordshire, Warwickshire, Worcestershire

YORKSHIRE — 88
East Yorkshire, North Yorkshire, South Yorkshire

NORTH EAST ENGLAND — 100
Northumberland, Tyne & Wear

NORTH WEST ENGLAND — 107
Cheshire, Cumbria, Lancashire, Greater Manchester

SCOTLAND

Aberdeen, Banff & Moray	136
Angus & Dundee	138
Argyll & Bute	139
Borders	144
Edinburgh & Lothians	145
Fife	147
Highlands	149
Perth & Kinross	153
Stirling & The Trossachs	156
Scottish Islands	157

WALES

Anglesey & Gwynedd	160
North Wales	162
Carmarthenshire	166
Ceredigion	167
Pembrokeshire	168
Powys	170
South Wales	173

THE FERRY BOAT INN &

THE FRIGATE

We welcome you to The Ferry Boat Inn on the shorefront in Ullapool. All of our 9 bedrooms are en suite and we offer Bar Meals or fine dining in our beautiful Restaurant.

**Ferry Boat Inn
Shore Street
Ullapool IV26 2UJ
Tel: 01854 612 366
www.ferryboat-inn.com**

THE FRIGATE CAFÉ & BISTRO

High quality licensed Bistro, Café, Outside Caterers, Deli, Bakery and Take Away

Frigate Café, Shore Street, Ullapool, IV26 2UJ
Tel: 01854 612 969
www.ullapoolcatering.co.uk

England and Wales • Counties

NORTHUMBERLAND
TYNE & WEAR
DURHAM
CUMBRIA
ISLE OF MAN
NORTH YORKSHIRE
LANCASHIRE
WEST YORKSHIRE
EAST RIDING OF YORKSHIRE
GREATER MANCHESTER
S. YORKSHIRE
ISLE OF ANGLESEY
CONWY
CHESHIRE
DERBYSHIRE
NOTTINGHAMSHIRE
LINCOLNSHIRE
GWYNEDD
STAFFORDSHIRE
SHROPSHIRE
LEICESTERSHIRE
RUTLAND
NORFOLK
WEST MIDLANDS
NORTHAMPTONSHIRE
CEREDIGION
POWYS
WARWICKSHIRE
CAMBRIDGESHIRE
SUFFOLK
WORCESTERSHIRE
HEREFORDSHIRE
BEDFORDSHIRE
CARMARTHENSHIRE
BUCKINGHAMSHIRE
ESSEX
PEMBROKESHIRE
GLOUCESTERSHIRE
HERTFORDSHIRE
OXFORDSHIRE
GREATER LONDON
WILTSHIRE
SURREY
KENT
SOMERSET
HAMPSHIRE
WEST SUSSEX
EAST SUSSEX
DEVON
DORSET
CORNWALL
ISLE OF WIGHT

NORTH WALES
a. Denbighshire
b. Flintshire
c. Wrexham

SOUTH WALES
d. Swansea
e. Neath & Port Talbot
f. Bridgend
g. Rhondda Cynon Taff
h. Merthyr Tydfil
i. Vale of Glamorgan
j. Cardiff
k. Caerphilly
l. Blaenau Gwent
m. Torfaen
n. Newport
o. Monmouthshire

1. Plymouth
2. Torbay
3. Poole
4. Bournemouth
5. Southampton
6. Portsmouth
7. Brighton & Hove
8. Medway
9. Thurrock
10. Southend
11. Slough
12. Windsor & Maidenhead
13. Bracknell Forest
14. Wokingham
15. Reading
16. West Berkshire
17. Swindon
18. Bath & Northeast Somerset
19. North Somerset
20. Bristol
21. South Gloucestershire
22. Luton
23. Milton Keynes
24. Peterborough
25. Leicester
26. Nottingham
27. Derby
28. Telford & Wrekin
29. Stoke-on-Trent
30. Warrington
31. Halton
32. Merseyside
33. Blackburn with Darwen
34. Blackpool
35. N.E. Lincolnshire
36. North Lincolnshire
37. Kingston-upon-Hull
38. York
39. Redcar & Cleveland
40. Middlesborough
41. Stockton-on-Tees
42. Darlington
43. Hartlepool

6 SOUTH WEST   Cornwall

Paul Ripley and Sarah Allen, tenants at St Kew Inn

THE SWEET TASTE OF SUCCESS

To find your nearest St Austell Brewery pub, visit www.staustellbrewery.co.uk

Enjoy award-winning food and beer in the South West's award-winning pubs

It's been a fruitful 12 months for St Austell Brewery. We were voted the UK's Best Pub Company at the Publican Food and Drink Awards; Admiral's Ale was awarded Supreme Champion in the International Beer Challenge and, to top it all, in March St Austell Brewery was crowned Regional Brewer of the Year at the Publican Awards.

So, the next time you go out, back a winner and choose a St Austell Brewery pub.

St Austell Brewery, 63 Trevarthian Road, St Austell, PL25 4BY t. 0845 2411122

Cornwall **SOUTH WEST ENGLAND** 7

Cornwall

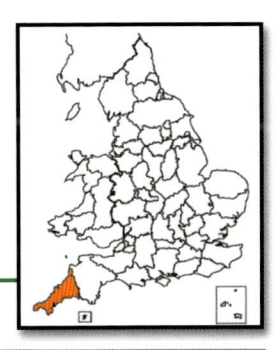

BULLERS ARMS HOTEL
Marhamchurch, Bude, EX23 0HB
Freehouse - Est Circa 1856

- Hunters Bar - all homemade fayre lunchtime and evening dining with daily specials
- Sunday Carvery - with a choice of 4 meats and 7 vegetables
- En - suite Accommodation - with a hearty full English breakfast
- Cask Marque accredited real ales
- Functions, Banquets, Parties
- Licensed to conduct civil ceremonies
- Business conferences, meetings (LCD projector, PA etc. available)

☎ **01288 361277**

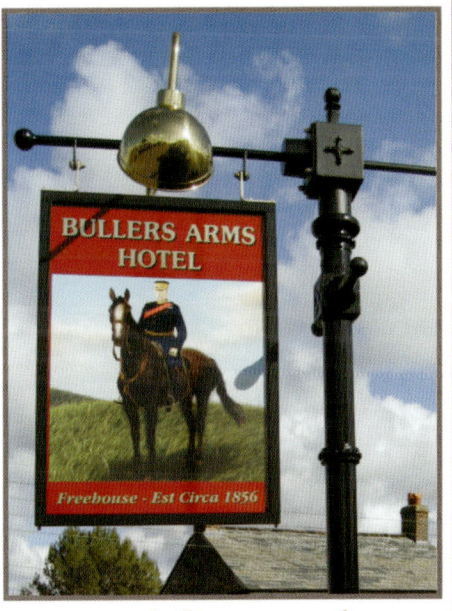

www.bullersarms.co.uk
enquiries@bullersarms.co.uk

ALL BEDROOMS WITH PRIVATE BATHROOM. FREE HOUSE WITH REAL ALE. CHILDREN AND PETS WELCOME. BAR AND RESTAURANT MEALS. LAUNCESTON 15 MILES.

RATES   S – SINGLE ROOM rate   D – Sharing DOUBLE/TWIN ROOM
S£ D£ =Under £35   S££ D££ =£36-£45   S£££ D£££ =£46-£55   S££££ D££££ =Over £55

This is meant as an indication only and does not show prices for Special Breaks, Weekends, etc.
Guests are therefore advised to verify all prices on enquiring or booking.

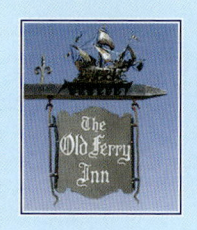

Why not come for a well deserved holiday to the family-run Old Ferry Inn, close to the edge of the beautiful River Fowey. There are many varied walks from country and riverside to breathtaking views along the Cornwall Coastal Path. The 400-year-old hotel has an excellent à la carte restaurant for evening meals and a comprehensive bar menu for lunch and evening. The Inn has 12 letting rooms with tea and coffee making facilities, colour TV and telephone. All rooms have en suite or private facilities, and most have river views.

The Old Ferry Inn

Bodinnick-by-Fowey PL23 1LX
Tel: (01726) 870237 • Fax: (01726) 870116
www.oldferryinn.com • e-mail: royce972@aol.com

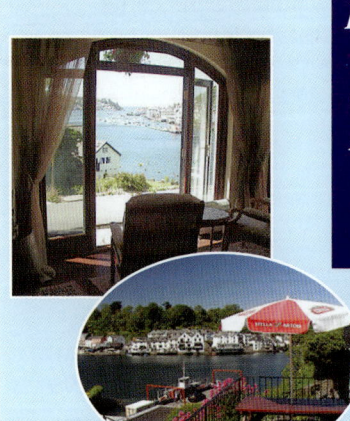

Prices are from £90-£130 per night for two people sharing

Cornwall   **SOUTH WEST ENGLAND** 9

Colliford Tavern   "AN OASIS ON BODMIN MOOR"
Colliford Lake, Near St Neot, Liskeard, Cornwall PL14 6PZ • Tel: 01208 821335
e-mail: info@colliford.com • www.colliford.com

Set in attractive grounds which include a children's play area, ponds and a working waterwheel, this delightfully furnished free house offers good food and bar snacks. Sprucely-appointed guest rooms are spacious and have en suite shower, colour television, radio alarm, beverage maker and numerous thoughtful extras.

An unusual feature of the tavern is a 37' deep granite well. In the midst of the scenic splendour of Bodmin Moor, this is a relaxing country retreat only a few minutes' walk from Colliford Lake, so popular with fly fishermen. Both north and south coasts are within easy driving distance and terms are most reasonable. Adjacent to Colliford Adventure Park - discounted entrance to indoor/outdoor attractions, lake/wood walks and animals.

★★★
INN

Campsite for touring caravans, motorhomes and tents - full electric hook-up etc available.

6 BEDROOMS, ALL WITH PRIVATE BATHROOM. FREE HOUSE WITH REAL ALE. CHILDREN WELCOME.
BAR SNACKS, RESTAURANT EVENINGS ONLY. TOTALLY NON-SMOKING. BODMIN 7 MILES. S££, D££.

ROYAL OAK INN   Duke Street, Lostwithiel PL22 0AG
Tel: 01208 872552/01208 872922

Full of character and with two beautifully kept bars, one of which does duty as a restaurant where splendid and reasonably priced meals are served daily, the 13th century Royal Oak is tucked away just off the main road. An underground tunnel is said to connect its cellar to the dungeons of nearby 12th and 13th century Restormel Castle, providing a smuggling and, possibly, an escape route. No-one will surely wish to escape from this warmly welcoming hostelry with its log fire and friendly atmosphere. Overnight guests are accommodated in attractively decorated bedrooms, all appointed with en suite facilities, television, radio and tea-makers.

6 BEDROOMS, ALL WITH PRIVATE BATHROOM. FREE HOUSE WITH REAL ALE. CHILDREN WELCOME.
BAR LUNCHES, RESTAURANT MEALS. NON-SMOKING AREAS. BODMIN 5 MILES. S£££, D£££.

OLD FERRY INN *(on facing page)*

12 BEDROOMS, ALL WITH PRIVATE BATHROOM. ALL BEDROOMS NON-SMOKING. REAL ALE. PETS WELCOME.
BAR MEALS, RESTAURANT EVENINGS ONLY. ST AUSTELL 9 MILES. D£/££.

Mount View Hotel

The Mount View is a detached Victorian hotel, built in 1894. This family-run public house is situated approximately 100 yards from the Mounts Bay beach, which runs between Penzance and Marazion.

There is an extensive menu including vegetarian choices, and the bar offers a good selection of wine, beer and spirits.

There are five letting rooms, three en suite, all with colour TV and tea/coffee making.

Dogs are welcome but they must be well behaved, and sociable with other dogs, and people.

Private parking • Open all year.

**Longrock, Penzance,
Cornwall TR20 8JJ
Tel: 01736 710416**

We are situated between Penzance and Marazion, approx. one mile from each, and half a mile from the heliport which provides an air link to the Isles of Scilly. The hotel is ideally situated to explore West Cornwall, with easy access to St Michaels Mount, St Ives, and Lands End. There are a number of easily accessible golf courses, sea and coarse fishing venues, and we are 100 yards from the South West Coastal Path. The local scuba diving centre is a short drive away, and nature lovers will find the nearby RSPB reserve at Marazion Marshes well worth a visit.

5 BEDROOMS, 3 WITH PRIVATE BATHROOM. CHILDREN AND PETS WELCOME. BAR MEALS. TRURO 24 MILES. S£.

The Crown Inn
Lanlivery, Near Bodmin, Cornwall PL30 5BT
Tel: 01208 872707

Charming free house, located on the 'Saints Way' in Cornwall and dating back to the 12th century. It has traditional low beams, open fires, and an inviting restaurant serving meat and fish dishes prepared daily from local produce. The inn is an ideal base for sightseeing in and around this Cornish area of natural beauty.

THE RISING SUN INN
Altarnun, Launceston, Cornwall PL15 7SN • Tel: 01566 86332

The Rising Sun is a country pub and has retained many features from its origins as a 16th century inn. It is the ideal place to escape to for a pint of your favourite ale, a game of dart or pool - and don't miss the home-cooked burgers, lasagne, fish dishes and meat pies.

PORT GAVERNE HOTEL (on facing page)

15 BEDROOMS, ALL WITH PRIVATE BATHROOM. ALL BEDROOMS NON-SMOKING. FREE HOUSE WITH REAL ALE. CHILDREN AND PETS WELCOME. BAR AND RESTAURANT MEALS. WADEBRIDGE 5 MILES. S£££, D£££.

Cornwall SOUTH WEST ENGLAND 11

This renowned 17th century inn is situated in an unspoilt fishing cove on the rugged North Coast of Cornwall. The beach is just 50 yards from the front door and the Coastal Path offers miles of breathtaking scenery.

For a relaxing break with a friendly atmosphere you need look no further. Golf, fishing, sailing and riding are all nearby.

All our rooms are en suite and centrally heated. We provide colour TV, radio, direct dial telephone, tea-making facilities and a hair dryer.

Pets welcome in the Inn and Self-catering accommodation available.

Port Gaverne Hotel
Near Port Isaac, Cornwall PL29 3SQ
Tel: 01208 880244 • Fax: 01208 880151
www.port-gaverne-hotel.co.uk

Traditional Family Pub and B&B

This former coaching inn lies at the centre of the village of Bugle, between Bodmin and St Austell.

- Comfortable bedrooms, all en suite, with colour TV, telephone and tea/coffee making.
- Good selection of ales, lagers, spirits and fine wines
- Bar snacks, daily specials and a full à la carte pub menu.

Authentic Indian cuisine available to eat in or takeaway. Non-smoking dining area.

The Bugle Inn

Fore Street, Bugle, St Austell PL26 8PB
Tel: 01726 850307 • e-mail: bugleinn@aol.com
www.bugleinn.co.uk

Ideal for attactions such as the Eden Project (three miles); the Cornish Riviera, Mevagissey and the Lost Gardens of Heligan are all within a short distance.

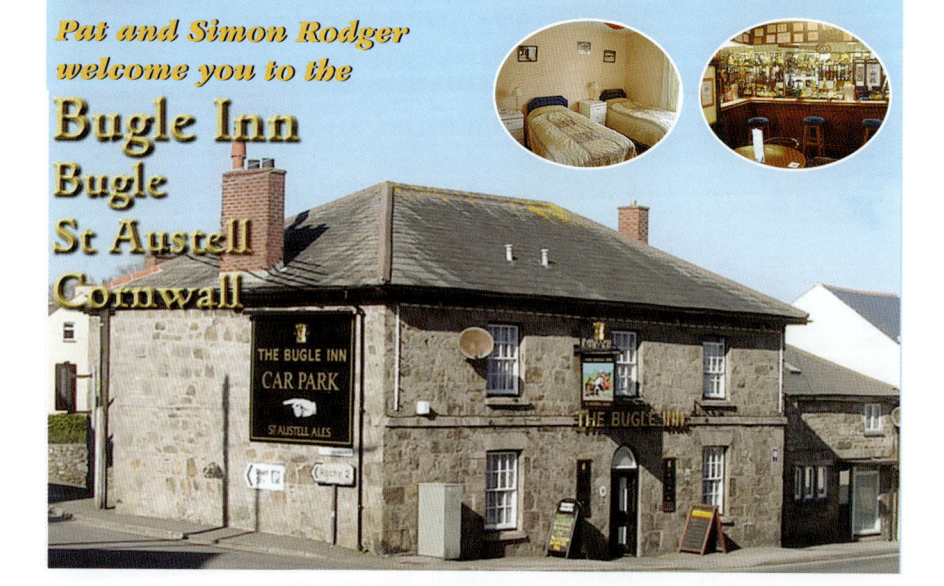

Pat and Simon Rodger welcome you to the

Bugle Inn
Bugle
St Austell
Cornwall

Devon — SOUTH WEST ENGLAND 13

Devon

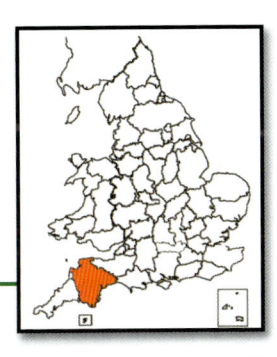

THE HOOPS INN
& COUNTRY HOTEL

Horns Cross, Near Clovelly,
Bideford, Devon EX39 5DL
Tel: 01237 451222 • Fax: 01237 451247

e-mail: sales@hoopsinn.co.uk   www.hoopsinn.co.uk

This picturebook thatched country inn blends 13th century charm with 21st century luxury and extends a warm welcome to its guests. Relax by one of the open log fires to soak up the olde worlde atmosphere while enjoying a real ale or wine before dining on the best of local fish, game or meat, including house favourites: seafood platters, half shoulder of lamb in onion gravy. Choose from over 200 wines. All bedrooms are en suite, individually furnished and well appointed. The superior rooms under the old thatch have romantic antique canopy beds. AA Red Rosette Restaurant. The Hoops is a splendid base for a combined sea, country or touring holiday, with opportunities for walking, cycling, fishing, golf, together with historic gardens, houses, and the world-famous fishing village of Clovelly on the doorstep, and Dartmoor and Exmoor within easy reach.

13 BEDROOMS, ALL WITH PRIVATE BATHROOM. .ALL BEDROOMS NON-SMOKING FREE HOUSE WITH REAL ALE. CHILDREN AND PETS WELCOME. BAR MEALS, RESTAURANT EVENINGS ONLY. DESIGNATED COVERED SMOKING AREA. CLOVELLY 5 MILES. S££££, D£££.

THE BUGLE INN (on facing page)

5 BEDROOMS, ALL WITH PRIVATE BATHROOM. ST AUSTELL BREWERY HOUSE WITH REAL ALE. CHILDREN WELCOME. BAR AND RESTAURANT MEALS. NON-SMOKING AREAS. ST AUSTELL 4 MILES. S£££, D££££.

The Tuckers Arms

Dalwood, Axminster, Devon EX13 7EG

This is a beautiful old English pub with a thatched roof, low beamed ceilings, flagstone floors and inglenook fireplaces. It is situated just off the A35 to the east of Honiton in the heart of Sir Francis Drake country.

The 800-year-old inn, built originally as a hunting lodge for the Duke of Beaulieu, nestles beside the babbling Cory brook, overlooked by Danes Hill, the site of a fort built by the marauding Vikings who came to these parts long before the Norman conquest. But Dalwood has not been invaded by tourists - this is rural England at its best and quietest!

Our rooms are extremely comfortable and have colour TV, tea & coffee making facilities, and en suite power showers.

At the Tucker's Arms we specialise in fresh fish and game; locally caught crab, lobster and lemon sole are regularly featured on our menu. These are supplemented by imaginative starters, and super home-made sweets. Local cheeses and clotted cream feature on the menu at all times.

01404 881342
www.tuckersarms.co.uk
reservations@tuckersarms.co.uk

Devon   SOUTH WEST ENGLAND   15

THE RED LION INN
Dittisham, Near Dartmouth, Devon TQ6 0ES
www.redliondittisham.co.uk

The Red Lion has been offering generous hospitality since 1750 when it was a Coaching House. Log fires and gleaming brass in a friendly old bar, hearty English breakfasts, terraced gardens overlooking the River Dart, and an exceptionally warm welcome all await you. Bedrooms are individually furnished, with comfortable beds, central heating, colour television, tea-making facilities and telephones. An extensive menu includes daily specials and features fresh produce, prime local meats, fresh fish and locally grown vegetables. Picturesque countryside and a mild climate make this a perfect holiday retreat.

Tel: 01803 722235

6 BEDROOMS, ALL WITH PRIVATE BATHROOM. ALL BEDROOMS NON-SMOKING. FREE HOUSE WITH REAL ALE. BAR MEALS. DARTMOUTH 5 MILES. S£££, D£££.

Dartmoor Lodge
Peartree Cross, Ashburton, Devon, TQ13 7JW
Tel: 01364 652 322 • 01364 653 990 • www.dartmoorlodge.com

There is no better place for walkers and lovers of wide-open spaces, with the attractions of the National Park on the doorstep. It is positioned equidistant between Plymouth and Exeter, both superb for culture and shopping. Dartmoor Lodge caters for every occasion, with modern facilities in both function suites as well as in the bedrooms.

The Cedars Inn
Bickington Road, Barnstaple, Devon EX31 2HE
Tel: 01271 371 784 • Fax: 01271 325 733 • www.cedarsinn-barnstaple.com

Just a short distance from the Devon coastline and ideal for cyclists taking the Tarka Trail, the inn is an ideal base for exploring or for observing the local wildlife. Accommodation is in lodge form, with single, double, twin and family rooms available. Each room is en suite, with a range of facilities including colour TV, stereo system and telephone.

The Weary Ploughman
Dartmouth Road, Churston Ferrers, Brixham, Devon TQ5 0LL
Tel: 01803 844 702 • www.wearyploughman.co.uk

Originally a railway hotel, this pub/ restaurant/ hotel provides locals and business persons with a relaxing sanctuary in which to eat, drink, and relax. There is a good selection of fine wines and ales in the bar, freshly prepared fare in the restaurant and de luxe accommodation at an affordable price.

THE TUCKERS ARMS (on facing page)

ALL BEDROOMS WITH PRIVATE BATHROOMS. REAL ALE. RESTAURANT MEALS. AXMINSTER 3 MILES.

16 SOUTH WEST ENGLAND   Devon

Mark and Judy Harrison
welcome you to

THE ROYAL OAK INN
Dunsford, Devon

The Royal Oak is a traditional village pub in the heart of the beautiful Devon village of Dunsford. It's a family-run place with a warm, friendly atmosphere and something for everyone.

Real ales from all over Britain. The kitchen serves generous portions of home-cooked good food with regular well-known specials.

The Royal Oak has a walled courtyard and a large Beer Garden with beautiful views across Dunsford and the Teign Valley

Dogs on leads are welcome and there are lots of animals to visit, great for children with our own play area. Plenty of off-road parking.

Quiet newly refurbished en suite bedrooms are available in the tastefully converted 400 year old granite and cob cob barn located to the rear of the Inn. All non-smoking. Each room has its own front door which opens out onto a pretty, walled courtyard. Ideal base for touring Dartmoor, Exeter and the coast

The Royal Oak Inn
Dunsford, Near Exeter, Devon EX6 7DA
TEL: 01647 252256 • e-mail:mark@troid.co.uk • www.royaloakd.com

Devon SOUTH WEST ENGLAND 17

Staghunters Inn/Hotel
Brendon, Exmoor EX35 6PS

- Family-run village inn with frontage to the East Lyn river, set in four acres of garden and paddock. This cosy hotel features log fires, fine wines and traditional ales.
- 12 en suite bedrooms with central heating, TV and tea/coffee making facilities.
- Meals are available in the bar and restaurant using fresh local produce; vegetarian dishes served.
- Fishing, shooting and riding available; own stables.
- Ample car parking.

Open all year. Terms on request.

Owners: The Wyburn Family.

e-mail: stay@staghunters.com
www.staghunters.com
Tel: 01598 741222
Fax: 01598 741352

12 BEDROOMS, ALL WITH PRIVATE BATHROOM. REAL ALE. BAR AND RESTAURANT MEALS. LYNTON 3 MILES. S£, D£.

The Anchor Inn
Fore Street, Beer, Near Seaton, Devon EX12 3ET
Tel: 01297 203 86 • www.anchorinn-beer.com

Visitors can expect a high standard of hospitality at The Anchor Inn, which has a specialist seafood restaurant and friendly staff. 8 en suite bedrooms provide all modern facilities, each overlooking the unspoilt East Devon fishing village. Why not curl up beside the bar's open log fire in winter or relax in the clifftop beer garden during the summer months?

Pet-Friendly
Pubs, Inns & Hotels
on pages 174-178
Please note that these establishments may not feature in the main section of this book

ROYAL OAK INN (on facing page)

5 ROOMS, ALL EN SUITE. REAL ALE; CHILDREN AND PETS WELCOME; MORETONHAMPSTEAD 4 MILES.

SOUTH WEST ENGLAND — Devon

The Foxhunters Inn
West Down, Near Ilfracombe EX34 8NU

- 300 year-old coaching Inn conveniently situated for beaches and country walks.
- Serving good local food.
- En suite accommodation.
- Pets allowed in bar areas and beer garden, may stay in accommodation by prior arrangement. Water bowls provided.

Tel: 01271 863757 • Fax: 01271 879313
www.foxhuntersinn.co.uk

8 BEDROOMS, ALL WITH PRIVATE BATHROOM. ALL BEDROOMS NON-SMOKING. CHILDREN AND PETS WELCOME. BAR AND RESTAURANT MEALS. ILFRACOMBE 4 MILES. S££££, D££.

RATES

Normal Bed & Breakfast rate per person
(single room)

PRICE RANGE	CATEGORY
Under £35	S£
£36-£45	S££
£46-£55	S£££
Over £55	S££££

Normal Bed & Breakfast rate per person
(sharing double/twin room)

PRICE RANGE	CATEGORY
Under £35	D£
£36-£45	D££
£46-£55	D£££
Over £55	D££££

This is meant as an indication only and does not show prices for Special Breaks, Weekends, etc. Guests are therefore advised to verify all prices on enquiring or booking.

BLUE BALL INN (on facing page)

16 BEDROOMS, ALL WITH PRIVATE BATHROOM. ALL BEDROOMS NON-SMOKING. FREE HOUSE WITH REAL ALE. CHILDREN AND PETS WELCOME. BAR AND RESTAURANT MEALS. LYNTON 2 MILES. S£££, D££.

… Devon … SOUTH WEST ENGLAND 19

Blue Ball Inn
formerly The Exmoor Sandpiper Inn

is a romantic Coaching Inn dating in part back to the 13th century, with low ceilings, blackened beams, stone fireplaces and a timeless atmosphere of unspoilt old world charm. Offering visitors great food and drink, a warm welcome and a high standard of accommodation.

The inn is set in an imposing position on a hilltop on Exmoor in North Devon, a few hundred yards from the sea, and high above the twin villages of Lynmouth and Lynton, in an area of oustanding beauty.
The spectacular scenery and endless views attract visitors and hikers from all over the world.

We have 16 en suite bedrooms, comfortable sofas in the bar and lounge areas, and five fireplaces, including a 13th century inglenook. Our extensive menus include local produce wherever possible, such as locally reared meat, amd locally caught game and fish, like Lynmouth Bay lobster; specials are featured daily. We also have a great choice of good wines, available by the bottle or the glass, and a selection of locally brewed beers, some produced specially for us.

Stay with us to relax, or to follow one of the seven circular walks through stunning countryside that start from the Inn. Horse riding for experienced riders or complete novices can be arranged. Plenty of parking. Dogs (no charge), children and walkers are very welcome!

Blue Ball Inn formerly The Exmoor Sandpiper Inn
Countisbury, Lynmouth, Devon EX35 6NE
01598 741263
www.BlueBallinn.com • www.exmoorsandpiper.com

20 SOUTH WEST ENGLAND   Devon

Situated in the pretty village of Mortehoe, The Smugglers offers luxury accommodation from twin rooms to family suites.
Treat yourselves and your pets to beautiful coastal walks and golden beaches, before you sample our delicious home-cooked meals, real ales and warm, year round hospitality.

**The Smugglers Rest Inn,
North Morte Road, Mortehoe,
North Devon EX34 7DR
Tel/Fax: 01271 870891**

info@smugglersmortehoe.co.uk
www.smugglersmortehoe.co.uk

THE SMUGGLERS

8 BEDROOMS, ALL WITH PRIVATE BATHROOM. FREE HOUSE WITH REAL ALE. CHILDREN AND PETS WELCOME. BAR AND RESTAURANT MEALS. NON-SMOKING AREAS. ILFRACOMBE 4 MILES. D£.

THE DARTBRIDGE INN
Totnes Road, Buckfastleigh, Devon TQ11 0JR
Tel: 01364 642 214 •01364 643 839 • www.dartbridgeinn.com

With a number of day-trip attractions nearby, this comfortable inn provides ground floor accommodation in a variety of double and twin rooms, with Z-beds and cots available on request. Fine wines and coffees, lunchtime snacks, and dishes featuring locally caught fish are obtainable all day everyday in the bar and restaurant.

RATES   S – SINGLE ROOM rate   D – Sharing DOUBLE/TWIN ROOM
S£ D£ =Under £35   S££ D££ =£36-£45   S£££ D£££ =£46-£55   S££££ D££££ =Over £55

This is meant as an indication only and does not show prices for Special Breaks, Weekends, etc.
Guests are therefore advised to verify all prices on enquiring or booking.

Devon   SOUTH WEST ENGLAND 21

The CASTLE INN
Bed & Breakfast
Lydford, Okehampton
Devon EX20 4BH
Tel: 01822 820241
info@castleinnlydford.co.uk
www.castleinnlydford.co.uk

One of the finest traditional wayside inns in the West Country, this romantic Elizabethan, family-run hotel simply oozes character. Featured in Conan Doyle's *'The Hound of the Baskervilles'*, it nestles on the western slopes of Dartmoor, offering first-class food in a bar and restaurant with slate floors, bowed ceilings, low, lamp-lit beams and fascinating antiques; dining by candlelight from imaginative à la carte menus is a memorable experience. Close by is Lydford Castle, built in 1195, and picturesque Lydford Gorge. Guest rooms, decorated in individual style, are beautifully furnished and equipped. This is a wonderful place to shake off the cobwebs of urban existence and appreciate the really worthwhile things of life.

9 BEDROOMS, ALL WITH PRIVATE BATHROOM. REAL ALES, BAR LUNCHES, RESTAURANT MEALS EVENINGS ONLY. TAVISTOCK 7 MILES.

Other specialised holiday guides from FHG

THE GOLF GUIDE • COUNTRY HOTELS OF BRITAIN
WEEKEND & SHORT BREAK HOLIDAYS IN BRITAIN
The bestselling and original **PETS WELCOME!**
500 GREAT PLACES TO STAY • SELF-CATERING HOLIDAYS IN BRITAIN
BED & BREAKFAST STOPS • CARAVAN & CAMPING HOLIDAYS
FAMILY BREAKS IN BRITAIN

Published annually: available in all good bookshops or direct from the publisher:
FHG Guides, Abbey Mill Business Centre, Seedhill, Paisley PA1 1TJ
Tel: 0141 887 0428 • Fax: 0141 889 7204
e-mail: admin@fhguides.co.uk • www.holidayguides.com

The Trout and Tipple is a quiet pub with a keen following for its real ale, real food and real welcome. It has four ales always available, Jail Ale permanently and a farmhouse cider plus two Beer Festivals a year – February & October.

It is a family-friendly pub and children are welcome, as are dogs. With a games room, patio area, dining room and large car park, there is room enough for everyone. All of this is just a mile out of Tavistock on the A386.

Trout features on the menu, with several options being sourced from the Tavistock Trout Fishery, complementing the otherwise traditional pub fare. Sunday's Roast is a two-course affair, with a roast (normally beef) and a traditional sweet.

Local Real Ale is very important to us. As a result Jail Ale from Princetown Brewery is always available and ales from Burrington Brewery, St Austell, Otter and Teignworthy have regular guest slots. Other guest ales are also brought in from breweries in the West Country and beyond. The pub is listed in the 2009 CAMRA Good Beer Guide and has Associate membership of the Society of Independent Brewers SIBA.

Parkwood Road, Tavistock, Devon PL19 0JS
Tel: 01822 618886 • www.troutandtipple.co.uk
info@thetroutandtipple.co.uk

The Trout & Tipple

THE GLOBE HOTEL
Fore Street, Topsham, Near Exeter, Devon EX3 0HR
Tel: 01392 873471 • Fax: 01392 873879

Dark oak panelling, comfortable leather settles and period prints all contribute to the traditional character of this sixteenth century coaching inn which stands on the main street of the ancient town of Topsham, on the estuary of the River Exe. Those seeking overnight accommodation will find comfortable bedrooms, all with private bathroom, colour television, direct-dial telephone, and tea and coffee making facilities. For an extra touch of luxury, rooms are available with four-poster or half-tester beds. The good value range of bar meals includes all the traditional favourites, and in the restaurant a full à la carte menu is served with courtesy and efficiency.

e-mail: sales@globehotel.com • www.globehotel.com

19 BEDROOMS, ALL WITH PRIVATE BATHROOM. ALL BEDROOMS NON-SMOKING. FREE HOUSE WITH REAL ALE. CHILDREN AND PETS WELCOME. BAR AND RESTAURANT MEALS. NON-SMOKING AREAS. EXETER 4 MILES. S££££, D£££.

A haven for walkers, riders, fishermen, canoeists or anyone just looking for an opportunity to enjoy the natural beauty of Dartmoor. We specialise in home-made food using local produce wherever possible. With the emphasis on Devon beers and ciders, you have the opportunity to quench your thirst after the efforts of the day with a drink at the bar or relaxing on the chesterfields in the lounge area, complete with log fire for winter evenings. Muddy paws, boots and hooves welcome.

THE FOREST INN
Hexworthy, Dartmoor
PL20 6SD
Tel: 01364 631211
Fax: 01364 631515
e-mail: info@theforestinn.co.uk

10 BEDROOMS, ALL EN SUITE OR WITH PRIVATE BATHROOM. ALL BEDROOMS NON-SMOKING. FREE HOUSE WITH REAL ALE. CHILDREN AND PETS WELCOME. BAR AND RESTAURANT MEALS. DESIGNATED COVERED SMOKING AREA. ASHBURTON 7 MILES. S£££, D££.

TROUT &TIPPLE (on facing page)

NO ACCOMMODATION. FREE HOUSE WITH REAL ALE. CHILDREN AND PETS WELCOME. BAR AND RESTAURANT MEALS. NON-SMOKING AREAS. PLYMOUTH 13 MILES.

Dorset

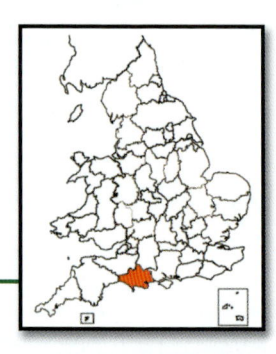

ANVIL INN
Salisbury Road, Pimperne, Blandford, Dorset DT11 8UQ 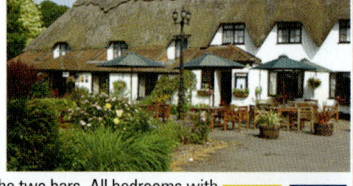
Tel: 01258 453431 • Fax: 01258 480182

A long, low thatched building set in a tiny village deep in the Dorset countryside – what could be more English? This typical Old English hostelry offering good old-fashioned English hospitality, a full à la carte menu with mouthwatering desserts in the charming beamed restaurant with log fire, together with specials of the day and light bites menu in the two bars. All bedrooms with private facilities; wi-fi available in all rooms. Ample parking. **From £75 single, £100 double/twin.**

e-mail: theanvil.inn@btconnect.com
www.anvilinn.co.uk

12 BEDROOMS, ALL WITH PRIVATE BATHROOM. ALL BEDROOMS NON-SMOKING. FREE HOUSE WITH REAL ALE. CHILDREN AND PETS WELCOME. BAR AND RESTAURANT MEALS. BLANDFORD FORUM 2 MILES. S£££, D£££.

Bridgehouse Hotel
2 Ringwood Road, Ferndown, Dorset BH22 9AN
Tel: 01202 578 828 • Fax: 01202 572 620 • www.thebridgehousehotel.co.uk

The Bridgehouse is convenient for Bournemouth International Airport; parking available for holidaymakers. Bedrooms are en suite with colour TV, coffee & tea tray, hairdryer and ironing facilities. Food is served throughout the day, and in the summer months, patrons can dine on the riverside terrace or island garden. Easy access to Poole Quay.

RATES   S – SINGLE ROOM rate   D – Sharing DOUBLE/TWIN ROOM
S£ D£ =Under £35   S££ D££ =£36-£45   S£££ D£££ =£46-£55   S££££ D££££ =Over £55

This is meant as an indication only and does not show prices for Special Breaks, Weekends, etc. Guests are therefore advised to verify all prices on enquiring or booking.

THE FISHERMAN'S HAUNT (on facing page)

12 BEDROOMS, ALL WITH PRIVATE BATHROOM. FULLERS HOUSE WITH REAL ALE. CHILDREN AND PETS WELCOME. BAR AND RESTAURANT MEALS. BOURNEMOUTH 5 MILES. S£££, D£££.

Dorset

SOUTH WEST ENGLAND 25

The Fisherman's Haunt

Salisbury Road, Winkton, Christchurch, Dorset BH23 7AS
Tel: (0)1202 477 283 • Fax: (0)1202 478 883
e-mail: fishermanshaunt@fullers.co.uk • www.fullershotels.com

Originally built as an inn dating back to 1673, this olde worlde property is full of period features, character and charm.

All 12 bedrooms are stylish and furnished to an excellent standard. We take great care in choosing our beds and bed linen, so that our guests have a comfortable and relaxing sleep. The restaurant enjoys an excellent reputation for good home-cooked food, using the finest local produce, good wines and Fuller's award-winning beers.

The Fisherman's Haunt is close to the New Forest, within easy reach of Christchurch and Bournemouth and is ideal for the country lover and angler, with the River Avon being close by.

All our Inns have been assessed and thoroughly inspected by the respected organisation of 'Quality in Tourism'.

Guest review - *A great place to stay. A very comfortable room with a high quality finish to both bedroom and bathroom. Great food for both breakfast and evening meals - good menu with a great selection on the 'specials' board for evening meals. Great location for both coast and New Forest. Would happily stay here again.*

FINDING US BY ROAD
From the M27 follow the signs to Ringwood. Take the B3347 to Sopley and Winkton for about 5 miles – the hotel in on the LH side

BANKES ARMS HOTEL
East Street, Corfe Castle,
Wareham, Dorset BH20 5ED
Tel: 01929 480206
Fax: 01929 480186
bankescorfe@aol.com
www.dorset-hotel.co.uk

In the shadow of historic Corfe Castle, this attractive, stone-built inn is ideally placed for a variety of holiday pleasures, being within easy reach of Swanage, Weymouth, Poole and Bournemouth.

Several real ales are on draught in company with light meals in the bar, and the à la carte restaurant specialises in fresh fish, game and traditional English fare.

There is a family room and a 200-seater beer garden with its own bar.

A delectable place in which to stay, providing comfortable and reasonably priced accommodation, all rooms having remote-control television and tea and coffee-making facilities.

10 BEDROOMS, 6 WITH PRIVATE BATHROOM. ENTERPRISE INNS HOUSE WITH REAL ALE. CHILDREN AND PETS WELCOME. BAR AND RESTAURANT MEALS. TOTALLY NON-SMOKING. WAREHAM 4 MILES. S£££, D£££.

St Leonards Hotel
185 Ringwood Road, St Leonards, Dorset BH24 2NP
Tel: 01425 471210 • Fax: 01425 480274 • www.st-leonardshotel.com

St Leonards is positioned on the edge of the New Forest, making visits to Ringwood, Bournemouth, and Poole easy and stress-free. The hotel restaurant features a seasonal menu, and guests can enjoy real ales, fine wines, and speciality teas and coffees. Accommodation is in 35 en suite bedrooms, all with modern facilities.

THE ANTELOPE INN, 8 High Street, Poole, Dorset BH15 1BP
Tel: 01202 672 029 • 01202 678 286 • www.antelopeinn.com
Just a stone's throw from Poole Quay, from where sightseeing trips to France and the Channel Islands leave frequently. But with so much natural beauty all around, you may not wish to leave this charming spot. 21 first and second floor bedrooms each have an en suite bathroom, plus modern facilities such as a stereo and widescreen DVD. Parking available.

Gloucestershire

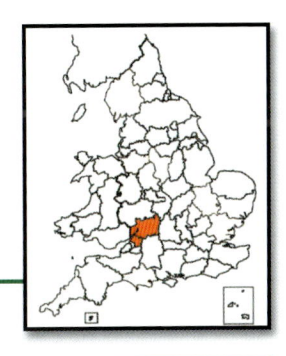

The Redesdale Arms was originally a 17th century coaching inn, on the road from Birmingham to London. Now a newly refurbished three star hotel which mixes the traditional concepts of inn keeping with the standards of a modern hotel. Set in delightful market town of Moreton-in-Marsh, you are in the heart of the Cotswolds and within 10-20 minutes of places such as Stow-on-the-Wold, Stratford-upon-Avon, Bourton-on-the-Water and Broadway. Log fires in the winter, patio garden in the summer and a short walk from the rolling Cotswold hills. Open all year. Privately owned and managed. Discounts often available midweek, throughout the year - please ask for details.

THE REDESDALE ARMS
High Street, Moreton-in-Marsh, Gloucestershire GL56 0AW
Tel: 01608 650308 • Fax: 01608 651843
e-mail: info@redesdalearms.com • www.redesdalearms.com

AA ★★★

24 BEDROOMS, ALL WITH PRIVATE BATHROOM. ALL BEDROOMS NON-SMOKING. FREE HOUSE WITH REAL ALE. CHILDREN WELCOME. BAR AND RESTAURANT MEALS. CHIPPING NORTON 8 MILES. S££££, D££££.

Old Manse House
Victoria Street, Bourton-on-the-Water, Gloucestershire GL54 2BX
Tel: 01451 820082 •Fax: 01451 810381• www.oldmansehotel.com

Ideally set in the centre of the Costwold village of Bourton-on-the-Water is this pretty country hotel, restaurant and pub. Real ales, fine wines and specialty cream teas and coffees are available. For a romantic getaway, book the four-poster room. All bedrooms are en suite, with a unique ambience, and full English breakfast is included in the room rate.

The Roo Bar
Clifton Down Station, Whiteladies Road, Bristol, Gloucestershire BS8 2PN
Tel: 0117 9237204

Just a short distance from the city centre, this Aussie theme pub is predominantly a sports bar with a number of screens showing live sporting fixtures. Other facilities include two American pool tables, a well stocked bar and an imaginative menu of pub favourites.

THE FOUNTAIN INN & LODGE
Parkend, Royal Forest of Dean, Gloucestershire GL15 4JD

Traditional village inn, well known locally for its excellent meals and real ales.

A Forest Fayre menu offers such delicious main courses as Lamb Shank In Redcurrant and Rosemary Sauce, and Gloucester Sausage in Onion Gravy, together with a large selection of curries, vegetarian dishes, and other daily specials.

Centrally situated in one of England's foremost wooded areas, the inn makes an ideal base for sightseeing, or for exploring some of the many peaceful forest walks nearby.

All bedrooms (including one specially adapted for the less able) are en suite, decorated and furnished to an excellent standard, and have television and tea/coffee making facilities.

Tel: 01594 562189 • Fax: 01594 564438
e-mail: thefountaininn@aol.com • www.thefountaininnandlodge.com

8 BEDROOMS, ALL WITH PRIVATE BATHROOM. ALL BEDROOMS NON-SMOKING. FREE HOUSE WITH REAL ALE. CHILDREN AND PETS WELCOME. BAR AND RESTAURANT MEALS. DESIGNATED COVERED SMOKING AREA. LYDNEY 4 MILES. S££, D££

The Bay Horse
1 Lewins Mead, Bristol, Gloucestershire BS1 2LJ • Tel: 01179 258287

Conveniently situated in Bristol's city centre, this drinking and dining venue offers tasty meals, plus fine wines and real ales. There is karaoke every Friday and facilities include a non-smoking area and a large screen TV.

THE CLOSE HOTEL
Long Street, Tetbury, Gloucestershire GL8 8AQ
Tel: 01666 502 272 • 01666 504 401 • www.theclose-hotel.com

This remarkable hotel stands second-to-none in terms of 16th century elegance, and enjoys a flawless reputation for atmosphere and comfort. There is a stylish restaurant offering a superb dining experience, and a well maintained garden with central fountain. All rooms are en suite; for an extra touch of luxury two have antique four-poster beds.

Somerset   SOUTH WEST ENGLAND 29

Somerset

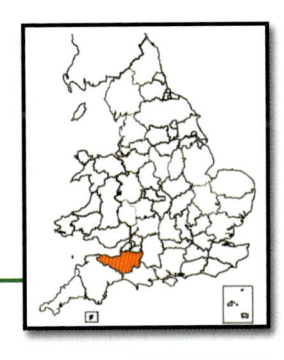

The Talbot 15th Century Coaching Inn
at Mells, Near Frome BA11 3PN

Set in the enchanting Somerset village of Mells, the historic Talbot Inn offers beautiful en suite accommodation, an award-winning restaurant and all the charm of a traditional English inn.

Close to some of the country's most popular attractions, including Bath, Longleat, Cheddar and Wells, the Talbot Inn is the perfect base for exploring this charming corner of England.

Traditional comforts and modern convenience combine to make the Talbot Inn the ideal place for a relaxing weekend break or a base for exploring the beautiful countryside and historic towns and villages around Somerset and Bath.

All our rooms are named after characters from the history of Mells - from Little Jack Horner to the poet Siegfried Sassoon, and offer supreme comfort and thoughtful amenities.

Dining here offers an award-winning à la carte menu of traditional English food with a delicate French influence, sourced from the best local ingredients. The informal restaurant offers a backdrop of extremes, with low oak beams and ceiling hops the alternative to a front room that would grace any country house hotel. Our overnight guests are served a freshly cooked English breakfast, whilst the Talbot's Sunday lunch has become a Mells institution.

Tel: 01373 812254
enquiries@talbotinn.com
www.talbotinn.com

8 BEDROOMS, ALL WITH PRIVATE BATHROOM. FREE HOUSE WITH REAL ALE. CHILDREN AND PETS WELCOME. BAR AND RESTAURANT MEALS. NON-SMOKING AREAS. BATH 10 MILES. S££££, D££££.

RATES

S – SINGLE ROOM rate   D – Sharing DOUBLE/TWIN ROOM

S£ D£ =Under £35   S££ D££ =£36-£45   S£££ D£££ =£46-£55   S££££ D££££ =Over £55

This is meant as an indication only and does not show prices for Special Breaks, Weekends, etc. Guests are therefore advised to verify all prices on enquiring or booking.

THE Hood Arms

A famous 17th century coaching Inn. Situated on the A39 at the foot of the Quantock Hills, close to the spectacular fossil beach at Kilve, a paradise for walkers, mountain bikers, dogs, sporting parties or simply relaxing.

The 12 recently refurbished en suite bedrooms include stylish four-posters. Stag Lodge in the courtyard garden has two luxury bedrooms and sitting room.

The beamed restaurant offers a relaxed dining experience whilst providing delicious locally sourced food. A full à la carte menu, chef's specials and bar snacks are available 7 days a week.

The bar is full of character and boasts an impressive array of real ales.

A warm welcome awaits locals and traveller alike. Dogs welcome.

Please look at our website for more details and prices.

Kilve Beach

The Hood Arms, Kilve, Bridgwater, Somerset TA5 1EA
01278 741210 • Fax: 01278 741477
e-mail: info@thehoodarms.com
www.thehoodarms.com

Somerset   **SOUTH WEST ENGLAND** 31

The Rest and be Thankful Inn

Early 19th century Coaching Inn at the heart of Exmoor National Park

This popular Inn and restaurant is in the centre of Wheddon Cross, the highest village on Exmoor, and a perfect base from which to explore the beautiful National Park.

The Inn was originally a staging post for travellers on their way between Dunster and Dulverton, and you will still find a warm welcome, good food and extremely comfortable accommodation awaiting you there today, almost 200 years later!

All our bedrooms are en suite with good quality furnishings. Our comfortable beds are made up with crisp cotton sheets. Soft white bathrobes and a basket containing good quality toiletries and face cloths provide extra touches of luxury.

Whether you are looking for bed and breakfast for a relaxing break in beautiful surroundings, or a more active holiday, the Rest and Be Thankful Inn and Exmoor are sure to meet your every need. There is a secure store at the Inn, where cycles and other equipment can be kept, and we also have a drying room for wet clothes and boots. Horse riding can be arranged with prior notice.

Tel: 01643 841 222
stay@restandbethankful.co.uk
www.restandbethankful.co.uk
Wheddon Cross, Minehead TA24 7DR

ALL BEDROOMS WITH PRIVATE BATHROOMS. REAL ALE. CHILDREN WELCOME.
BAR AND RESTAURANT MEALS. ££££

The Boathouse

Newbridge Road, Bath, Somerset BA1 3NB • Tel: 01225 482584

The Boathouse is situated by the water's edge and features a well maintained garden, perfect for outdoors enthusiasts in summer months. The interior layout is contemporary and open-plan in style, and the bar stocks a good choice of wines, beers, and real ales. The main menu offers a variety of home cooked meals and pub snacks are available.

The George Inn

Mill Lane, Bathampton, Bath, Somerset BA2 6TR • Tel: 01225 425079

Situated near the River Avon and the Tennyson Avon Canal, the George affords delightful views of the river and boats. The interior is traditional in style, with oak beams, open fires and little alcoves, nooks and crannies. The menu offers a good range of specials including fish dishes, and the Sunday roast lunch is deservedly popular.

THE HOOD ARMS *(on facing page)*

12 BEDROOMS, ALL WITH PRIVATE BATHROOM. ALL BEDROOMS NON-SMOKING. FREE HOUSE WITH REAL ALE. CHILDREN AND PETS WELCOME. BAR AND RESTAURANT MEALS. DESIGNATED COVERED SMOKING AREA. NETHER STOWEY 3 MILES. S££££, D££££.

**Glastonbury Road,
West Pennard,
Glastonbury
BA6 8NH
Tel: 01458 832941**

The Lion at Pennard is a 15th century coaching inn, complete with deep inglenook fireplaces, flagstone floors and oak beams. Accommodation is available in seven comfortable en suite bedrooms, making this an ideal base for visiting the many places of interest in the area, including the historic towns of Wells and Glastonbury.

Delicious bar and restaurant meals can be enjoyed each lunchtime and evening.

Children are welcome; high chairs are available if required.

THE LION
at Pennard

The lounge bar offers an excellent range of refreshments, and visitors will receive a warm welcome from the friendly staff – and perhaps from the resident ghost who is believed to sit there!

Bed and breakfast rates are most reasonable.

Dogs welcome.

e-mail: d.pennard@btconnect.com

Somerset

SOUTH WEST ENGLAND 33

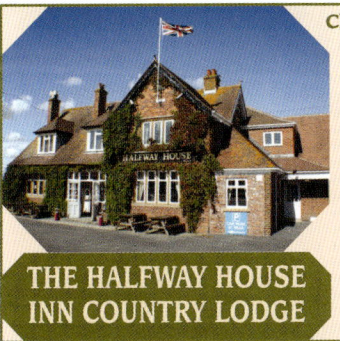

Chilthorne Domer, Near Yeovil, Somerset BA22 8RE
Tel: 01935 840350 • Fax: 01935 849006
paul@halfwayhouseinn.com • www.halfwayhouseinn.net

Offering you the very best in country hospitality and an ideal base from which to tour Somerset and Dorset, The Halfway House Inn Country Lodge has 20 en suite rooms available, including a disabled-friendly lodge and a charming four-poster Bridal Suite with jacuzzi and luxury steam/shower cabinet. Good pub food is available in the restaurant, with a menu to suit all tastes and a frequently changing specials board.

Set within the grounds of The Halfway and with delightful views of the surrounding countryside, there is a fishing and model boating lake. Guests who stay at The Halfway are welcome to sail or fish for free.

THE HALFWAY HOUSE INN COUNTRY LODGE

20 BEDROOMS, ALL EN SUITE. ALL BEDROOMS NON-SMOKING. FREE HOUSE WITH REAL ALE. WELL BEHAVED CHILDREN AND PETS WELCOME. BAR AND RESTAURANT MEALS. DESIGNATED OUTDOOR COVERED SMOKING AREA. YEOVIL 3 MILES. S£££, D££.

West Somerset shares in the wild, heather-covered moorland of Exmoor, along with the Quantock Hills to the east, for walking, mountain biking, horse riding, fishing and wildlife holidays. Stretching inland from the Bristol Channel, historic villages and towns like medieval Dunster, the ancient harbour town of Watchet with its marina and pretty villages like Porlock all provide ideal bases for exploring the area. Visit Glastonbury Tor, steeped in myths and legends, with its associations with King Arthur, and Cadbury Castle, the site of Camelot.

The forty miles of coastline with cliffs, sheltered bays and sandy beaches includes family resorts like Weston-super-Mare, with its famous donkey rides and all the other traditional seaside attractions, as well as the world's largest dedicated helicopter museum. More family fun can be found at Minehead, the start of the South West Coast Path, Burnham-on-Sea and quieter Clevedon.

The city of Bath has all the features of a major 21st century centre, festivals, theatres, museums, galleries, gardens, sporting events and of course, shopping. Attracting visitors from all over the world, this designated World Heritage Site boasts wonderful examples of Georgian architecture and of course, the Roman Baths. The opening in 2006 of the Thermae Bath Spa, using the only natural hot springs in Britain, has ensured the revival of the spa tradition which began here over 2000 years ago.

THE LION AT PENNARD (on facing page)

7 BEDROOMS, ALL WITH PRIVATE BATHROOM. ALL BEDROOMS NON-SMOKING. REAL ALE. CHILDREN AND DOGS WELCOME. BAR AND RESTAURANT MEALS. GLASTONBURY 3 MILES. D£.

The Wheatsheaf
Combe Hay, Bath, Somerset BA2 7EG • Tel: 01225 833504

Wooden beams and a roaring log fire contribute to this pub's traditional atmosphere. With large terraced gardens, lawns and stunning landscape views, it has an excellent reputation for serving delicious meals, ideal for the whole family. Facilities include a large beer garden, and BBQs are held during summer months.

The Dustan House Inn
8-10 Love Lane, Burnham on Sea, Somerset TA8 1EU • Tel: 01278 784343

Situated just a short walk from the centre of Burnham on Sea, this friendly inn serves delicious food freshly prepared by the highly skilled chef, and the bar is stocked with a good selection of real ales, beers and wines. Accommodation is in six en suite bedrooms with modern facilities. Children and dogs are welcome.

The Bristol Inn
Chapel Hill, Clevedon, Somerset BS21 7NL • Tel: 01275 872073

There's never a dull day here at the Bristol Inn, located in the heart of Clevedon village and just a short walk from the beach. A wide choice of beers and ales is available behind the bar, and there is regular entertainment, with live music/disco on Fridays. Facilities include a pool table, dart board, terraced seating and a snug area.

The Who'd A Thought It Inn
Northload Street, Glastonbury, Somerset BA6 9JJ
Tel: 01458 834460 • Fax: 01458 834460 • www.whodathoughtit.co.uk

Interestingly named inn located in the pretty market town of Glastonbury. The smart bar is stocked with a variety of chilled draught beers and the elegant restaurant serves classic English cuisine - diners are advised to book in advance to avoid disappointment.

RATES

Normal Bed & Breakfast rate per person **(single room)**

PRICE RANGE	CATEGORY
Under £35	S£
£36-£45	S££
£46-£55	S£££
Over £55	S££££

Normal Bed & Breakfast rate per person **(sharing double/twin room)**

PRICE RANGE	CATEGORY
Under £35	D£
£36-£45	D££
£46-£55	D£££
Over £55	D££££

This is meant as an indication only and does not show prices for Special Breaks, Weekends, etc. Guests are therefore advised to verify all prices on enquiring or booking.

Wiltshire

The Lamb Inn
High Street, Hindon, Wiltshire SP3 6DP
Tel: 01747 820573 • Fax: 01747 820605
www.lambathindon.co.uk

The fascinating history of this ancient inn is related in its brochure, which reveals among other intriguing facts that it was once the headquarters of a notorious smuggler. No such unlawful goings-on today – just good old-fashioned hospitality in the finest traditions of English inn-keeping. Charmingly furnished single, double and four-poster bedrooms provide overnight guests with cosy country-style accommodation, and the needs of the inner man (or woman!) will be amply satisfied by the varied, good quality meals served in the bar and restaurant. Real ales can be enjoyed in the friendly bar, where crackling log fires bestow charm and atmosphere as well as warmth.   ETC/AA ★★★★

17 BEDROOMS, ALL WITH PRIVATE BATHROOM. ALL BEDROOMS NON-SMOKING. YOUNGS HOUSE WITH REAL ALE. CHILDREN AND PETS WELCOME. BAR AND RESTAURANT MEALS. DESIGNATED COVERED SMOKING AREA. SHAFTESBURY 7 MILES. S££££, D££££.

The Rowden Arms
Rowden Hill, Chippenham, Wiltshire SN15 2AW
Tel: 01249 653870 • Fax: 01249 460755

A welcoming family food house, voted number one by the local newspaper. The bar stocks a good range of draught beers, ales and wines and there is a regular programme of entertainment.

The Green Dragon
26 High Street, Market Lavington, Devizes, Wiltshire SN10 4AG
Tel: 01380 813375 • www.greendragonlavington.co.uk

An award-winning inn, with a good selection of real ales, lagers, beers and fine wines, and a superior reputation for food and accommodation. Facilities include an enclosed garden with a pets section and a BBQ area.

The Wheatsheaf Inn
Oaksey, Near Malmesbury, Wiltshire SN16 9TB
Tel: 01666 577348 • Fax: 01666 575067

Set in this beautifully rural part of Wiltshire, the inn retains traditional features such as low beams and a chimney with carved crosses on it to fend off witches. Facilities include a skittle alley, quoits, bar skittles and dominoes, and there is a popular restaurant. A holiday cottage is available to rent - telephone for further details.

The Carpenter's Arms
Easton Town, Sherston, Malmesbury, Wiltshire SN16 0LS
Tel: 01666 840665

'Simple is as simple does' – and never has such a motto been as true as in this pub, which has no jukebox, satellite TV or one-arm bandits. Food is served throughout the day, and facilities include a beer garden and a cosy conservatory.

The Horse & Groom Inn
Charlton, Near Malmesbury, Wiltshire SN16 9DL • Tel: 01666 823904

A rare treat for regular patrons of country inns, this privately owned inn has recently undergone a major refurbishment and now boasts an outstanding interior with delightful countryside features: an original fireplace, flagstone floor, and solid oak tables. Accommodation is in five airy en suite bedrooms with all modern facilities.

THE SMOKING DOG
62 High Street, Malmesbury, Wiltshire SN16 9AT
Tel: 01666 825823

A cosy pub built from Cotswold stone, where the popular menu is prepared from fresh ingredients, and a wide range of fine wines and real ales is available.

RATES

Normal Bed & Breakfast rate per person **(single room)**

PRICE RANGE	CATEGORY
Under £35	S£
£36-£45	S££
£46-£55	S£££
Over £55	S££££

Normal Bed & Breakfast rate per person **(sharing double/twin room)**

PRICE RANGE	CATEGORY
Under £35	D£
£36-£45	D££
£46-£55	D£££
Over £55	D££££

This is meant as an indication only and does not show prices for Special Breaks, Weekends, etc. Guests are therefore advised to verify all prices on enquiring or booking.

London   **LONDON & SOUTH EAST ENGLAND** 37

London (Central & Greater)

London Eye

The Royal Oak
Longbridge Road, Barking, Greater London IG11 8UF
Tel: 020 8507 1600 • www.pub-explorer.com/gtlondon/pub/royaloakbarking.htm
An friendly establishment offering a wide range of draught beers and real ales, plus DJs every Friday and Saturday and regular 70s/80s nights. There are BBQs in summer and live sporting fixtures shown on plasma screens. Over 18s only.

The Coach & Horses
Burnhill Road, Beckenham, Greater London BR3 3LA • Tel: 0208 6509142
www.pub-explorer.com/gtlondon/pub/coach&horsesbeckenham.htm
A small likeable pub situated near the beautiful gardens in Kelsey Park. It offers a great selection of draught beers including Guinness and Strongbow, as well as regular and guest real ales. Patio area; wheelchair access throughout.

The Blue Anchor
Bridgen Road, Bexley, Greater London DA5 1JE
Tel: 01322 523582 • www.pub-explorer.com/gtlondon/pub/blueanchorbexley.htm
Good honest beer, real ales and hearty meals are served in this lively pub restaurant. Facilities include an IT box, jukebox, dartboard and pool tables. plus live sporting fixtures shown on plasma screens for that all-important match. A children's menu is available.

The George
74 Bexley High Street, Bexley, Greater London DA5 1AJ
Tel: 01322 523523 • www.pub-explorer.com/gtlondon/pub/georgebexley.htm
A sports bar with a wide selection of cold draught beers and real ales. There's no chance of missing out on an important match, with live sporting fixtures shown on the numerous TVs positioned throughout. Enjoy the quality burger menu and live monthly entertainment. Outdoor eating area available.

The King's Arms
156 The Broadway, Bexleyheath, Greater London DA6 7DW • Tel: 020 8303 1173
All on one level, this busy pub serves breakfast, steaks and a variety of other meals throughout the day. The bar stocks a wide selection of draught beers and fine wines. Regular events include a Monday dart team, Tuesday quiz night and Wednesday poker league. Wifi throughout and a jukebox.

The Yacht
Long Lane, Bexleyheath, Greater London DA7 5AE
Tel: 020 8303 4889 • www.pub-explorer.com/gtlondon/pub/yachtbexleyheath.htm
Customers can expect faultless service at this Steak and Ale house, famed for its airy, open plan arrangement as well as the mouth-watering dishes on offer. Children can amuse themselves in the designated play area while you relax over a fine wine or real ale. Activities include pool night on Tuesday, quiz night on Thursday and two pool tables.

The Crown
155 Bromley Common, Bromley, Greater London BR2 9RJ
Tel: 020 8460 1472 • www.pub-explorer.com/gtlondon/pub/crownbromley.htm
Situated just 2.5 miles from Bromley town centre, the pub restaurant's contemporary interior attracts a large variety of customers in search of a chilled pint, ale, coffee, or food from the full à la carte menu; children's menu also available. Facilities include a quiet area, patio area, baby changing facilities and disabled toilet.

Freelands Tavern
31 Freelands Road, Bromley, Greater London BR1 3HZ • Tel: 020 8464 2296 •
www.pub-explorer.com/gtlondon/pub/freelandstavernbromley.htm
The Freelands is known for its firm commitment to sport, screening all major fixtures on impressive plasma screens. A great selection of hot and cold food is also available – toasties, jacket potatoes, rib-eye steaks etc. The bar serves a good selection of draught beers, wines and real ales. A popular beer garden is perfect during the summer months.

London

LONDON & SOUTH EAST ENGLAND

Shortlands Tavern
Station Road, Shortlands, Bromley, Greater London BR2 0EY
Tel: 020 8460 2770 • www.pub-explorer.com/gtlondon/pub/shortlandstavern.htm

Shortlands is situated next to the railway station and overlooks the platform. Relax in the beer garden over one of the carefully selected wines, beers and ales, or get involved in one of the pub's weekly activities – quiz night, speed pool, or dart. Sports fans can watch that all-important match on the big screen. Children are welcome (till 7pm).

The Rose & Crown
55 High Street, Wimbledon Village, London SW19 5BA
Tel: 020 8947 4713 • Fax: 020 8947 4994 • www.roseandcrownwimbledon.co.uk

Situated within walking distance of the All England Lawn Tennis Club, Wimbledon Theatre and Wimbledon Common, with good train links to central London. Enjoy a cold draught beer or real ale at the friendly bar, dine in comfort inside the snug restaurant or in the airy, heated courtyard. 13 en suite rooms, all with plasma Sky TV, and coffee/tea making facilities.

The Windmill on The Common
Clapham, London SW4 9DE
Tel: 020 8673 4578 • www.windmillclapham.co.uk

A friendly public house blended with a modern hotel, the newly furbished Windmill serves a good range of beers and lagers on tap and boasts a new à la carte menu, with specials changed daily. Accommodation is in 29 luxurious en suite air-conditioned rooms, equipped with king-size beds, plasma screens, freeview TV, fresh milk and wifi.

White Cross Hotel Pub
Riverside (Off Waterlane), Richmond, Surrey TW9 1TH
Tel: 020 8940 6844 • www.youngs.co.uk

Patrons are eagerly encouraged to sample the wide range of Young's award-winning real ales, wines and food. This is the ideal place to go for a cool pint and light bite after the rugby. Facilities include wifi, a beer garden, and log fire

RATES

Normal Bed & Breakfast rate per person
(single room)

PRICE RANGE	CATEGORY
Under £35	S£
£36-£45	S££
£46-£55	S£££
Over £55	S££££

Normal Bed & Breakfast rate per person
(sharing double/twin room)

PRICE RANGE	CATEGORY
Under £35	D£
£36-£45	D££
£46-£55	D£££
Over £55	D££££

This is meant as an indication only and does not show prices for Special Breaks, Weekends, etc. Guests are therefore advised to verify all prices on enquiring or booking.

Wheatsheaf Pub

6 Stoney Street, Borough, London SE1 9AA • Tel: 020 7407 7242 • www.pubs.com

Young's have refurbished this tiny market pub and stocked it with a good range of beer. Its two-bar concept has been retained - public and saloon. Enjoy a tipple by the crackling log fire on a winter evening. It is within walking distance of Clink Prison Museum and Southwark Cathedral, as well as the new art-house clubs by London Bridge station.

Westminster Arms

Storey's Gate, Westminster, London SW1P 3AT • Tel: 020 7222 8520 • www.pubs.com

Take a trip to the heart of Westminster for one of many real ales stocked at this pub-restaurant-wine bar. This three-floored establishment, located near to Big Ben, is popular with local office workers. Snacks are available at the bar but for a more relaxing meal, dine upstairs or outside at street level and people watch. The pub is reputedly haunted by the ghost of a boy who died in the Great Fire of London!

The Warrington Hotel

93 Warrington Crescent, Maida Vale, London W9 1EH
Tel: 020 7286 2929 • www.gordonramsay.com/thewarrington

When this pub became an object of chef Gordon Ramsay's affections, there was no turning back ... and who would want to? Guests are of course guaranteed a feast from the exquisite menu. For lovers of fine wine and beer (and a casual dress code) – make the Warrington your next destination.

London has everything to offer! With a range of accommodation at prices to suit every pocket, it's easy to spend a weekend here or take a longer break. Among the most popular places for visitors are the museums and art galleries. The National Gallery houses one of the largest collections in the world, while the Tate Modern concentrates on the work of artists from the beginning of the 20th century. Except for some special exhibitions, entry to both is free, and this also applies to the Natural History Museum, where a new Darwin Centre is opening, and the Victoria and Albert Museum, with such a wide range of exhibits of art and design from different cultures. Smaller, more specialised museums exist too, including the Old Operating Theatre and Herb Garret, a real operating theatre dating from 1821, the Movieum of London, the film museum where you have the opportunity to shoot your own film, and to see props used in Superman and other favourite films.

London   **LONDON & SOUTH EAST ENGLAND**

Viaduct Tavern
126 Newgate St, Holborn, London EC1A 7AA
Tel: 020 7600 1863 • www.pubs.com
Located opposite the Holborn Viaduct, this little corner pub offers customers a relaxed environment away from the hustle and bustle in which to enjoy real ales, wines and beers. Sandwiches are available Monday to Friday at lunchtimes. Original features date back to 1869, the year Queen Victoria opened the Holborn Viaduct. Nearest Tube – St Paul's.

Trafalgar Tavern
Park Row, Greenwich, London SE10 9NW • Tel: 020 8858 2909
Charles Dickens, William Gladstone and several senior Members of Parliament frequented this Regency-style drinking house in the mid-19th century. After a major refurbishment the Trafalgar is now much more than just a pub, with a restaurant, bar and banqueting suites. Bar snacks are available at the Duncan Bar and mouth-watering fish dishes are a 'must try' in the Collingwood Restaurant.

Town of Ramsgate
62 Wapping High Street, London E1W 2PN • Tel: 020 7481 8000 • www.pubs.com
This narrow pub has a murky but interesting past. Situated next to the Wapping Old Stairs, an alleyway that leads down to the riverside, one can quite believe that convicts would use the narrow path as an escape route all those years ago. Now it is a welcoming local for East Londoners and visiting friends.

THE TOTTENHAM
6 Oxford Street, London W1D 1AN • Tel: 020 7636 7201 • www.pubs.com
Believe it or not, the Tottenham is the last remaining pub out of the 38 that used to exist on London's famous Oxford Street, and was built by the famous Baker Brothers. This is the ideal place to go after work for a quick pint to unwind from the day's stresses.

Tom Cribb
36 Panton Street, London SW1Y 4EA • Tel: 020 7839 3601 • www.pubs.com
Come to Tom Cribb's and spot performers from the local 'luvvie' hinterland. Named after Tom Cribb himself, the bare-knuckle fighter turned publican, this traditional Piccadilly pub serves a good range of beers and ales on tap. Come in for a hearty meal, light sandwich or jacket potato. Facilities include TV and air-conditioning.

The Tipperary
66 Fleet St, London EC4Y 1HT
Tel: 020 75836470 • www.pubs.com
Situated on London's Fleet Street, this authentic Irish pub serves Guinness with a smile. The pub is open all day, with wheelchair access and real ales!

The Ship
116 Wardour Street, Soho, London W1F 0TT
Tel: 020 7437 8446 • www.pubs.com

Come and immerse yourself in the creative atmosphere of this Soho pub - Wardour Street is the centre of the TV and film-making industry and The Ship is popular with many in the business. The bar is well stocked with Fuller's draught and real ales.

RED LION PUB
48 Parliament Street, Whitehall, London SW1A 2NH
Tel: 020 7930 5826 • www.pubs.com

Situated between the House of Commons and Downing Street, The Red Lion is popular with politicians, civil servants and journalists. An upstairs dining room and cellar bar provide extra space for busy times of day.

Richard I Pub
52 Royal Hill, Greenwich, London SE10 8RT
Tel: 020 8692 2996 • www.pubs.com

Located on a quiet back street in Greenwich is this charming 1920s conversion, offering two bar areas, and a beer garden for BBQs, al fresco drinking and dining in summer months. The menu ranges from ciabattas and sandwiches to big burgers, jacket potatoes, fish and chips and chilli con carne. Children are welcome till 8.30pm.

Red Lion
Crown Passage, Off Pall Mall, St James's, London SW1Y 6PP
Tel: 020 7930 4141 • www.pubs.com

This pub can get very busy but it is deservedly popular. The bar stocks a good selection of whiskies and beers, and for a light bite, filling sandwiches at affordable prices. The surrounding are area retains a genial Dickensian ambience, particularly as it is still gas lit!

Punch Bowl Pub
41 Farm St, Mayfair, London W1J 5RP
Tel: 020 7493 6841 • www.pubs.com

The Punch Bowl is a enjoyably understated little pub situated in London's Mayfair. Simple decorations outside and inside mean there's no risk of pretentiousness or over-priced drinks and food - ideal for time out whether working or sightseeing.

Prince Alfred Pub
5a Formosa Street, Maida Vale, London W9 1EE • Tel: 020 7286 3287

This is one of the last remaining authentic Victorian pubs, Grade II Listed, and now in competition with Gordon Ramsay's Warrington, round the corner. So class conscious were the Victorians that pubs such as this were built compartmentally, each of the five bars having a separate entrance. At the back, there is a dining room with a bar.

Berkshire LONDON & SOUTH EAST ENGLAND 43

Berkshire

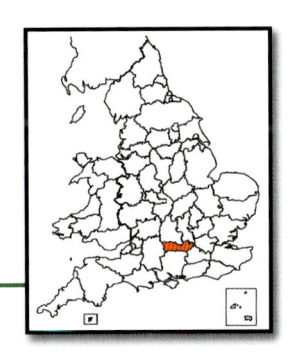

The Bell at Boxford

**Lambourn Road
Near Newbury
Berkshire RG20 8DD**
01488 608721 • Fax 01488 658502

AA ★★★ Inn

info@bellatboxford.com • www.bellatboxford.com

The Bell at Boxford is a traditional 'Inn of distinction' with 10 en suite bedrooms. Paul and Helen Lavis have been your hosts for the past 24 years serving real ales, fine wines and award-winning food. Ideal for weddings and parties

We pride ourselves in being more than just a pub or hostelry. With free WiFi throughout, we strive to be the complete home away from home in the heart of the idyllic Lambourn Valley.

We are situated only 3 miles from Newbury town centre, and 4 miles from Newbury Racecourse. 4 miles from Lambourn and 5 minutes from the A4 and M4.

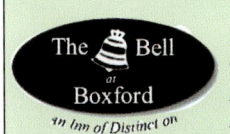

The Bell at Boxford
An Inn of Distinction

11 en suite bedrooms in total, all with power shower, high definition TV, radio, tea and coffee making facilities, hairdryers, trouser press.

*Pets are welcome by arrangement.
Long stay rates are available upon request.*

10 BEDROOMS, ALL WITH PRIVATE BATHROOM. ALL BEDROOMS NON-SMOKING. FREE HOUSE WITH REAL ALE. CHILDREN AND PETS WELCOME. BAR AND RESTAURANT MEALS. DESIGNATED COVERED SMOKING AREA. NEWBURY 3 MILES. S££££, D££££.

THE WEE WAIF

**Old Bath Road, Charvil, Near Reading, Berkshire RG10 9RJ
Tel: 0118 9440 066 • Fax: 0118 9691 525 • www.weewaif.tablesir.com**

Situated in the tranquil village of Charvil, with easy access to Reading, London and Heathrow. The restaurant is open seven days a week and features a daily-changing specials board. A range of accommodation will suit all requirements, with Sky TV, en suite bath and shower, and extra linen. Newbury racecourse is just 40 minutes away.

44 LONDON & SOUTH EAST ENGLAND   **Berkshire**

THE SWAN INN
Craven Road, Lower Green, Inkpen, Hungerford, Newbury, Berkshire RG17 9DX • enquiries@theswaninn-organics.co.uk
Tel: 01488 668326 • Fax: 01488 668306 • www.theswaninn-organics.co.uk

The Swan Inn Hotel & Organic Food Restaurant at Inkpen is a perfect venue for an evening meal, a conference, a weekend exploring the Berkshire countryside, or a longer stay. The tastefully extended 17th century village inn has 10 en suite bedrooms, and is located in an area of outstanding natural beauty on the North Wessex Downs. The hotel restaurant and bar food feature organic produce as well as beef from the farm. Our famous home-cured bacon, gammons and range of sausages are on sale in the farm shop.

10 BEDROOMS, ALL WITH PRIVATE BATHROOM. FREE HOUSE. CHILDREN WELCOME. BAR AND RESTAURANT MEALS. HUNGERFORD 4 MILES.

The Wellington Arms
203 Yorktown Road, Sandhurst, Berkshire GU47 9BN
Tel: 01252 872408
www.thewellingtonarms.co.uk

★★★ INN

The Wellington Arms is a friendly, inviting local pub with en suite B&B accommodation, situated in the heart of Sandhurst.
Public bar, spacious lounge bar and spacious gardens; large car park.
Here at the Wellington Arms we provide a large selection of foods to cater for most tastes and appetites. We source the majority of our meats and vegetables from the local area, ensuring optimum quality whilst also helping reduce our carbon footprint.

Welcome to The Wellington Arms and enjoy your visit!

6 BEDROOMS, ALL WITH PRIVATE BATHROOM. ALL BEDROOMS NON-SMOKING. BRAKSPEAR HOUSE WITH REAL ALE. CHILDREN WELCOME, PETS IN FRONT BAR ONLY. BAR MEALS. DESIGNATED COVERED SMOKING AREA. CAMBERLEY 3 MILES. S£££, D££££.

RATES
S – SINGLE ROOM rate   D – Sharing DOUBLE/TWIN ROOM
S£ D£ =Under £35   S££ D££ =£36-£45   S£££ D£££ =£46-£55   S££££ D££££ =Over £55

This is meant as an indication only and does not show prices for Special Breaks, Weekends, etc. Guests are therefore advised to verify all prices on enquiring or booking.

Buckinghamshire LONDON & SOUTH EAST ENGLAND 45

Buckinghamshire

The Five Arrows Hotel
Waddesdon, Near Aylesbury, Buckinghamshire HP18 0JE
Tel: 01296 651727 • Fax: 01296 655716
e-mail: five.arrows@nationaltrust.org.uk • www.thefivearrows.co.uk

This charming small country hotel and restaurant stands at the gates of Waddesdon Manor. It was originally built by Baron Ferdinand de Rothschild to house the craftsmen and architects working on the Manor. There are nine en suite bedrooms and two suites. The bar and restaurant are open seven days a week. Lunch or dinner is a relaxed, informal experience, and on fine days may be enjoyed in the pretty courtyard and garden. It has a reputation for imaginative modern European food, with a wine list featuring a wide range of Rothschild wines.

Open for breakfast, morning coffee, lunch, afternoon tea and dinner
Sunday lunches are served from 12 noon to 3.30pm • Children welcome

11 BEDROOMS, ALL WITH PRIVATE BATHROOM. ALL BEDROOMS NON-SMOKING. FREE HOUSE WITH REAL ALE. AYLESBURY 5 MILES. S££££, D££££.

Ye Old Jug
Lower Rd, Hardwick, Aylesbury, Buckinghamshire HP22 4DZ
Tel: 01296 641303 • www.yeoldejug.com

With easy links to nearby London and Oxford, this delightful establishment offers a wide variety of activities throughout the year. Facilities include a beer garden, indoor and outdoor function areas, a large plasma TV and wifi access throughout.

The Saracen's Head Inn
38 Whielden Street, Amersham Old Town, Bucks HP7 0HU
Tel: 01494 721958 • www.thesaracensheadinn.com

Hear the chilling tale of the two ghosts who reputedly roam this 17th century inn at night. With an outdoor area for BBQs and an open log fire in the bar area, this charming English pub provides a unique ambience. Lunch and evening meals are available in the restaurant and accommodation includes single, double and family size rooms.

LONDON & SOUTH EAST ENGLAND — Buckinghamshire

Church House Hotel
www.churchhousehotel.co.uk

50 Rowsham Dell, Giffard Park
Milton Keynes
Buckinghamshire
MK14 5SJ

- All rooms en suite, with Sky TV, tea/coffee making, radio alarm, hairdryer and direct-dial telephone.
- Homely atmosphere
- TV Lounge • Games room
- Restaurant/Bar
- Functions and parties
- Conferences
- Ample car parking

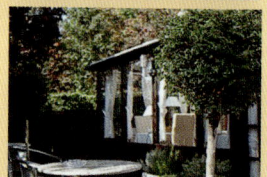

Tel: 01908 216030 • Fax: 01908 216332 • info@churchhousehotel.co.uk

10 BEDROOMS, ALL WITH PRIVATE BATHROOM. ALL BEDROOMS NON-SMOKING. FREE HOUSE. CHILDREN AND PETS WELCOME. BAR AND RESTAURANT MEALS. LONDON 45 MILES. S£££, D££££.

Gatehanger's Freehouse
Lower End, Ashendon, Aylesbury, Bucks HP18 0HE
Tel: 01296 651296 • www.gatehangers.co.uk

This traditional countryside inn is situated just a short drive from Aylesbury village, with neighbouring Oxford close by. The five en suite bedrooms offer coffee and tea making facilities, and the restaurant serves home-cooked food made from local produce, with bar snacks available Friday lunchtimes and a weekly Sunday roast.

BROUGHTON HOTEL
Broughton, Milton Keynes, Buckinghamshire MK10 9AA
Tel: 01908 667726 Fax: 01908 604844 www.thebroughton.com

Ideal for a stopover and fully equipped with amenities to keep the whole family entertained, with five plasma screens, a beer garden/patio area and children's play area. The restaurant provides an extensive menu, with a Wednesday curry night. All rooms have recently been decorated and have an en suite shower and bath.

Buckinghamshire LONDON & SOUTH EAST ENGLAND 47

DIFFERENT DRUMMER HOTEL
High Street, Stony Stratford, Milton Keynes, Bucks MK11 1AH
Tel: 01908 564733 • Fax: 01908 260646
info@hoteldifferentdrummer.co.uk
www.hoteldifferentdrummer.co.uk

Until 1982 known as 'The Swan with Two Necks', this ancient inn has been transformed into a superbly furnished hotel, where the comfortable guest rooms have en suite bathrooms, colour television with satellite channels, free wireless internet access, tea/coffee making etc. In the magnificent, oak-panelled Al Tamborista Restaurant diners may experience by candlelight Italian and seafood cuisine at its very best and most inventive. Also very deserving of mention is the recently opened wine bar and restaurant, The Vine, where top international cuisine and quality wines combine with London-style contemporary chic. An absolute must for those looking for something different in style and cuisine.

19 BEDROOMS, ALL EN SUITE. ALL BEDROOMS NON-SMOKING. CHILDREN WELCOME. BAR AND RESTAURANT MEALS. LONDON 45 MILES. S£££/££££, D££££.

RATES

Normal Bed & Breakfast rate per person
(single room)

PRICE RANGE	CATEGORY
Under £35	S£
£36-£45	S££
£46-£55	S£££
Over £55	S££££

Normal Bed & Breakfast rate per person
(sharing double/twin room)

PRICE RANGE	CATEGORY
Under £35	D£
£36-£45	D££
£46-£55	D£££
Over £55	D££££

This is meant as an indication only and does not show prices for Special Breaks, Weekends, etc. Guests are therefore advised to verify all prices on enquiring or booking.

Hampshire

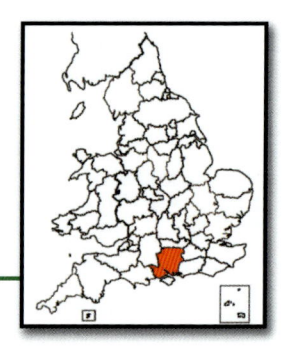

The Swan Hotel
High Street, Alton, Hampshire GU34 1AT
Tel: 01420 83777 • Fax: 01420 87975 • www.swanalton.com

Jane Austen afficionados can enjoy a visit to her cottage in nearby Chawton, now a museum displaying her life's work. With a lavishly decorated interior and well furnished bedrooms, The Swan is an ideal place to stay. Thes 36 en suite rooms have colour TV, tea/coffee making facilities, and wifi throughout.

The Hen & Chicken
Upper Froyle, Alton, Hampshire GU34 4JH
Tel: 01420 22115 • www.henandchicken.co.uk

On the A31, a friendly establishment where children are welcome, with their own special play area. Traditional features include an inglenook fireplace and a large beer garden, and the food menu includes classic dishes and pub meals. The well stocked bar offers wines, beers and real ales.

The Danebury Hotel
2 High Street, Andover, Hampshire SP10 1NX
Tel: 01264 323 332 • 01264 335 440 • www.thedaneburyhotel.com

Just a short drive from Stonehenge is this luxurious town house hotel which dates back centuries. These days it is the place to go at weekends, with a busy disco and late bar. Relax after lunch or dinner with a glass of wine on one of the soft leather sofas in the The Market Bar. Guests can expect high quality accommodation with amenities including satellite TV.

RATES S – SINGLE ROOM rate   D – Sharing DOUBLE/TWIN ROOM

S£ D£ =Under £35   S££ D££ =£36-£45   S£££ D£££ =£46-£55   S££££ D££££ =Over £55

This is meant as an indication only and does not show prices for Special Breaks, Weekends, etc. Guests are therefore advised to verify all prices on enquiring or booking.

THE WHITE BUCK (on facing page)

7 BEDROOMS, ALL WITH PRIVATE BATHROOM. FULLERS HOUSE WITH REAL ALE. CHILDREN AND PETS WELCOME. BAR AND RESTAURANT MEALS. RINGWOOD 4 MILES. S££££, D££££.

Hampshire

LONDON & SOUTH EAST ENGLAND 49

The White Buck

FULLER'S Inns — Quality and Character

Bisterne Close,
Burley, Ringwood,
Hampshire BH24 4AT
Tel:(0) 1425 402 264 • Fax:(0)1425 403 588
e-mail: whitebuck@fullers.co.uk • www.fullershotels.com

A former country house with seven stylish refurbished bedrooms, The White Buck is set in two and a half acres in the heart of the New Forest, a wonderful location for a relaxing stay. Well known for fine food and Fuller's cask ales, the inn combines rustic charm with a traditional atmosphere and attractive period-style bars. Wedding receptions, dinner parties and small social events catered for. Please call the inn for further information or menus.

All our Inns have been assessed and thoroughly inspected by the respected organisation of 'Quality in Tourism'.

Guest review – *"I cannot commend the staff of the White Buck inn enough. Everyone we had contact with from reception to bar staff seemed to have one aim in common which was to ensure that their guests were well looked after. Superb place."*

enjoyEngland.com ★★★★ INN

FINDING US BY ROAD... Situated between A31 & A35. Follow signs for Burley Village. The White Buck is signposted just on the outskirts of the village.

The New Forest Breakfast

LONDON & SOUTH EAST ENGLAND — Hampshire

Three Lions
Stuckton, near Fordingbridge, Hampshire SP6 2HF
Tel: 01425 652489
Fax: 01425 656144

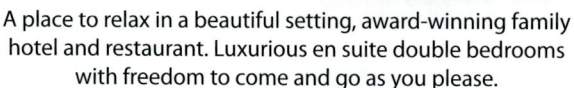

A place to relax in a beautiful setting, award-winning family hotel and restaurant. Luxurious en suite double bedrooms with freedom to come and go as you please.
··pet-friendly·· See our website for full details.

www.thethreelionsrestaurant.co.uk

ALL ROOMS WITH PRIVATE BATHROOM. REAL ALE. CHILDREN AND PETS WELCOME. BAR AND RESTAURANT MEALS. FORDINGBRIDGE 1 MILE.

The Bear Hotel
15-17 East Street, Havant, Hampshire PO9 1AA
Tel: 02392 486 501 • Fax: 02392 470 551 • www.thebear-hotel.com

The Bear is positioned close to the town centre, and boasts a host of famous past guests, including Queen Victoria, Churchill and Eisenhower. Accommodation and food are matched in terms of quality and comfort; the restaurant is renowned in the area for serving excellent traditional fare. Single, double, twin and family rooms are available, all en suite.

The Raven Hotel
Station Road, Hook, Hampshire RG27 9HS
Tel: 01256 762 541 • Fax: 01256 768 677 • www.theraven-hotel.com

Former guests of this elegant hotel include Enid Blyton and Edward VIII. It enjoys a convenient position half an hour away from Windsor Castle, the New Forest, Bird World, Ascot, Windsor and Newbury racecourses, and Reading Football Club. Accommodation is in 38 en suite bedrooms, each with modern facilities.

The Farmhouse Inn Lodge
Burrfields Road, Portsmouth, Hampshire PO3 5HH
Tel: 023 92650510 • www.farmhouseinnlodge.com

Five miles from Goodwood Racecourse and Portsmouth's historic Dockyard, this is an ideal place to relax - and best of all – play, with an 18-hole golf course and driving range nearby. Guests can dine in the lounge or outside on the patio. Two honeymoon suites and 74 other rooms are available, as well as executive and leisure suites.

THE GROSVENOR HOTEL
23 High Street, Stockbridge, Hampshire SO20 6EU
Tel: 01264 810 606 • Fax 01264 810 747 • www.thegrosvenor-hotel.com

This Georgian-style hotel is situated between the cathedral cities of Winchester and Salisbury. Dishes featuring local produce such as the chef's speciality Test Trout are on the menu in The Tom Cannon Restaurant. The wood panelled Bankside Bar also offers an à la carte menu and a range of snacks. A new wing provides accommodation with modern facilities.

Isle of Wight

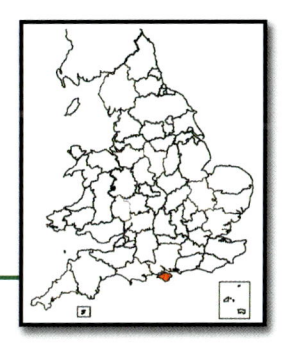

The Fountain Inn
High Street, Cowes, Isle of Wight PO31 7AW
Tel: 01983 292 397 • 01983 299 554 • www.fountaininn-cowes.com
This Isle of Wight 'must-see' is famous in yachting circles as home to the Royal Yacht Club. It offers panoramic views of the harbour and shoreline, an early-bird buffet breakfast and a famous 'kilo of mussels' dinner. 20 en suite rooms all have direct-dial telephone, TV, hairdryer, trouser press and CD player.

Ryde Castle
Esplanade, Ryde, Isle of Wight PO33 1JA
Tel: 01983 563 755 • Fax: 01983 566 906 • www.rydecastle.co.uk
Visiting the Ryde Castle is like diving into a history textbook. This regal looking establishment has been a hospital and army HQ during both World Wars. Indulge in a pre-dinner drink and then dine in style in the brasserie. 18 en suite bedrooms have all modern facilities. Blackgang Chine and Fantasy Theme Park are nearby.

RATES   S – SINGLE ROOM rate   D – Sharing DOUBLE/TWIN ROOM
S£ D£ =Under £35   S££ D££ =£36-£45   S£££ D£££ =£46-£55   S££££ D££££ =Over £55

This is meant as an indication only and does not show prices for Special Breaks, Weekends, etc. Guests are therefore advised to verify all prices on enquiring or booking.

The Isle of Wight, only a short ferry ride away from the Southern mainland, is the ultimate holiday destination, with award-winning beaches, water sports centres, seakayaking, diving, sailing and windsurfing. For land-based activites there are over 500 miles of interconnected footpaths, historic castles, dinosaur museums, theme parks and activity centres, while resorts like Sandown, Shanklin, Ryde and Ventnor offer all that is associated with a traditional seaside holiday. There is a thriving arts community, and of course two internationally renowned music festivals held every year. Something for everyone!

Kent

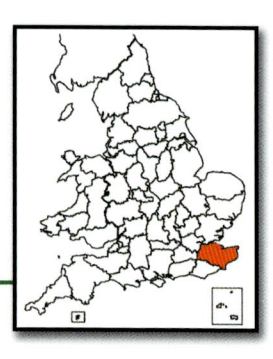

The Orchard Spot
Spot Lane, Otham, Maidstone, Kent ME15 8SE
Tel: 01622 861802 • Fax: 01622 861801 • www.theorchardspot.co.uk
The interior is stylish and contemporary, and it enjoys a spectacular location amongst open fields in this beautiful area of Kent. The restaurant serves delicious food at affordable prices and the bar stocks an impressive choice of real ales and beers.

The Flagship
115 Snargate St Dover, Kent CT17 9DA
Tel: 01322 862087
A stylish Kentish establishment offering menu classics such as seafood and mature steaks, plus carefully selected wines, guest beers and real ales. Parking available.

Kings Arms Hotel
Market Square, Westerham, Kent TN16 1AN
Tel: 01959 562 990 • Fax: 01959 561 240 • www.the-kingsarms.com
Take full advantage of the sales at Blue Water Shopping Centre, which is located only 20 minutes away. Enjoy some chilled entertainment over a light lunch or early evening tipple in The Conservatory, light and airy for summer relaxation. All rooms are en suite, with satellite TV and music centre.

Pet-Friendly
Pubs, Inns & Hotels
on pages 174-178
Please note that these establishments may not feature in the main section of this book

Oxfordshire　　　　　　　　　　**LONDON & SOUTH EAST ENGLAND** 53

Oxfordshire

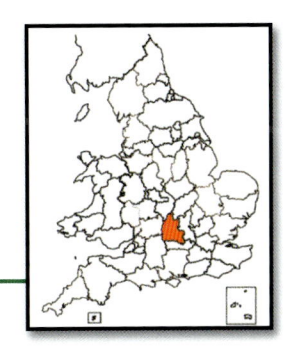

The Inn for all Seasons

Dog owners themselves, Matthew and Heather Sharp extend a warm welcome to others who wish to bring their pets to visit the Cotswolds and stay in a genuinely dog-friendly Inn with dedicated ground floor rooms with direct access to gardens, exercise area and country walks.

The Inn for all Seasons is a family-owned and run ★★ Hotel based on a traditional 16th century English Coaching Inn. Character en suite bedrooms, inglenooks, log fires and a genuinely friendly inn atmosphere provide the perfect setting to enjoy a Rosetted menu prepared by Chef/Proprietor, Matthew, and his English-led kitchen team. An ideal base for touring, walking, garden visiting.

The Barringtons, Near Burford, Oxfordshire OX18 4TN • 01451 844324
e-mail: sharp@innforallseasons.com • www.innforallseasons.com
B&B from £65.00pppn • Dinner, B&B from £70.00pppn.

9 BEDROOMS, ALL WITH PRIVATE BATHROOM. ALL BEDROOMS NON-SMOKING. PETS WELCOME. BAR AND RESTAURANT MEALS. BURFORD 3 MILES. S££££, D££££.

RATES　　S – SINGLE ROOM rate　　　D – Sharing DOUBLE/TWIN ROOM
S£ D£ =Under £35　　S££ D££ =£36-£45　　S£££ D£££ =£46-£55　　S££££ D££££ =Over £55

This is meant as an indication only and does not show prices for Special Breaks, Weekends, etc. Guests are therefore advised to verify all prices on enquiring or booking.

Surrey

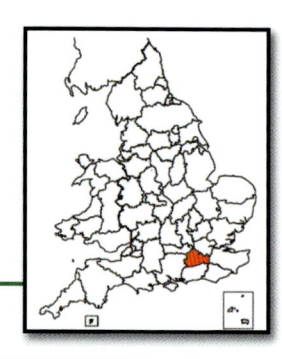

THE COMPASSES INN
Station Road, Gomshall, Surrey GU5 9LA
Tel: 01483 202506

This attractive inn was once known as the 'God Encompasses' but through time and mispronunciation is now simply known as the 'Compasses'. Known for its appetising selection of home-cooked dishes and supporting local Surrey Hills Brewery, this friendly hostelry has a warm ambience accentuated by its exposed oak beams and horse brasses. There is good home-cooked food in the bar and the restaurant; à la carte menu available in the evenings. Situated beneath the North Downs, there is a popular beer garden through which runs the Tillingbourne Stream. A tranquil port of call amidst delightful countryside.

2 BEDROOMS, ALL WITH PRIVATE BATHROOM. REAL ALES. CHILDREN WELCOME, PETS ALLOWED IN BAR ONLY. BAR AND RESTAURANT MEALS. GUILDFORD 6 MILES. ££££ PER ROOM PER NIGHT.

The Ely
London Road (A30), Blackwater, Camberley, Surrey GU17 9LJ
Tel: 01252 860 444 • Fax: 01252 878 265 • www.theely.com

The Ely is simply perfect for motorists looking for a cosy and traditional stopover on the M3. With an alluring redbrick exterior and outdoor terrace, passersby can't resist taking a break for refreshment. Children are well catered for in the hotel's restaurant and outdoor play area. Rooms are en suite, with TV, hairdryer and trouser press facilities.

White Cross Hotel Pub
Riverside (Off Waterlane), Richmond, Surrey TW9 1TH
Tel: 020 8940 6844 • www.youngs.co.uk

Patrons are eagerly encouraged to sample the wide range of Young's award-winning real ales, wines and food. This is the ideal place to go for a cool pint and light bite after the rugby. Facilities include wifi, a beer garden, and log fire.

www.holidayguides.com

East Sussex

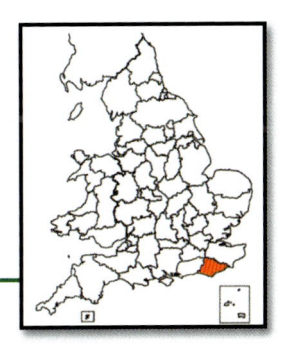

West and East Sussex share with neighbouring Kent an attractive coastline with cliffs and sandy beaches, and the countryside of the High Weald and the North Downs. In addition the gently rolling chalk hills and heathland of the South Downs stretch from Eastbourne on the Sussex coast almost to Winchester in Hampshire. Here there are endless possibilities for outdoor pursuits – walking, cycling, horse riding, golf, and if you're looking for something more adventurous, hanggliding and paragliding! In the Seven Sisters Country Park which covers most of the downland you can try canoeing, or enjoy the flora and fauna of the local wildlife habitats. Not only are there a number of major walking trails like the South Downs Way, the Wey-South Path, and the Cuckoo Trail, you can also follow the many shorter public rights of way, with plenty of inviting country pubs where you can take a well earned break.

The Druid's Head
9 Brighton Place, Brighton, East Sussex BN1 1HJ
Tel: 01273 325490

A popular Sussex Coast pub and diner with an unpretentious atmosphere. Some of the outside brickwork dates all the way back to 1510, with sash windows and other period features. The cuisine is varied and of a very high standard, and beers and ales are well kept.

The Franklin Tavern
158 Lewes Road, Brighton, East Sussex BN2 3LF
Tel: 01273 602995 • Fax: 01273 698535

The pub is close to Brighton University and is popular with family and friends visiting students. Food and drinks are reasonably priced, and live sporting fixtures are shown on large plasma screens.

The Buccaneer
10 Compton Street, Eastbourne, East Sussex BN21 4BW • Tel: 01323 732 829

Located in the heart of theatreland and popular with patrons for a pre- or post-theatre tipple, this majestic building was built in the style of the Pavilion at Brighton. It offers a good selection of hand-pulled real ales and other refreshments. Pub food is served every day from a varied menu, and Sunday lunch is particularly popular.

The Farm@Friday Street
Friday Street, Langney, Eastbourne, East Sussex BN23 8AP
Tel: 01323 766049 • www.whitingandhammond.co.uk

After an extensive refurbishment, oak beams, stone-flagged floors, authentic log fires and leather sofas create a welcoming pub atmosphere. Food and drink is reasonably priced, with the emphasis on fresh local produce wherever possible.

THE WHEEL INN
Heathfield Road, Burwash Weald, Etchingham, East Sussex TN19 7LA
Tel: 01435 882758 • Fax: 01435 883625

The Wheel Inn is situated in an area of outstanding natural beauty and offers a good choice of lagers, beers, spirits and mixers. This free house stocks its own British cask conditioned real ales. Facilities include a pool table and dart board.

The Swan Mountain
Lewes Road, Forest Row, East Sussex RH18 5ER • Tel: 01342 822318

The Swan Mountain is well worth seeking out. The interior is very cosy, with open log fires, low-beamed ceilings and a snug – all the traditional features one hopes to find in a friendly family pub. Other delightful features include a restaurant area and a sun terrace for outdoor dining in summer months.

The Roebuck
Wych Cross, Forest Row, East Sussex RH18 5JL
Tel: 01342 823 811 • Fax: 01342 824 790 • www.theroebuck.co.uk

Winnie the Pooh fans may remember hearing about Forest Row as it borders Royal Ashdown Forest, where the famous bear lived! Summers are delightful at the Roebuck with its outdoor patio and restaurants. Accommodation is in 30 en suite bedrooms, all with modern facilities. Brighton and Royal Tunbridge Wells are a short drive away.

The White Hart
Winchelsea Road, Guestling, Near Hastings, East Sussex TN35 4LW
Tel: 01424 813187

The White Hart is a Beefeater pub in an Grade II Listed building with a country house atmosphere. Log fires and traditional furnishings and fittings create a charming olde worlde ambience, and the bar is stocked with a good variety of beers, lagers, ales and fine wines. Children are welcome at this establishment, and there is a large beer garden.

East Sussex

The Blind Busker
75- 7 Church Road, Hove, East Sussex BN3 2BB • Tel: 01273 749110

Great staff and a stylish interior with comfy seating areas, rugs, drapes and a modern colour scheme are the basis of this friendly pub's first class reputation. Food is very popular here and Sunday lunches on the outdoor decking area are a firm favourite, with a choice of burgers, swordfish and a variety of other tasty delights.

The Green Man
Lewes Road, Ringmer, East Sussex BN8 5NA
Tel: 01343 812422 • www.greenmanringmer.co.uk

The new decked patio area makes outdoor dining a real treat here at the Green Man in Ringmer. The restaurant has a reputation for good service and even better food - the Sunday Carvery is especially popular and is a great excuse for a family day out. The bar is stocked with a varied selection of beers, lagers, real ales and fine wines.

The White Horse
Marine Drive, Rottingdean, East Sussex BN2 7HR
Tel: 01273 300 301 • Fax: 01273 308 716 • www.whitehorsehotelrottingdean.com

Enjoy a scrumptious lunch outside on the decked patio/ terrace and afterwards take a short trip along the coast to explore the many delights of Brighton. The 19 newly decorated bedrooms have exquisite sea views, en suite facilities and all mod cons.

Looking for Holiday Accommodation?

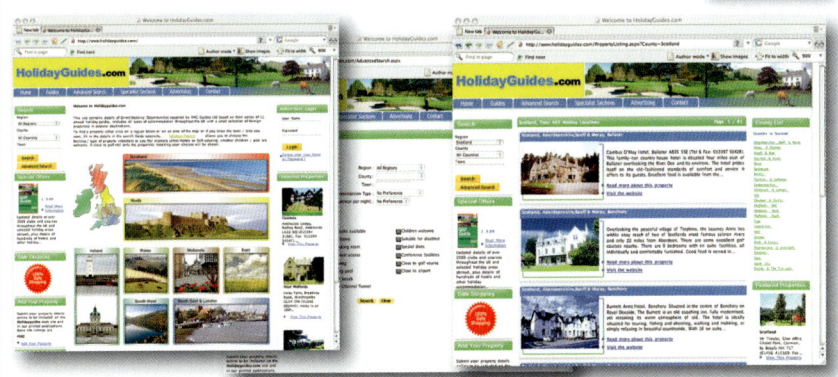

FHG
·K·U·P·E·R·A·R·D·

for details of hundreds of properties throughout the UK, visit our website

www.holidayguides.com

West Sussex

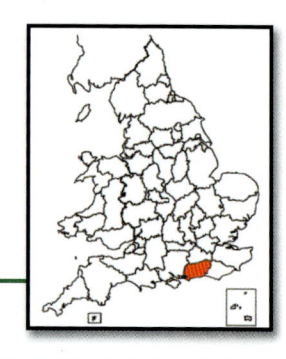

The HALFWAY BRIDGE
PETWORTH

With the South Downs as a backdrop, Paul and Sue Carter welcome you to their fabulous retreat in the heart of classic Polo country.

Bar, Restaurant & Luxury Rooms

www.thesussexpub.co.uk

For reservations and enquiries ring

01798 861281

Halfway Bridge, Petworth
West Sussex GU28 9BP

6 BEDROOMS/SUITES, ALL WITH PRIVATE BATHROOM. CHILDREN AND PETS WELCOME. BAR LUNCHES AND RESTAURANT MEALS. CHICHESTER 13 MILES.

RATES S – SINGLE ROOM rate   D – Sharing DOUBLE/TWIN ROOM

S£ D£ =Under £35   S££ D££ =£36-£45   S£££ D£££ =£46-£55   S££££ D££££ =Over £55

This is meant as an indication only and does not show prices for Special Breaks, Weekends, etc. Guests are therefore advised to verify all prices on enquiring or booking.

Bedfordshire EAST OF ENGLAND

Bedfordshire

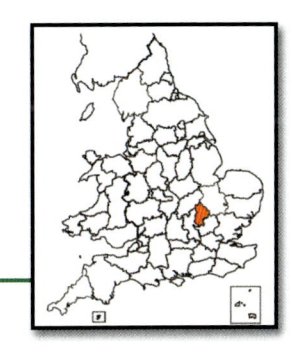

THE KNIFE & CLEAVER

Deep in the heart of rural Bedfordshire, this friendly country inn offers a warm welcome to locals and visitors alike, and proves equally popular with both.

One of the main reasons for its enviable reputation is the quite exceptional Victorian-style conservatory restaurant, where the finest of fresh ingredients are prepared with care and imagination by first-class chefs and where the accompanying wine list has been selected with quality and value as the highest priorities.

Nine well-appointed en suite bedrooms, all with power shower, satellite television and a full range of amenities, provide comfortable accommodation for those wishing to explore this lovely area.

The Grove, Houghton Conquest, Bedford, Bedfordshire MK45 3LA
Tel: 01234 740387 • Fax: 01234 740900
e-mail: info@knifeandcleaver.com • www.knifeandcleaver.co.uk

9 BEDROOMS, ALL WITH PRIVATE BATHROOM. ALL BEDROOMS NON-SMOKING. FREE HOUSE WITH REAL ALE. CHILDREN WELCOME. PETS WELCOME IN ROOMS ONLY. BAR AND RESTAURANT MEALS. DESIGNATED COVERED SMOKING AREA. AMPTHILL 2 MILES. S££££, D££££.

The Bull
259 London Road, Bedford, Bedfordshire MK42 0PX
Tel: 01234 355719 • www.myspace.com/thebullbedford

The Bull with its mock Tudor exterior offers an extensive selection of weekly activities, including a quiz night, pool tournament, and Thursday night curry club. With a wide range of pub snacks, food deals and drinks offers, wifi, and live sport on plasma screens, there is something for everyone. Children and dogs are welcome in the outdoor area.

The Castle
Newham Street, Bedford, Bedfordshire MK40 3JR • Tel: 01234 353295
Located in a popular area of Bedford, The Castle dates back 200 years, and is a perfect place for post-work get-togethers over an ale or fine wine. Home-made, hearty meals are of great value and size – Punjabi dishes are on the menu Fridays and Saturdays for the more adventurous palate. B&B accommodation is available in one single and three twin rooms.

The Fox and Hounds
178 Goldington Road, Bedford, Bedfordshire MK40 3EB • Tel: 01234 353993
Enjoy the drinks offers and entertainment in this modern-style pub, situated close to the University. Weekly activities include pool, karaoke (and bingo if no football on TV!). Pub snacks and main meals are available as well as a children's menu.

The Pheasant
300 Kimbolton Road, Bedford, Bedfordshire MK41 8YR
Tel: 01234 409301 • www.pub-explorer.com/beds/pub/pheasantbedford.htm
A Bedfordshire pub for all the family, with live sport shown on two large-screen TVs, a children's play area, pool table and dart board. The lunchtime menu offers freshly prepared pub favourites accompanied by teas, coffees, real ales and fine wines. In summer months the beer garden is popular with locals and visitors alike.

RATES

Normal Bed & Breakfast rate per person
(single room)

PRICE RANGE	CATEGORY
Under £35	S£
£36-£45	S££
£46-£55	S£££
Over £55	S££££

Normal Bed & Breakfast rate per person
(sharing double/twin room)

PRICE RANGE	CATEGORY
Under £35	D£
£36-£45	D££
£46-£55	D£££
Over £55	D££££

This is meant as an indication only and does not show prices for Special Breaks, Weekends, etc. Guests are therefore advised to verify all prices on enquiring or booking.

THE GLOBE INN (on facing page)
NO ACCOMMODATION. GREENE KING HOUSE WITH REAL ALE. CHILDREN WELCOME. BAR AND RESTAURANT MEALS. LUTON 11 MILES.

★ Canal-side location with access over own bridge.
★ Beer garden with outdoor eating facilities
★ Bar/Lounge open all day, every day
★ Children welcome ★ Children's play area
★ Dining area fully non-smoking
★ Excellent choice of food served 12 noon-10pm daily
★ Cask Marque Accredited 2005
★ Booking Highly Recommended

THE Globe INN

Globe Lane, Stoke Road, Old Linslade, Leighton Buzzard, Bedfordshire LU7 2TA
Tel: 01525 373338
www.pub-explorer.com
e-mail: 6458@greeneking.co.uk

NOW ON FACEBOOK become a fan!

Cambridgeshire

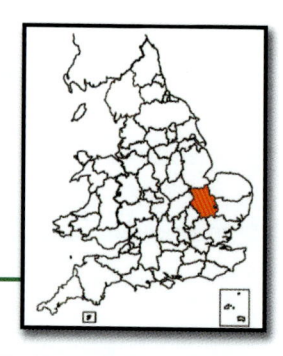

The Boathouse
14 Chesterton Road, Cambridge, Cambridgeshire CB4 3AX • Tel: 01223 460905

Pleasant, waterside establishment set in beautiful Cambridgeshire surroundings, serving real ales, Continental lagers, soft drinks and Costa coffee. Amenities include a games room, plasma screen TVs, a pool table, beer garden, and a varied food menu offering English, Thai, Mexican and Italian cuisine.

The Fox
Gladeside Bar Hill, Cambridge, Cambridgeshire CB3 8DY • Tel: 01954 780305

Bar Hill's pride and joy – a stylish, well maintained venue with a sociable layout. Children are welcome, and amenities include an outdoor children's play area, pool table and jukebox.

The George
High Street, Spaldwick, Huntingdon, Cambridgeshire PE28 0TD • Tel: 01480 890293

This pub's high street setting means that it is a firm favourite with locals as well as passers by. The mixture of olde world and contemporary is well balanced - spotlights in the ceiling and leather sofas, yet open fires for winter cosiness. The restaurant has a great reputation, with a choice of Mediterranean, New World and English cuisine.

The Waggon & Horses
39 High Street, Milton, Cambridgeshire CB4 6DF • Tel: 01223 860313

Listed in *The Good Beer Guide* is this prominent mock-Tudor style venue with an interesting preoccupation with hats and pictures - and an impressive collection of both! In the beer garden are swings, a slide and chickens too! Regular features include bar billiards, a quiz night, balti night, a dart board and piano.

Cambridgeshire

EAST OF ENGLAND 63

Palmerston Arms
82 Oundle Road, Peterborough, Cambridgeshire PE2 9PA
Tel: 01733 565865 • www.palmerston-arms.co.uk

'The Palmy' is an olde world pub steeped in traditional pub values. Behind the bar is a selection of good quality real ales, draught ciders and perry, direct from the cask. When hunger strikes, try a Cornish pasty or freshly made pie.

THE WOODMAN
Thorpe Wood, Peterborough, Cambridgeshire PE3 6SQ • Tel: 01733 267601

Situated in the Longthorpe area is this golfing themed inn, furnished with suede and leather seats and sofas. Early breakfast is available for dedicated golfers and the regular food menu is available from noon onwards. Wifi access, TV, pool table, large beer garden and patio area.

The Harrier
184 Gunthorpe Road, Peterborough, Cambridgeshire PE4 7DS
Tel: 01733 575362 • Fax: 01733 575364

A modern family pub, a member of the Hungry Horse group, where the menu is a major attraction. The staff are particularly helpful and work tirelessly behind the well stocked bar. Facilities include a pool table, big screen TV and decked chill-out area for adults.

The Halcyon
Atherstone Avenue, Peterborough, Cambridgeshire PE3 9TT
Tel: 01733 263801

After an extensive makeover, The Halcyon offers a Hungry Horse food menu – affordable and varied! Regular activities include live bands and a poker night, and there is a dart board, pool table and a smoking shelter with TV installed!

Milton Arms
205 Milton Road, Cambridge, Cambridgeshire CB4 1XG • Tel: 01223 505012

Situated in a residential area north of Cambridge, the Milton Arms is a member of the Hungry Horse hospitality scheme, with a large dining area and a peaceful lounge area with comfy furniture. Amenities include wifi access, a new outdoor children's play area, a sports bar with a pool table, flat screen TVs, and a beer garden and alfresco dining area.

The Red Lion
33 High Street, Grantchester, Cambridgeshire CB3 9NF • Tel: 01223 840121

Traditional, thatched pub located in an idyllic area by the river in Grantchester; a path in the garden leads to the tranquil River Cam, an ideal after-dinner walk. The first-class menu offers seafood and game dishes, plus a vegetarian option, and there is also a children's menu.

Essex

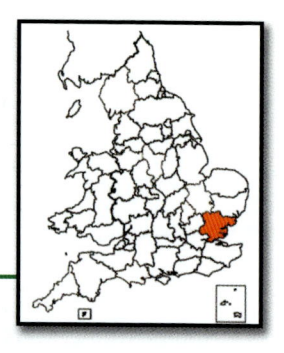

The Lion & Lamb
Stortford Road, Little Canfield, Near Takeley, Dunmow, Essex CM6 1SR
Tel: 01279 870257 • Fax: 01279 870423 • www.lionandlamb.co.uk

Bar and restaurant providing customers with the perfect setting for that romantic evening for two, or a long awaited catch-up drink with friends. Tradition prevails when it comes to decor, with blackened oak beams, a huge open fire and soft lighting.

The Bull Hotel
Bridge Street, Halstead, Essex, CO9 1HU
Tel: 01787 472144 • 01787 472496 • www.bullhotel-halstead.com

The Bull is a lively and very popular high street pub/inn, suitable for just about every occasion. Whether you're looking for a stopover, some live music or a beautiful garden to dine 'al fresco' in the summer months, look no further. All 19 rooms are en suite, with colour TV and coffee/tea making facilities.

RATES

Normal Bed & Breakfast rate per person
(single room)

PRICE RANGE	CATEGORY
Under £35	S£
£36-£45	S££
£46-£55	S£££
Over £55	S££££

Normal Bed & Breakfast rate per person
(sharing double/twin room)

PRICE RANGE	CATEGORY
Under £35	D£
£36-£45	D££
£46-£55	D£££
Over £55	D££££

This is meant as an indication only and does not show prices for Special Breaks, Weekends, etc. Guests are therefore advised to verify all prices on enquiring or booking.

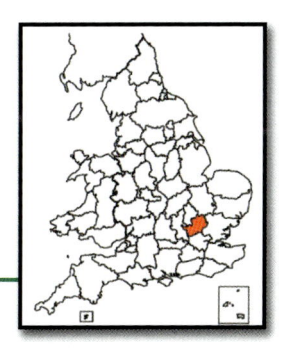

Hertfordshire

The Mitre Inn
58 High Street, Barnet, Hertfordshire EN5 5SJ
Tel: 020 8449 6582 • www.pub-explorer.com/herts/pub/mitrebarnet.htm
This dog-friendly (on leads!) pub is positioned on Barnet's popular and busy high street. The bar stocks a wide range of draught beers, real ales and cocktails (to order), all of which can be enjoyed in the bar, living area or restaurant. Live sporting fixtures on plasma screens.

The Duke Of York
Ganwick Corner, Barnet Road, Barnet, Hertfordshire EN5 4SG
Tel: 0208 4490297 • www.pub-explorer.com/herts/pub/dukeofyorkbarnet.htm
Superbly refurbished gastro bar and dining room, with easy access to Barnet High Street and Arkley countryside. It offers draught beers and regularly changing guest ales at the bar, and an imaginative menu in the restaurant.

THE SUN HOTEL
Sun Street, Hitchin, Hertfordshire SG5 1AF
Tel: 01462 432 092 • Fax: 01462 431 488 • www.sunhotel-hitchin.com
The Sun, with its delightful interior, is situated in Hitchin and dates back to the 16th century. Enjoy an excellent meal in the hotel's restaurant, which features dishes from around the world as well as traditional English cuisine. Real ales and fine wines are also available. 32 en suite bedrooms have wifi, CD player and colour TV.

The Valiant Trooper
Trooper Road, Aldbury, Tring, Hertfordshire HP23 5RW
Tel: 01442 851203 • www.valianttrooper.co.uk/
This Valiant Trooper offers many traditional feaures such as beamed ceilings, an inglenook fireplace, exposed brickwork, and a woodburning stove. The converted barn at the rear (now a restaurant) completes this beautifully positioned establishment.

Norfolk

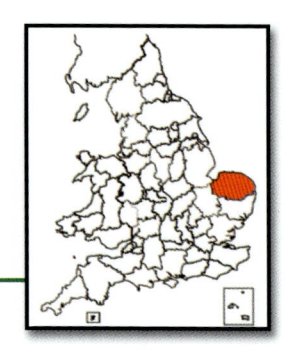

The Feathers Hotel

Manor Road, Dersingham, King's Lynn, Norfolk PE31 6LN
Tel & Fax: 01485 540207

In the gently undulating countryside of north-west Norfolk, this solid and welcoming stone-built inn stands on the fringe of Sandringham Estate, one of the Queen's favourite country homes. While not claiming to compete with that offered to Her Majesty, the Feathers provides comfortable and reasonably priced en suite accommodation with bedrooms simply furnished in the modern style and each having colour television. Real ale is served in the two popular bars, the Saddle Room and the Sandringham, and a right royal cuisine is provided with both à la carte and table d'hôte menus available. Well-tended gardens make a most pleasant setting for this attractive hostelry.

e-mail: info@thefeathershotelnorfolk.co.uk
www.thefeathershotelnorfolk.co.uk

ALL ROOMS WITH PRIVATE BATHROOM. REAL ALE. CHILDREN WELCOME. BAR AND RESTAURANT MEALS. HUNSTANTON 7 MILES. S££££, D££££.

Pet-Friendly
Pubs, Inns & Hotels
on pages 174-178
Please note that these establishments may not feature in the main section of this book

Norfolk

THE *Hill House*
Happisburgh NR12 0PW
Tel & Fax: 01692 650004

This attractive free house on the lonely Norfolk coast at Happisburgh (pronounced 'Hazeborough') was once the favourite haunt of the remarkable Sir Arthur Conan Doyle, creator of Sherlock Holmes. Clues may be found in that the coastline here is renowned for its ghosts and has been a graveyard for ships over the years which have foundered on the formidable Haisborough Sands, some seven miles off-shore. However, conviviality and good fare is provided by a visit to the inn's beamed bar and restaurant.

Excellent accommodation is available in spacious rooms and there is a large garden in which a double en suite room has been created in a converted signal box overlooking the sea. Different!

4 BEDROOMS, 2 WITH PRIVATE BATHROOM. FREE HOUSE WITH REAL ALE. CHILDREN AND PETS WELCOME. BAR MEALS LUNCHTIME AND EVENINGS, RESTAURANT MENU EVENINGS ONLY NON-SMOKING AREAS. WALSHAM 6 MILES. S£, D£

The Bull
25 High Street, Dereham, Norfolk NR19 1DZ • Tel: 01362 697771

Situated in the town centre on the main High Street is this Listed pub, with open fires and original oak beams. The Bull is an ideal lunchtime retreat, with reasonably priced food and facilities including plasma screens, a pool table and dart board.

The Otter
12 The Square, Thorpe Marriot, Drayton, Norfolk NR8 6XE • Tel: 01603 260455

Located just a short distance from Norwich, this fully refurbished family pub has an open-plan layout, where patrons can enjoy a delicious meal from the Sizzler menu. Live sporting fixtures are shown on screens in the sports bar downstairs. Free wifi access throughout.

EAST OF ENGLAND — Norfolk

THE OLD HALL INN is an old world character freehouse/restaurant situated on the coast road between Cromer and Great Yarmouth. It is in the middle of the village and just five minutes' walk from one of the best beaches along the Norfolk coast. There are six letting rooms, three of which are en suite, all have tea/coffee making facilities and TV.

THE OLD HALL INN
Sea Palling
NR12 0TZ
Tel: 01692 598323
Fax: 01692 598822

There is a non-smoking à la carte restaurant and bar meals are also available.

Well behaved children and pets are welcome.

Prices start at £35 for a single room, inclusive of full English breakfast, and £50 for a double room (two persons) per night.

THE OLD HALL INN — Freehouse & Restaurant

6 BEDROOMS, 3 WITH PRIVATE BATHROOM. ALL BEDROOMS NON-SMOKING. FREE HOUSE WITH REAL ALE. CHILDREN AND PETS WELCOME. BAR AND RESTAURANT MEALS. DESIGNATED COVERED SMOKING AREA. HAPPISBURGH 4 MILES. S£, D£££.

The Rushcutters Arms
Thorpe-St-Andrew, Norwich, Norfolk NR7 0HE
Tel.: 01603 435403 • Fax: 01603 439790

On the outskirts of Norwich in the peaceful village of Thorpe St Andrew, this Grade II Listed venue offers guests a traditional pub experience, with open fires, large oak beams and charming alcoves, nooks and crannies. The food is popular here and prepared from fresh ingredients. Facilities include an outdoor patio overlooking the Norfolk Broads.

THE WHEATSHEAF
Church Road, West Beckham, Near Holt, Norfolk NR25 6NX
Tel: 01263 822110 • www.wheatsheaf.org.uk

This beautiful pub is steeped in history and situated in West Beckham, near Holt. Inside, there are two separate dining rooms and a beamed bar area with a log fire. The food is home cooked, with a range of dishes from light snacks to main meals. Self-catering accommodation is available all year round.

RATES
S – SINGLE ROOM rate   D – Sharing DOUBLE/TWIN ROOM

S£ D£ =Under £35   S££ D££ =£36-£45   S£££ D£££ =£46-£55   S££££ D££££ =Over £55

This is meant as an indication only and does not show prices for Special Breaks, Weekends, etc. Guests are therefore advised to verify all prices on enquiring or booking.

The Lifeboat Inn

16th Century Smugglers' Ale House

Ship Lane, Thornham, Norfolk PE36 6LT
Tel: 01485 512236 • Fax: 01485 512323
e-mail: lifeboatinn@maypolehotels.com

THE LIFEBOAT INN has been a welcome sight for the weary traveller for centuries – roaring open fires, real ales and a hearty meal awaiting. The Summer brings its own charm – a cool beer, gazing over open meadows to the harbour, and rolling white horses gently breaking upon Thornham's sandy beach.

Dogs are welcome in all our bars and we provide the sort of breakfast that will enable you to keep up with your four-legged friend on the way to the beach!

Guests arriving at reception are greeted by our grand old fireplace in the lounge – ideal for toasting your feet after a day walking the coastal path – if you can coax your sleeping dog out of prime position! The restaurant (AA Rosette) opens every evening offering a varied selection of dishes to suit all tastes. Our extensive bar snack menu is also available if guests wish their pets to join them in the bar.

There are numerous and varied walks along miles of open beaches, across sweeping sand dunes, through pine woods or along chalk and sandstone cliff tops. It is truly a walker's paradise – especially if you're a dog.

We hope you will come and visit us. For our brochure and tariff which includes details of breaks please ring 01485 512236 **or visit our website**

www.maypolehotels.com

14 BEDROOMS, ALL WITH PRIVATE BATHROOM. PETS WELCOME. BAR AND RESTAURANT MEALS. HUNSTANTON 4 MILES.

The Banningham Crown

Colby Road, Banningham, Norwich, Norfolk NR11 7DY
Tel: 01263 733534 • Fax: 01263 733082

Located opposite the village green in the quiet village of Banningham is this CAMRA listed pub and restaurant. It offers a full à la carte menu, bar snacks and a great selection of real ales. Entertainment includes live jazz nights, BBQs, Morris dancers and quiz nights.

THE BELL HOTEL

King Street, Thetford, Norfolk IP24 2AZ
Tel: 01842 754 455 • Fax: 01842 755 552 • www.bellhotel-thetford.com

Thetford, an old cathedral town, is a tranquil Norfolk getaway. The Bell featured regularly in the popular sitcom 'Dad's Army', playing second home to cast and crew. Standard rooms are en suite, with colour TV and coffee/tea making amenities; special feature rooms also available.

70 EAST OF ENGLAND — **Norfolk**

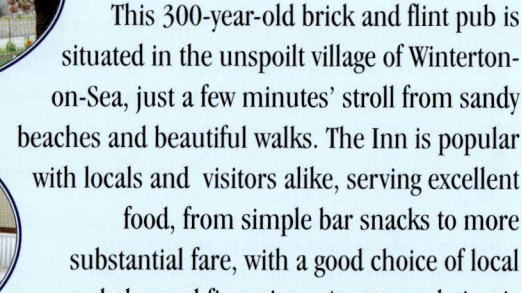

Fishermans Return

This 300-year-old brick and flint pub is situated in the unspoilt village of Winterton-on-Sea, just a few minutes' stroll from sandy beaches and beautiful walks. The Inn is popular with locals and visitors alike, serving excellent food, from simple bar snacks to more substantial fare, with a good choice of local real ales and fine wines. Accommodation is available on a B&B basis, in three tastefully furnished en suite double bedrooms.

The Lane, Winterton-on-Sea NR29 4BN
Tel: 01493 393305
e-mail: fishermansreturn@yahoo.co.uk
www.fishermans-return.com

3 ROOMS, ALL WITH PRIVATE BATHROOM. FREE HOUSE WITH REAL ALE. BAR MEALS. GREAT YARMOUTH 8 MILES.

RATES

Normal Bed & Breakfast rate per person **(single room)**

PRICE RANGE	CATEGORY
Under £35	S£
£36-£45	S££
£46-£55	S£££
Over £55	S££££

Normal Bed & Breakfast rate per person **(sharing double/twin room)**

PRICE RANGE	CATEGORY
Under £35	D£
£36-£45	D££
£46-£55	D£££
Over £55	D££££

This is meant as an indication only and does not show prices for Special Breaks, Weekends, etc. Guests are therefore advised to verify all prices on enquiring or booking.

www.holidayguides.com

Suffolk

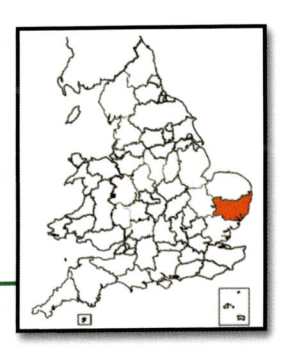

THE BROME GRANGE HOTEL
Norwich Road, Brome, Near Eye, Suffolk IP23 8AP
Tel: 01379 870456 • www.bromegrange.co.uk • bromegrange@fastnet.co.uk
Set amid the Suffolk countryside, The Grange boasts 22 ground floor en suite rooms, all with views of the beautiful hotel gardens. Single, double, twin or family size rooms are available. The stylish Knight's Restaurant serves à la carte international and English dishes with produce from the hotel's own organic free-range farm.

The Beehive
The Street, Horringer, Bury St Edmunds, Suffolk IP29 5SN • Tel: 01284 735260
This beautiful pub boasts an award-winning restaurant serving fresh, home-made dishes prepared from local ingredients. The building has exposed flint walls, and inside is traditional in style, with pine furniture, oak beams and a number of charming little nooks and crannies.

The Dog & Partridge
29 Crown Street, Bury St Edmunds, Suffolk IP33 1QU • Tel: 01284 764792
Put your overnight bag down at the adjacent inn and pop in to the pub next door for a nightcap. Drink and dine in peace, play some pool, watch the football highlights, or simply pull up a pew outside in either of the two courtyards. Accommodation is nine non-smoking bedrooms. Wifi hotspot available.

The Mill Inn
Market Cross Place, Aldeburgh, Suffolk IP15 5BJ
Tel: 01728 452563 • www.themillinnaldeburgh.com
On the sea front at Aldeburgh, this popular pub provides comfortable accommodation and easy access to the beach, as well as to shopping amenities, cinema and theatre. Drop in for a delicious bar snack or a glass of real ale. Rooms have colour TV, tea/coffee tray, and hairdryer.

The Bull Inn & Restaurant

The Street,
Woolpit
Bury St Edmunds
IP30 9SA
Tel: 01359 240393

A family-run pub, ideal for touring the beautiful county of Suffolk

- Traditional food and daily specials lunchtime and evenings (not Sunday pm).
- Good choice of real ales and wines
- Excellent en suite accommodation (single, double and family)
- Large garden and car park

www.bullinnwoolpit.co.uk • info@bullinnwoolpit.co.uk

8 BEDROOMS, ALL WITH PRIVATE BATHROOM. ALL BEDROOMS NON-SMOKING. PUNCH TAVERNS HOUSE WITH REAL ALE. CHILDREN WELCOME. BAR AND RESTAURANT MEALS. NON-SMOKING AREAS. STOWMARKET 5 MILES. S££, D£££.

The Spread Eagle

Out Westgate, Bury St Edmunds, Suffolk IP33 2DE • Tel: 01284 754523

'A pub for all ages' is this establishment's slogan. Food is served throughout the week, with an unbeatable Sunday roast lunch as a highlight. Facilities include quiz nights with free buffets, three plasma screens and a children's play area.

The Ship Inn at Dunwich

St James Street, Dunwich, Suffolk IP17 3DT
Tel: 01728 648219 • info@shipindunwich.co.uk • www.shipinndunwich.co.uk

The Inn is positioned just a short drive away from neighbouring seaside towns, Southwold and Aldeburgh. Single, double and family rooms are available, each en suite, with coffee/tea making facilities and colour TV. The pub's dining room is renowned for its adventurous menu and helped gain the pub a rave review in *The Good Pub Guide*.

Suffolk   EAST OF ENGLAND

THE GROSVENOR
25/31 Ranelagh Road, Felixstowe, Suffolk IP11 7HA • Tel: 01394 284137

This authentic public house has retained most of its original features, and the interior includes comfortable lounges, a pool room and a bar area. Live sporting fixtures are shown on a large screen TV, with a jukebox and a dart board for patrons' enjoyment.

The Huntsman & Hound
Stone Street, Spexhall, Halesworth, Suffolk IP19 0RN • Tel: 01986 781341

Traditional 15th century Inn close to the Suffolk coast, with the Norfolk Broads just a short drive away. Stay in one of three bedrooms, each en suite, with colour TV and coffee/tea making facilities. Enjoy a pint of real ale in the bar area and some freshly home-cooked food. Pets welcome by arrangement.

The Thrasher
Nacton Road, Ipswich, Suffolk IP3 9RZ • Tel: 01473 723355

Having undergone a major refurbishment, the pub is now a focal point of the local community. The stylish interior is elegantly decorated, with impressive LCD TV screens in the restaurant's seating area. The cuisine is particularly popular, with something for everyone on the imaginative menu.

The Crown
9 Ipswich Road, Claydon, Ipswich, Suffolk IP6 0AA
Tel: 01473 830289 • Fax: 01473 832986

Standing proudly in Claydon village on the edge of Ipswich, this attractive establishment offers a good value Hungry Horse menu. Oak beams and a beer garden make this an attractive spot to stop off for refreshment on a day out.

RATES

Normal Bed & Breakfast rate per person
(single room)

PRICE RANGE	CATEGORY
Under £35	S£
£36-£45	S££
£46-£55	S£££
Over £55	S££££

Normal Bed & Breakfast rate per person
(sharing double/twin room)

PRICE RANGE	CATEGORY
Under £35	D£
£36-£45	D££
£46-£55	D£££
Over £55	D££££

This is meant as an indication only and does not show prices for Special Breaks, Weekends, etc. Guests are therefore advised to verify all prices on enquiring or booking.

Derbyshire

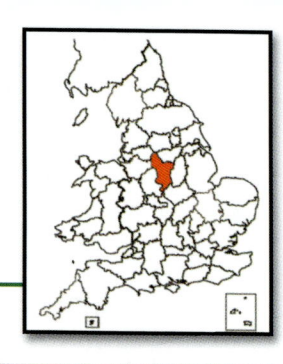

DOG & PARTRIDGE
· COUNTRY INN ·

Mary and Martin Stelfox welcome you to a family-run 17th century Inn and Motel set in five acres, five miles from Alton Towers and close to Dovedale and Ashbourne. We specialise in family breaks, and special diets and vegetarians are catered for. All rooms have private bathrooms, colour TV, direct-dial telephone, tea-making facilities and baby listening service.

Ideal for touring Stoke Potteries, Derbyshire Dales and Staffordshire Moorlands. Open Christmas and New Year.

'Staffs Good Food Winners 2003/2004'.

Restaurant open all day, non-residents welcome

e-mail: info@dogandpartridge.co.uk
Tel: 01335 343183 • www.dogandpartridge.co.uk
Swinscoe, Ashbourne DE6 2HS

MOST BEDROOMS WITH PRIVATE BATHROOM. REAL ALE. CHILDREN AND PETS WELCOME. BAR MEALS. ASHBOURNE 3 MILES. S£££/££££, D££.

YORKSHIRE BRIDGE INN (on facing page)

14 BEDROOMS, ALL WITH PRIVATE BATHROOM. FREE HOUSE WITH REAL ALE. CHILDREN AND PETS WELCOME. BAR AND RESTAURANT MEALS. NON-SMOKING AREAS. HATHERSAGE 2 MILES. S£££, D££.

Derbyshire

THE MIDLANDS 75

The Yorkshire Bridge Inn
1826

- Glorious Peak District location
- Fantastic real ales
- Fine food prepared to order
- Fresh local produce
- 14 comfortable bedrooms
- Friendly atmosphere for all

Freehouse of the year
finalist 2000, 2001 & 2004

enjoyEngland.com
★★★★ INN

AA
★★★★
Inn

Call 01433 651361 for a brochure
web: www.yorkshire-bridge.co.uk

Derbyshire

Tel: 01298 23875 • www.devarms.com
e-mail: lesleywoodward@tiscali.co.uk

Set in the pictureque village of Peak Forest in the heart of the Peak District, the Devonshire Arms was once a coaching Inn, but today is a pub/hotel where our prime concern is your comfort, relaxation and enjoyment. The staff are here to ensure your visit exceeds your expectations and everyone can be certain of a warm welcome.

We have a large variety of rooms, all of which are en suite and individually styled and refurbished regularly. We are able to cater for couples, single people or families. Each bedroom has remote-control colour television, tea and coffee making facilities and hair dryer.

Dogs are welcome to stay and there is no extra charge.

The Inn is privately owned, personally managed and has an enviable reputation for staff service, food and the accommodation we offer.

Prices from £32.50.

The Devonshire Arms
Peak Forest,
Near Buxton,
Derbyshire
SK17 8EJ

Derbyshire THE MIDLANDS

THE LITTLE JOHN INN
**Station Road, Hathersage
Hope Valley
Derbyshire S32 1DD**

This handsome stone building which dates from the 19th century is popular with locals and visitors alike. It has won awards for its ale and carries a good selection of refreshments. This is just the place for a relaxing drink or meal after a day walking on the high moors. Home-cooked food is served in the bar, and there are two plasma screen TVs. The pub is mainly non-smoking. Accommodation is available in five en suite rooms and two charming cottages

Owner Stephanie Bushell offers all guests a warm welcome.

Tel: 01433 650225 • • Fax: 01433 659831

5 BEDROOMS, ALL WITH PRIVAE BATHROOM. TWO COTTAGES. REAL ALE. BAR MEALS. CHILDREN AND PETS WELCOME. BAKEWELL 8 MILES.

Family-Friendly
Pubs, Inns & Hotels
See the Supplement on pages 179-182 for establishments which really welcome children

RATES

Normal Bed & Breakfast rate per person **(single room)**		Normal Bed & Breakfast rate per person **(sharing double/twin room)**	
PRICE RANGE	CATEGORY	PRICE RANGE	CATEGORY
Under £35	S£	Under £35	D£
£36-£45	S££	£36-£45	D££
£46-£55	S£££	£46-£55	D£££
Over £55	S££££	Over £55	D££££

This is meant as an indication only and does not show prices for Special Breaks, Weekends, etc. Guests are therefore advised to verify all prices on enquiring or booking.

THE DEVONSHIRE ARMS (on facing page)

7 BEDROOMS, ALL WITH PRIVATE BATHROOM. ALL BEDROOMS NON-SMOKING. FREE HOUSE WITH REAL ALE. CHILDREN AND PETS WELCOME. BAR AND RESTAURANT MEALS. DESIGNATED COVERED SMOKING AREA. CHAPEL-EN-LE-FRITH 4 MILES. S££, D££.

Herefordshire

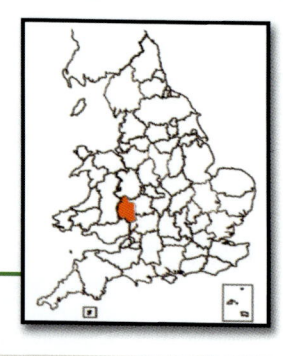

THE Rhydspence Inn

**Whitney-on-Wye,
Near Hay-on-Wye HR3 6EU
Tel: 01497 831262
Fax: 01497 831751**

Built for the medieval pilgrims and used by the cattle drovers, this beautiful 14th century inn can claim to have provided food and accommodation for 600 years.

Today it has an excellent reputation for top quality exciting food served in the dining room overlooking the Wye Valley, or bar and brasserie meals in the very atmospheric eating areas.

It is a genuine inn where you can enjoy a drink, have a light snack or sumptuous meal with wines from the extensive list.

All bedrooms are en suite, tastefully furnished, decorated in traditional style, and all have 21st century facilities.

e-mail: info@rhydspence-inn.co.uk
www.rhydspence-inn.co.uk

7 BEDROOMS, ALL WITH PRIVATE BATHROOM. ALL BEDROOMS NON-SMOKING. FREE HOUSE WITH REAL ALE. CHILDREN WELCOME. BAR AND RESTAURANT MEALS. DESIGNATED COVERED SMOKING AREA. HAY-ON-WYE 4 MILES. S£££, D£££.

The Royal Hotel

**Palace Pound, Ross-on-Wye, Herefordshire HR9 5HZ
Tel: 01989 565 105 • Fax: 01989 768 058 • www.theroyal-ross.com**

Charles Dickens and Queen Victoria are former visitors at the eye-catching Royal Hotel. Browse through the shops in the local market town or relax at the hotel with a cream tea and scone on the Riverside Terrace. Later, sample the extensive menu, perhaps with a real ale or fine wine. Accommodation is in 42 en suite rooms, each with a truly astonishing view.

Leicestershire & Rutland

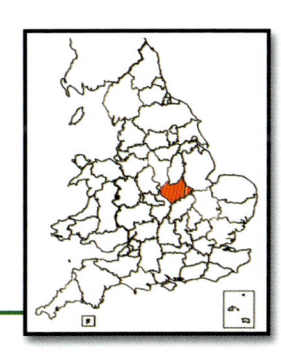

The Mill on the Soar
Coventry Road, Broughton Astley, Leicestershire LE9 6QA
Tel: 01455 282419 • Fax: 01455 285937

This friendly inn is ideal for a variety of purposes - romantic breaks, long weekends or business trips. Conferences are well catered for, with two delegate packages providing all modern facilities. A variety of room tariffs are offered – a family room accommodates two adults and one child. There is easy access to Birmingham, NEC and Rugby.

Fieldhead Hotel
Markfield Lane, Markfield, Leicester, Leicestershire LE67 9PS
Tel: 01530 245 454 • 01530 243 740 • www.thefieldhead.com

The perfect meeting place for a reunion, wedding or birthday, with three function rooms, each capable of creating a unique atmosphere. The pub has an 'all day, every day' food policy and offers delicious seasonal menus. Accommodation is available in 28 en suite rooms, each with colour TV, wifi and coffee/tea making facilities.

The Wheatsheaf Inn
Brand Hill, Woodhouse Eaves, Leicestershire LE12 8SS
Tel: 01509 890320 • Fax: 01509 890891 • www.wheatsheafinn.net

Newly refurbished Inn, pub and restaurant offering the very best wines, real ales and beers, plus high quality cuisine, and luxurious accommodation in a cosy cottage annexe with twin and double rooms.

Pet-Friendly Pubs, Inns & Hotels
on pages 174-178
Please note that these establishments may not feature in the main section of this book

Rothley Court Hotel
Westfield Lane, Rothley, Leicestershire LE7 7LG
Tel: 0116 237 4141 • Fax: 0116 237 4483 • www.rothleycourt.com

Rothley Court is deservedly popular for the vast array of luxuries and activities on offer, with its own trout-filled river as well as 'Karmaroma' Beauty & Holistic Therapy. Expect quality meals in the restaurant and a fine selection of ales and fine wines at the bar. Accommodation is in 30 en suite rooms, all with modern facilities.

The Windmill Inn & Brascote Restaurant
Brascote, Newbold Verdon, Leicestershire LE9 9LE • Tel: 01455 824433

You can't miss the ivy-clad Windmill Inn, standing majestically in Leicestershire's Brascote. It is stylish yet traditional, with low beams, an open log fire and a good choice of real and guest ales.

Looking for Holiday Accommodation?

FHG
KUPERARD

for details of hundreds of properties throughout the UK, visit our website

www.holidayguides.com

Northamptonshire

THE FALCON HOTEL
Castle Ashby, Northampton, Northamptonshire NN7 1LF
Tel: 01604 696 200 • Fax: 01604 696 673 • www.falconhotel-castleashby.com

With Silverstone and Stratford-upon-Avon only a short distance away, one can be assured of an outstanding level of modern English cuisine and excellent service at The Falcon. Accommodation can be found in the hotel itself or in one of the cottages next door. Each room is en suite with a full range of modern facilities.

The Swan at Lamport
Harborough Road, Lamport, Northamptonshire NN6 9EZ
Tel: 01604 686 555 • theswanlamport@tiscali.co.uk

The Swan at Lamport is the ideal place to come on sunny days and rainy afternoons! It features a stylish interior and offers a carefully selected stock of wines and real ales. All dishes on the varied menu are prepared from fresh ingredients.

The Talbot Hotel
New Street, Oundle, Northamptonshire PE8 4EA
Tel: 01832 273 621 • Fax: 01832 274 545 • www.thetalbot-oundle.com

Much of this fine building was built from the ruins of Fotheringhay Castle, which has associations with Mary, Queen of Scots, and it is rumoured that her spirit haunts the hotel. Accommodation is in 35 uniquely designed en suite bedrooms, each with modern facilities and modem plug-in points.

Saracens Head Hotel
219 Watling Street West, Towcester, Northants NN12 6BX
Tel: 01327 350 414 • Fax: 01327 359 879 • www.saracenshead-towcester.com

This sturdy hotel dates back to the 19th century and is mentioned in Dickens' first novel, 'The Pickwick Papers'. Very popular in the town, it is renowned for wholesome meals such as fish and chips, and steaks cooked to your liking. Accommodation is in 21 en suite bedrooms. There is easy access to Towcester and Silverstone racecourses.

Nottinghamshire

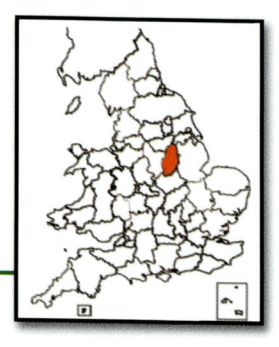

The Chesterfield at Bingham
Church Street, Bingham, Nottinghamshire NG13 8AL
Tel: 01949 837342 • www.thechesterfield.co.uk

A gastro pub retaining several original features, the Chesterfield offers an imaginative menu of dishes prepared from locally sourced ingredients, and diners may eat alfresco in the delightful beer garden. For a pint of your favourite draught beer or real ale, The Chesterfield is the ideal place.

THE CHESTERFIELD ARMS
Main Road, Gedling, Nottingham, Nottinghamshire NG4 3HL • Tel: 01159 878686

Located in the peaceful village of Gedling, with pretty hanging baskets outside, this eye-catching pub is devoted to sport, with live fixtures shown on screens throughout. Food is affordably priced and entertainment includes quiz and race nights.

The Travellers Rest
Mapperley Plains, Nottingham, Nottinghamshire NG3 5RT
Tel: 0115 9264412 • Fax: 0115 9203134

This superb pub is set in rural surroundings, yet with easy access to Nottingham town centre. Chef & Brewer pubs are known for serving mouthwatering dishes at affordable prices; the speciality here is a fresh fish supper. Why not sample one of the pub's quality wines or real ales to accompany your meal?

The Fiveways
Edwards Lane, Nottingham, Nottinghamshire NG5 3HU • Tel. 0115 9265612

Edwardian-style woodcarvings enhance the traditional exterior of this old coaching house, where refreshment is reasonably priced and the choice is extensive. Facilities include a piano room, a beer garden and two smoking shelters.

Nottinghamshire

The Goose at Gamston
Gamston, Nottingham, Nottinghamshire NG2 6NA • Tel: 0115 9821041

The Goose is positioned in idyllic surroundings in Gamston and is an ideal family retreat, especially during summer months. The interior is elegant, with high ceilings and traditional wooden beams. The menu offers a wide range of tasty dishes, and for children (or big kids), there is ice cream!

THE THREE PONDS
Kimberley Road, Nuthall, Nottingham, Nottinghamshire NG16 1DA
Tel: 0115 9383170 • Fax: 0115 9382153

A friendly pub with an extensive menu of home-made dishes served in generous portions. The bar is stocked with a good selection of high quality real ales and draught beers. Regular activities include a popular quiz night and a poker night.

The Windsor Castle
Carlton Hill, Carlton, Nottingham, Nottinghamshire NG4 1EB • Tel: 0115 9871374

Since its refurbishment two years ago, this lively pub now boasts its very own stage and dance floor. Sport is important here, with live matches shown on the big screen, and customers can enjoy watching the game with a pint of their favourite ale and a tasty snack.

The Rose & Crown
Derby Road, Lenton, Nottingham, Nottinghamshire NG7 2GW • Tel: 0115 9784958

Situated in Lenton, Nottingham's student area, the Rose & Crown is a lively pub where good food is served and great company is free! Amenities include a beer garden, DJs, live music, a pool table, dart board, five TVs and a big screen for live sporting fixtures.

The Tree Tops
Plains Road, Mapperley, Nottingham, Nottinghamshire NG3 5RF
Tel: 0115 9558989 • Fax: 0115 9674031

Located just outside Nottingham in rural surroundings, and ideal for a peaceful lunchtime drink, the Tree Tops is cosy, with printed wallpaper and comfy sofas. The bar is stocked with real ales kept to a first class standard, and traditional pub food is available throughout the day.

The Ferry Inn
Main Road, Wilford, Nottingham, Nottinghamshire NG11 7AA
Tel: 0115 981 1441 • Fax: 0115 982 5089

Wilford is a quaint little village with a river flowing through it, and the pub is like something out of a fairytale, with low ceilings, real inglenook fires, wood-panelled recesses and attractive hanging baskets. Chef & Brewer pubs are renowned for serving superb food made from fresh ingredients, plus a good selection of quality beers, real ales and fine wines.

84 **THE MIDLANDS** — Shropshire

Shropshire

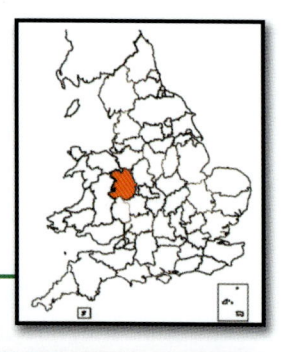

The Four Alls Inn & Motel
Newport Rd, Woodseaves, Market Drayton TF9 2AG

A warm welcome is assured at the Four Alls, situated in a quiet location of Woodseaves yet only a mile from the town of Market Drayton, and within easy reach of Shropshire's premier attractions.

Relax in our spacious bar, sample our home-cooked food and excellent traditional beers, then enjoy a good night's sleep in one of our nine en suite chalet-style rooms with central heating, TV and tea/coffee making facilities. The function room is available for weddings, celebrations or as a conference venue and can accommodate 50-100. Large car park.

Tel: 01630 652995 • Fax: 01630 653930
e-mail: inn@thefouralls.com • www.thefouralls.com

AA ★★★ Inn

9 BEDROOMS, ALL WITH PRIVATE BATHROOM. ALL BEDROOMS NON-SMOKING. REAL ALE. BAR AND RESTAURANT MEALS. SHREWSBURY 18 MILES. S££, D££££.

RATES

Normal Bed & Breakfast rate per person
(single room)

PRICE RANGE	CATEGORY
Under £35	S£
£36-£45	S££
£46-£55	S£££
Over £55	S££££

Normal Bed & Breakfast rate per person
(sharing double/twin room)

PRICE RANGE	CATEGORY
Under £35	D£
£36-£45	D££
£46-£55	D£££
Over £55	D££££

This is meant as an indication only and does not show prices for Special Breaks, Weekends, etc. Guests are therefore advised to verify all prices on enquiring or booking.

THE CROWN COUNTRY INN (on facing page)

3 BEDROOMS, ALL WITH PRIVATE BATHROOM. ALL BEDROOMS NON-SMOKING. FREE HOUSE WITH REAL ALE. CHILDREN WELCOME. BAR AND RESTAURANT MEALS. TOTALLY NON-SMOKING. LUDLOW 8 MILES. S£££, D££.

THE Crown COUNTRY INN

Set below the rolling hills of Wenlock Edge, the Crown Country Inn is an ideal place to stay and explore the area. This Grade II Listed Tudor inn retains many historic features, including oak beams and flagstone floors.

Here you can sample traditional ales, fine food and a warm welcome from hosts, Richard and Jane Arnold.

The menu offers a tempting variety of traditional and more exotic dishes, plus daily 'specials', all freshly prepared using the finest ingredients.

Accommodation is available in three large bedrooms, all en suite, with television and tea/coffee making facilities.

• Shropshire Good Eating Awards • Restaurant of the Year •

Munslow, Near Craven Arms, Shropshire SY7 9ET
Tel: 01584 841205
www.crowncountryinn.co.uk
info@crowncountryinn.co.uk

Warwickshire

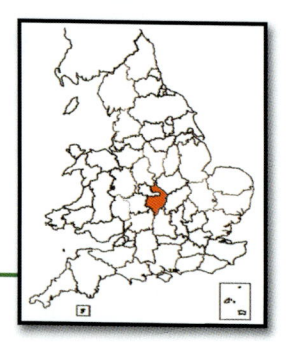

The Coleshill Hotel
152-156 High Street, Coleshill, Warwickshire B46 3BG
Tel: 01675 465 527 • Fax: 01675 464 013 • www.coleshillhotel.com

The Coleshill is a popular haunt, with a heated outdoor terrace and delightfully named fireside 'Nook'. Birmingham NEC is just three miles away, and the city centre is convenient for a burst of retail therapy. Accommodation is spread over two buildings, with a Georgian annexe across the road. Each room is en suite, and rates include a full English breakfast.

The Clarendon House
High Street, Kenilworth, Warwickshire CV8 1LZ
Tel: 01926 857 668 • Fax: 01926 850 669 • www.clarendonhouse-hotel.com

With Warwick Castle and Shakespeare's Stratford nearby, The Clarendon is an ideal point from which to enjoy great family days out. Outdoor types will marvel at the choice of sporting activities in the area. Rooms are en suite, with direct-dial telephone and other standard facilities; rates include full English breakfast.

THE MILLERS HOTEL
Twycross Road, Sibson, Nuneaton, Warwickshire CV13 6LB
Tel: 01827 880 223 • Fax: 01827 880 990 • www.millershotel-sibson.com

Sibson's former village bakery is now a superb conference and training centre and is perfect for weddings and birthday celebrations. Accommodation is en suite with all modern facilities. The Bar/Restaurant serves modern and traditional snacks and meals, real ale and carefully selected wines. Easy access to East Midlands Airport and Birmingham NEC.

Pet-Friendly
Pubs, Inns & Hotels
on pages 174-178
Please note that these establishments may not feature in the main section of this book

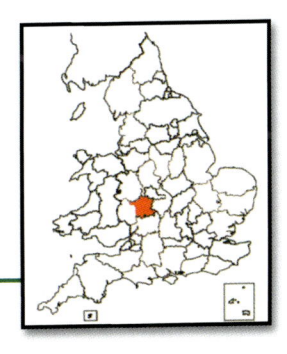

Worcestershire

The Anchor Inn
Main Road, Wyre Piddle, Pershore, Worcestershire WR10 2JB
Tel: 01386 556059
Formerly boatmen's cottages, the Anchor Inn has gardens overlooking the beautiful South Worcestershire countryside and a terraced area by the waterside. Draught beers, real ales and wines are available, and the menu features dishes prepared from locally sourced ingredients.

Perdiswell House
Droitwich Road, Worcester, Worcestershire WR3 7JU • Tel: 01905 451311
Popular pub and diner situated on the outskirts of Worcester, with lots of delightful features and facilities to make your visit as relaxing and enjoyable as possible. A children's play area called Fuzzy Ed's Fun House will keep the kids entertained while mum and dad relax.

The Talbot
8-10 Barbourne Road, Worcester, Worcestershire WR1 1HT • Tel: 01905 723744
The Talbot is a candidate for the best pub in town, with a whole host of facilities and weekly entertainment including live music, a pool table, dart board and a beer garden – perfect for alfresco dining in summer months. Dishes on the menu are of a high standard and are prepared from the freshest ingredients.

THE MARWOOD
The Tything, Worcester, Worcestershire WR1 1JL
Tel: 01905 330 460 • www.themarwood.co.uk
Stunning Georgian establishment located in the tranquil Worcestershire countryside, with all traditional features including open log fires, a cosy restaurant and a lavish Champagne Terrace. This pub has character and stands out because of this, offering a good selection of beers, real ales and European lagers.

88 YORKSHIRE   East Yorkshire

East Yorkshire

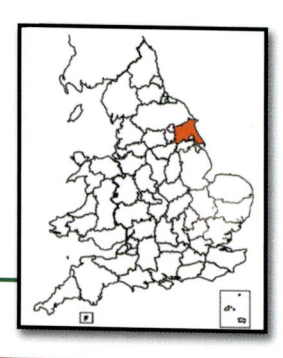

THE WOLDS INN

Driffield Road, Huggate, East Yorkshire YO42 IYH
Tel: 01377 288217

huggate@woldsinn.freeserve.co.uk

A peaceful country inn in farming country high in the Wolds, the hostelry exudes an atmosphere well in keeping with its 16th century origins. Panelling, brassware and crackling fires all contribute to a mood of contentment, well supported in practical terms by splendid food served either in the convivial bar, where meals are served daily at lunchtimes and in the evenings, or in the award-winning restaurant where choice may be made from a mouth-watering à la carte menu. Sunday roasts are also very popular.

Huggate lies on the Wolds Way and the inn is justly popular with walkers, whilst historic York and Beverley and their racecourses and the resorts of Bridlington, Hornsea and Scarborough are within easy reach.

First-rate overnight accommodation is available, all rooms having en suite facilities, central heating, colour television and tea and coffee tray.

3 BEDROOMS, ALL WITH PRIVATE BATHROOM. ALL BEDROOMS NON-SMOKING. FREE HOUSE WITH REAL ALE. CHILDREN WELCOME. BAR MEALS, A LA CARTE MENU IN EVENINGS. POCKLINGTON 6 MILES. S££, D£.

RATES S – SINGLE ROOM rate   D – Sharing DOUBLE/TWIN ROOM
S£ D£ =Under £35   S££ D££ =£36-£45   S£££ D£££ =£46-£55   S££££ D££££ =Over £55

This is meant as an indication only and does not show prices for Special Breaks, Weekends, etc. Guests are therefore advised to verify all prices on enquiring or booking.

North Yorkshire

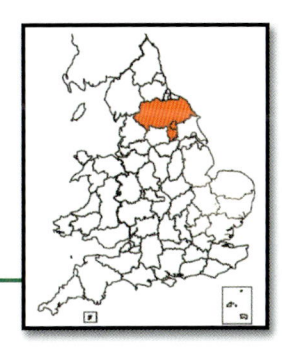

Just a few minutes' drive from the A1, The Green Dragon in the attractive little village of Exelby dates back to the early 18th century and boasts an excellent restaurant, comfortable, well appointed accommodation and a large car park. The Green Dragon is a family run, independent country inn taking pride in its friendly welcoming service. In winter the open log fires provide a warm, cosy atmosphere, whilst in the summer visitors can enjoy the decked area for alfresco eating. Inside the recently refurbished inn you can choose to eat in the bar or the spacious and attractive restaurant. Daily specials are also available every lunchtime and evening, and food is home cooked and locally sourced wherever possible. Food is served until 9pm (8pm Sundays).

To accompany your meal, there's a good selection of fine wines and excellent real ales, up to three of them on tap at any one time, with Black Sheep Best Bitter and Theakston's Black Bull as the regular brews, plus a guest ale. Live music and Theme Nights, plus Quiz Nights on Tuesdays.

There are four tastefully decorated and furnished rooms, (two doubles, one twin and one single), all en suite, with colour television and hospitality tray.

Exelby village is approximately two miles from the delightful market town of Bedale, the "Gateway to Wensleydale", which has a good range of shops, pubs, restaurants and a leisure centre.

The Green Dragon
High Row, Exelby, Bedale DL8 2HA
tel: 01677 422233
e-mail: jean@thegreendragonexelby.com
www.thegreendragonexelby.com

4 BEDROOMS, ALL EN SUITE. CHILDREN WELCOME. REAL ALE. RESTAURANT MEALS. BEDALE 2 MILES.

Pet-Friendly
Pubs, Inns & Hotels
on pages 174-178
Please note that these establishments may not feature in the main section of this book

The Dog & Gun at Potto

Welcome to The Dog & Gun Country Inn at Potto...

The Dog & Gun is located in the picturesque village of Potto, at the foot of the Cleveland Hills. With stunning views overlooking Roseberry Topping, our country inn offers a unique blend of exquisite cuisine, all hand prepared by our chefs, five luxury guest rooms, a restaurant and bar serving a wide range of local ales.

Our five guest rooms at The Dog & Gun all feature king-size beds and en suite facilities. They come complete with wifi connection and wall-mounted satellite TV.

Dog & Gun Country Inn, Cooper Lane, Potto, North Yorkshire DL6 3HQ • Tel: 01642 700232
mail@thedogandgunpotto.com • www.thedogandgunpotto.com

The Suite is our largest room which is perfect for both business and wedding guests. This room comes complete with its own sofa, table and chairs, but also a fantastic free-standing half-egg shaped bath in the middle of the room which is separate from the en suite!

We now have two private dining rooms available for up to 20 guests, the larger of which comes with its own dedicated bar and also waiting staff.

North Yorkshire **YORKSHIRE** 91

THE WHEATSHEAF IN WENSLEYDALE

Excellent en suite accommodation, including four posters, at this comfortable family owned hotel offering the best of local cuisine and comfort.

The Wheatsheaf, Carperby, Near Leyburn DL8 4DF
Tel: 01969 663216 • Fax: 01969 663019
e-mail: info@wheatsheafinwensleydale.co.uk
www.wheatsheafinwensleydale.co.uk

ALL ROOM WITH PRIVATE BATHROOM. CHILDREN WELCOME. BAR AND RESTAURANT MEALS.
AYSGARTH 1 MILE.

New Inn *Clapham – 'As relaxed as you like'*
Quality Accommodation in the Yorkshire Dales.

A comfortable hotel in the Yorkshire Dales National Park, The New Inn has been lovingly and carefully refurbished, with a fine blend of old and new to retain the characteristics of this fine 18th Century Coaching Inn.

This traditional Village Inn has 19 en suite bedrooms, including ground floor and disabled bedrooms. Residents' lounge, Restaurant, two comfortable bars serving a selection of local ales, fine wines and a large selection of malt whiskies. Our food offers a mix of traditional and modern cooking.

New Inn, Clapham, Near Ingleton, North Yorkshire LA2 8HH
e-mail: info@newinn-clapham.co.uk
www.newinn-clapham.co.uk

Tel: 015242 51203
Fax: 015242 51824

19 BEDROOMS, ALL WITH PRIVATE BATHROOM. ENTERPRISE INNS HOUSE WITH REAL ALE.
CHILDREN AND PETS WELCOME. BAR MEALS, RESTAURANT EVENINGS ONLY. SETTLE 6 MILES. S£££, D£££.

DOG & GUN COUNTRY INN *(on facing page)*

5 ROOMS, ALL WITH ORIVATE BATHROOM. REAL ALE. BAR & RESTAURANT MEALS.
STOKESLEY 5 MILES.

The Fox & Hounds Inn

Former 16th century coaching inn, now a high quality residential Country Inn & Restaurant set amidst the beautiful North York Moors. Freshly prepared dishes, using finest local produce, are served every lunchtime and evening, with selected quality wines and a choice of cask ales. Excellent en suite acccommodation is available.
Open all year. Winter Breaks available November to March.

For bookings please Tel: 01287 660218
Ainthorpe, Danby, Yorkshire YO21 2LD
e-mail: info@foxandhounds-ainthorpe.com
www.foxandhounds-ainthorpe.com

★★★★ INN

7 BEDROOMS, ALL WITH PRIVATE BATHROOM. ALL BEDROOMS NON-SMOKING. FREE HOUSE WITH REAL ALE. CHILDREN AND PETS WELCOME. BAR AND RESTAURANT MEALS. WHITBY 12 MILES. S£££, D££.

The Fox Inn

Bow Street, Guisborough, North Yorkshire TS14 6BP • Tel: 01287 632958

Situated just off the main street in the little town of Guisborough near the North Yorkshire Moors. With a wide range of food available, this family-friendly venue is a local favourite. The layout is open-plan, and regular entertainment includes a karaoke evening and DJs. Accommodation is in eight en suite bedrooms, all with modern facilities.

The Three Fiddles

34 Westgate, Guisborough, North Yorkshire TS14 6BA • Tel: 01287 63241

The Three Fiddles is situated in the busy market town of Guisborough. Food is prepared from fresh ingredients and served throughout the day, and amenities include a children's bouncy castle and a beer garden. Accommodation is in five rooms, all with colour TV and tea/coffee making facilities.

www.holidayguides.com

The Foresters Arms

MAIN STREET, GRASSINGTON, SKIPTON, NORTH YORKSHIRE BD23 5AA

The Foresters Arms, Grassington, once an old coaching inn, is situated in the heart of the Yorkshire Dales. An ideal centre for walking or touring. A family-run business for over 40 years, serving hand-pulled traditional ales. Home made food served lunchtime and evening.

All bedrooms are en suite, with satellite TV and tea/coffee making facilities.

Prices £35 single; £70 double. *Proprietor: Rita Richardson*

Tel: 01756 752349 • Fax: 01756 753633
e-mail: theforesters@totalise.co.uk
www.forestersarmsgrassington.co.uk

7 BEDROOMS, ALL WITH PRIVATE BATHROOM. FREE HOUSE WITH REAL ALE. CHILDREN AND PETS WELCOME. BAR AND RESTAURANT MEALS. SKIPTON 8 MILES. S££, D££.

The Cross Keys
Middlesbrough Road, Upsall, Guisborough, North Yorkshire TS14 6RW
Tel: 01287 610035

The Cross Keys is the meeting point for the local branch of CAMRA, and offers all the traditional attractions of the classic English pub, such as low oak beams, wood-panelled recesses and a beer garden where guests have the option of dining alfresco. 20 bedrooms with all modern facilities provide comfortable accommodation.

The Claro Beagle
Ripon Road, Harrogate, North Yorkshire HG1 2JJ • Tel: 01423 569974

A modern-style community pub, with a contemporary bright, fresh look. There is a sports area with pool tables, a dart board and a plasma screen showing live sporting fixtures. Free wifi facility throughout.

RATES   S – SINGLE ROOM rate   D – Sharing DOUBLE/TWIN ROOM
S£ D£ =Under £35   S££ D££ =£36-£45   S£££ D£££ =£46-£55   S££££ D££££ =Over £55
This is meant as an indication only and does not show prices for Special Breaks, Weekends, etc.
Guests are therefore advised to verify all prices on enquiring or booking.

Royal Oak Hotel

**Great Ayton
North Yorkshire**

The Best in Yorkshire Hospitality

The Monaghan family have run The Royal Oak Hotel since 1978. This 18th Century rural hostelry is at the heart of the village. Original features include the beamed ceilings and welcoming log fires, and add to the charm and character of this traditional inn.

The Best Ales in Yorkshire

The lively public bar is popular with visitors and locals alike.

Good ales on tap include Theakston's Old Peculiar, Theakston's bitter, Along with keg ales, lager, cider and a good range of wines and spirits.

The extensive choice of menu at the Royal Oak is not one for the indecisive. Ditherers will find themselves at closing time still unable to choose from the excellent choice.

Food is also available in the tastefully decorated, comfortably rustic bars, and guest bedrooms provide well appointed overnight accommodation, all being en suite, with central heating, colour television and tea-making facilities.

**Royal Oak Hotel
High Green, Great Ayton,
North Yorkshire TS9 6BW
Tel: 01642 722361 • Fax: 01642 724047
e-mail: info@royaloak-hotel.co.uk
www.royaloak-hotel.co.uk**

Derek and Linda Monaghan

The New Inn
BURNT YATES

★★★★ for Accommodation, Food and Service

Situated on the doorstep to the Yorkshire Dales, in the village of Burnt Yates, this beautifully maintained, traditional inn first opened its doors as a hostelry in 1810; today it combines the perfect ingredients for an enjoyable lunch or evening out: a genuine warm welcome, expertly kept real ales, fine wines and delicious food, all home-cooked using high quality local produce.

Comfortable en suite bedrooms make an ideal base for a truly memorable stay.

The beautiful spa town of Harrogate is only a ten minute drive away and you are within easy reach of some of the finest countryside in Britain.

Burnt Yates, Harrogate, North Yorkshire HG3 3EG
Tel: 01423 771070 • Fax: 01423 772360

e-mail: newinnharrogate@btconnect.com
www.thenewinnburntyates.co.uk

8 BEDROOMS, ALL WITH PRIVATE BATHROOM. REAL ALE. CHILDREN AND PETS WELCOME. RESTAURANT MEALS. RIPLEY 2 MILES. S££££. D££-££££.

THE TRAVELLER'S REST
Crimple Lane, Crimple, Harrogate, North Yorkshire HG3 1DF
Tel: 01423 883960

An old fashioned, traditional public house near Harrogate town centre, with low oak beams, a delightful stone-floored section and a charming conservatory leading to the garden area, where alfresco diners can enjoy views of sheep, ducks and swans. Real ales and draught beers are served chilled during summer months.

The Squinting Cat
Lund House Green, Pannal Ash, Harrogate, North Yorkshire HG3 1QF
Tel: 01423 565650

The Squinting Cat is a Two For One public house set in rural surroundings just south of the town centre. Families love to come here for mouth-watering dishes at affordable prices, and facilities include a children's 'Wacky Warehouse' play area and a large beer garden.

ROYAL OAK INN (on facing page)

5 BEDROOMS, ALL WITH PRIVATE BATHROOM. REAL ALE. CHILDREN WELCOME. BAR AND RESTAURANT MEALS. THIRSK 23 MILES, MIDDLESBROUGH 9. S££. D££.

Nestling beneath the rising fells of Langstrothdale, the inn stands in a stunning location overlooking the River Wharfe.

This traditional Dales Inn with flagged floors, stone walls and mullioned windows is the last remaining family-owned freehouse in the parish of Buckden, Upper Wharfedale.

Comfortable accommodation, quality home-cooked food, well kept cask beers from Black Sheep and Copper Dragon Breweries, together with an excellent selection of wines and malts, are on offer in our unique inn.

The George is centrally located in the Yorkshire Dales National Park and is ideal for touring or walking.

GEORGE INN
Kirk Gill, Hubberholme,
Near Skipton,
North Yorkshire BD23 5JE
Tel: 01756 760223
www.thegeorge-inn.co.uk

We have three rooms located in the main pub building on the first floor and three more rooms in the annex building. All rooms are en suite and strictly non smoking. Dogs are not allowed. We have no family rooms and cannot accept children less than 14 years of age.

6 BEDROOMS, ALL WITH PRIVATE BATHROOM. REAL ALE. BAR MEALS. KETTLEWELL 8KM. D££££.

The Crown Inn
High Street, Knaresborough, North Yorkshire HG5 0HB • Tel: 01423 862122

A friendly venue showing live sporting fixtures and hosting regular pool tournaments, the Crown is perfect for a relaxed lunchtime outing or an early evening meal with family or friends. Live music and regular entertainment are popular features.

The Coulby Farm
Coulby Newham, Middlesbrough, North Yorkshire TS8 9DZ
Tel: 01642 594140 • Fax: 01642 590404

The Coulby is a family pub, with good children's facilities and a Two For One food menu to suit all ages. The decor is a pleasant mix of creams and browns with leather sofas, and facilities include a large Fun House with ball pits, slides, and climbing frames.

THE FORRESTERS ARMS HOTEL

Dating from the 12th century, this is one of England's oldest inns. The Henry Dee Bar still retains evidence of the days when it was the stable and the cosy lower bar has an unusual rounded stone chimney breast where log fires exude cheer in chilly weather.

Both bars are furnished with the work of Robert Thompson (the 'Mouseman') who carved a tiny mouse on every piece of furniture produced.

Real ale is available in convivial surroundings and ample and well-presented Yorkshire fare will more than satisfy the healthiest appetite.

This is the heart of James Herriot Country, within the North York Moors National Park, and the hotel is well recommended as a touring base, having outstanding accommodation.

The Forresters Arms, Kilburn, North Yorkshire YO61 4AH
Tel: 01347 868386 • e-mail: admin@forrestersarms.com • www.forrestersarms.com

9 BEDROOMS, ALL WITH PRIVATE BATHROOM. FREE HOUSE WITH REAL ALE. CHILDREN AND PETS WELCOME. BAR AND RESTAURANT MEALS. THIRSK 6 MILES. S££, D££.

The Rudd's Arms

Marton, Middlesbrough, North Yorkshire TS7 8BG • Tel: 01642 315262

After a substantial makeover, the Rudd's Arms features chic furnishings and fittings and a new open-plan layout. The pub is well known for its good quality food, including tapas and breakfast menus and for serving an extensive range of drinks. There are regular quiz nights, plus free wifi and a decked seating area.

The Norman Conquest

Flatts Lane, Middlesbrough, North Yorkshire TS6 0NP • Tel: 01642 454000

A family pub where food is served throughout the day from an inventive menu; customers can dine anywhere in the open plan layout or in the beer garden. Activities include a weekly quiz, karaoke and live entertainment. Children welcome.

THE NEW INN MOTEL
Main Street, Huby, York YO61 IHQ
Tel: 01347 810219

Nine miles north of York in the village of Huby in the Vale of York, the Motel is an ideal base for a couple of nights away to visit York (15 minutes to the nearest long-stay car park), or a longer stay to visit the East Coast of Yorkshire, the Dales, the Yorkshire Moors, Herriot Country, Harrogate and Ripon.

The Motel is situated behind the New Inn (a separate business) which, contrary to its name, is a 500-year old hostelry, originally an old coaching inn, and full of character. All rooms are en suite (singles, doubles, twin and family rooms), and have colour television and tea-making facilities. Good home cooking is served, including vegetarian meals, and a full English breakfast is a speciality.

Pets are welcome (by arrangement)
Special breaks always available
Telephone for brochure

www.newinnmotel.co.uk
enquiries@newinnmotel.freeserve.co.uk

£35-£50 (single)
£60-£70 (double)
Special rates for Short Breaks and weekly rates

AA ★★★
Highly Commended
Guest Accommodation

8 BEDROOMS (NON-SMOKING), ALL WITH PRIVATE BATHROOM. FREE HOUSE WITH REAL ALE. CHILDREN WELCOME. RESTAURANT MEALS. YORK 9 MILES. S££, D£.

THE SOUTHERN CROSS
Dixons Bank, Middlesbrough, North Yorkshire TS7 8NX • Tel: 01642 317539

A large pub situated on a main road in the suburbs of Middlesbrough. Downstairs is a sports bar with four plasma screens, so there's no chance of missing that all important football match. The Two for One Menu is very popular amongst the locals at lunchtimes, and there are regular quizzes and live music.

The Three Jolly Sailors
Burniston, Scarborough, North Yorkshire YO13 0HJ • Tel: 01723 871628

Situated in the quaint village of Burniston just north of Scarborough is this Grade II Listed pub, an ideal stopoff point for ramblers on the Smugglers Walk between Scarborough and Whitby. All dishes are freshly prepared from locally sourced ingredients whenever possible.

The Scarborough
Market Lane, Eastfield, Scarborough, North Yorkshire YO11 3YN
Tel: 01723 582444 • Fax: 01723 582443

A Hungry Horse pub serving food and drink over four floors, with a children's play area on the top floor – a safe and secure place to keep youngsters entertained while parents relax. There is a beer garden, and regular events include pool competitions, karaoke and DJ/fun nights.

The Griffin
42 Micklegate, Selby, North Yorkshire YO8 0EQ
Tel: 01757 703227 • Fax: 01757 704574

A popular spot on the market square in Selby, recently refurbished to create an uplifting atmosphere, with contemporary lighter shades and stylish furnishings. Regular activities include three pool tables, a weekly quiz, karaoke and a live DJ at weekends.

The Londesborough Hotel
Market Place, Selby, North Yorkshire YO8 4NS
Tel: 01757 707355 • Fax: 01757 701607

Brimming with tradition, this friendly bar stocks a good selection of beers, ales and wines, and the kitchen brigade prepares quality meals to suit all tastes. Accommodation is in 23 Laura Ashley-style luxury bedrooms, almost all en suite.

The Windmill
16 - 20 Blossom Street, York, North Yorkshire YO24 1AJ • Tel: 01904 624834

This is a popular and contemporary venue situated in York centre. The menu offers an ample choice of delicious dishes and the bar is stocked with a wide range of drinks. Comfortable accommodation and good service make this an even more attractive prospect.

THE KNAVESMIRE
Albemarke Road, York, North Yorkshire YO23 1ER • Tel: 01904 655927

Located 200 yards from York racecourses, this attractive sports and entertainment bar is well equipped to satisfy all requirements, with four pool tables, a video jukebox, and a bar stocked with a wide range of beers, lagers, ales and wines.

Lendal Cellars
26 Lendal, York, North Yorkshire YO1 8AA • Tel: 01904 623121

Traditional cellar bar situated in the picturesque city of York, with food available from an exciting menu including burgers and other pub food favourites. The bar is well stocked, with guest real ales, lagers, beers and wines. Features include an open-mic night, live bands and an outdoor pool table. Children welcome when dining.

100 NORTH EAST ENGLAND — Northumberland

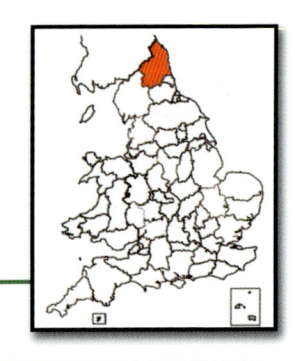

Northumberland

The Rob Roy
Tel & Fax: 01289 306428

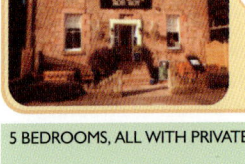

- Situated close to the River Tweed and just five minutes from the centre of the historic town of Berwick-upon-Tweed.
- Fully licensed bar area serving real ales and a good selection of wines. Beer garden with stunning river views.
- Harbour Lights Restaurant offering a superb range of tempting food, with local produce used where possible.

Hosts: Linda & Ian Woods

The Rob Roy, Dock Road • Tweedmouth
Berwick-upon-Tweed • Northumberland • TD15 2BE
e-mail: therobroy@hotmail.co.uk

5 BEDROOMS, ALL WITH PRIVATE BATHROOM. BAR AND RESTAURANT MEALS. NEWCASTLE 58 MILES. S££, D£.

THE COTTAGE INN
CRASTER

- Charming country inn just a short walk from the rugged Northumberland coastline.
- All bedrooms have been renovated, and offer comfortable accommodation overlooking the gardens.
  - En suite facilities • Flat Screen TV with Sky
  - Garden views • Pocket sprung beds
  - Tea and coffee tray • Full central heating
- Easy access for disabled guests (all rooms on ground level)
- Food and ales are sourced locally, and offer a real taste of Northumberland

Dunstan Village, Craster, Alnwick NE66 3SZ
Tel: 01665 576658
e-mail: enquiry@cottageinnhotel.co.uk
www.cottageinnhotel.co.uk

10 BEDROOMS, 8 WITH PRIVATE BATHROOM. REAL ALE. BAR MEALS. CHILDREN WELCOME. ALNWICK 6 MILES.

Family-Friendly
Pubs, Inns & Hotels
See the Supplement on pages 179-182 for establishments which really welcome children

Northumberland NORTH EAST ENGLAND 101

The Bay Horse Inn
West Woodburn, Hexham NE48 2RX
Tel: 01434 270218 • Fax: 01434 270274

A delightful 18thC coaching inn, nestling by a stone bridge over the River Rede. On the A68, 6 miles from Otterburn, 20 miles from Corbridge, 24 miles from Newcastle Airport; ideally placed for Hadrian's Wall, Kielder Water, Alnwick and the Scottish Borders.

- Excellent home-cooked cuisine
- Lounge bar

7 bedrooms, 5 en suite, all individually decorated in a delightful cottage style, with colour TV, tea and coffee making facilities, hairdryer, ironing facilities and a trouser press.

★★★ INN

enquiry@bayhorseinn.org
www.bayhorseinn.org

7 BEDROOMS, 5 WITH PRIVATE BATHROOM. CHILDREN WELCOME. BAR AND RESTAURANT MEALS. OTTERBURN 6 MILES, CORBRIDGE 20 MILES.

Bay Horse Inn
Main Street, West Woodburn, Hexham, Northumberland NE48 2RX
Tel : 01434 270218 • enquiry@bayhorseinn.org • www.bayhorseinn.org

Get active at The Bay Horse, a starting point for touring cyclists/walkers. Try your hand at fishing, horseriding, quad biking or clay target shooting. There are five log cabin-style rooms to choose from; for a romantic weekend away, book the honeymoon suite with its four-poster bed. All pub/restaurant meals prepared from local produce.

Pet-Friendly
Pubs, Inns & Hotels
on pages 174-178
Please note that these establishments may not feature in the main section of this book

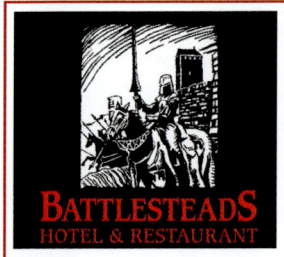

Wark Hexham Northumberland NE48 3LS
01434 230209

Dating from 1747, this stone-built inn and restaurant features excellent bar meals and à la carte menus, good choice of wines, and cask and conditioned beers. A friendly, family-run hotel, with 17 en suite bedrooms, including ground floor rooms with disabled access, it is ideally placed for Hadrian's Wall, Kielder and Border Reiver Country.
• Pets are very welcome by prior arrangement.

From £50-£60pppn

e-mail: info@battlesteads.com
www.battlesteads.com

17 BEDROOMS, ALL WITH PRIVATE BATHROOM. ALL BEDROOMS NON-SMOKING. PETS WELCOME. BAR MEALS. NEWCASTLE 20 MILES. S££££, D£££.

RATES

Normal Bed & Breakfast rate per person
(single room)

PRICE RANGE	CATEGORY
Under £35	S£
£36-£45	S££
£46-£55	S£££
Over £55	S££££

Normal Bed & Breakfast rate per person
(sharing double/twin room)

PRICE RANGE	CATEGORY
Under £35	D£
£36-£45	D££
£46-£55	D£££
Over £55	D££££

This is meant as an indication only and does not show prices for Special Breaks, Weekends, etc. Guests are therefore advised to verify all prices on enquiring or booking.

Northumberland NORTH EAST ENGLAND 103

The Anglers Arms
A Legend in the very Heart of Northumberland

This traditional Coaching Inn is situated only 6 miles from Morpeth, beside picturesque Weldon Bridge on the River Coquet. Bedrooms are cosy and welcoming, with a touch of olde worlde charm. Be prepared for a hearty Northumbrian breakfast!

Meals can be be enjoyed in the friendly bar, or outdoors on sunny summer days; alternatively dine in style and sophistication in the à la carte Pullman Railway Carriage restaurant. Ideal for exploring both coast and country, the Inn also caters for fishermen, with its own one-mile stretch of the River Coquet available free to residents.

The Anglers Arms
Weldon Bridge, Longframlington,
Northumberland NE65 8AX
Tel: 01665 570271/570655
Fax: 01665 570041
info@anglersarms.fsnet.co.uk
www.anglersarms.com

8 BEDROOMS, ALL WITH PRIVATE BATHROOM. FREE HOUSE WITH REAL ALE. CHILDREN WELCOME. BAR AND RESTAURANT MEALS. NON-SMOKING AREAS. ROTHBURY 5 MILES. S£££, D££.

There really is something to suit everyone in **NORTHUMBERLAND**. Hadrian's Wall is one of the best examples of the Roman occupation, the turmoil of the wars with the Scots has left fortresses and castles to visit, while the advent of Christianity on Holy Island leaves a more peaceful image. Learn more about British history and enjoy the freedom of the open spaces of this lovely region.

Rambling over the heather-clad Cheviot moorlands, exploring the castles and pele towers built to ward off invading Scots, watching the feast of wildlife on the coast and in the countryside, breathing in the wonderful sea air on a golden sandy beach, you'll find it all in Northumberland. Rare and endangered wildlife is found all along the coast and the ultimate destination for enthusiasts is the Farne Islands, with boat trips from the family resort of Seahouses to watch the grey seals and seabirds, including puffins, in the breeding seasons. Stormy weather may delay the crossing, and the Grace Darling Museum at Bamborough is a reminder of the dangers of this sometimes tempestuous sea.

www.holidayguides.com

104 **NORTH EAST ENGLAND** Northumberland

THE OLDE SHIP HOTEL

**Main Street,
Seahouses,
Northumberland
NE68 7RD
Tel: 01665 720200
Fax: 01665 720383**

A former farmhouse dating from 1745, the inn stands overlooking the harbour in the village of Seahouses.

The Olde Ship, first licensed in 1812, has been in the same family for 100 years and is now a fully residential hotel. All guest rooms, including three with four-poster beds, and executive suites with lounges and sea views, are en suite, with television, refreshment facilities and direct-dial telephone. The bars and corridors bulge at the seams with nautical memorabilia. Good home cooking features locally caught seafood, along with soups, puddings and casseroles

www.seahouses.co.uk • e-mail: theoldeship@seahouses.co.uk

18 BEDROOMS, ALL WITH PRIVATE BATHROOM. ALL BEDROOMS NON-SMOKING. FREE HOUSE WITH REAL ALE. CHILDREN OVER 10 YEARS WELCOME IF STAYING IN HOTEL. BAR AND RESTAURANT MEALS. BAMBURGH 3 MILES. S££, D££££.

The Northumberland coast is a designated Area of Outstanding Natural Beauty, and keen walkers can take the Coast Path from the walled Georgian market town
of Berwick-on-Tweed to Cresswell, stopping at little fishing villages on the way. For a shorter route, follow the section along Embleton beach from Craster, best known for its traditionally smoked kippers, to get the best views of the ruins of Dunstanburgh Castle. The award-winning beach and village of Bamburgh are dominated by the castle, rebuilt on a rocky headland site inhabited since prehistoric times. View the castle collections, and even take part in an archaeological dig.
Just to the north is the causeway access (beware of the tides!) to the Holy Island of Lindisfarne where St Aidan introduced Christianity to England. A visit to the lively market town of Alnwick and the castle, Hogwarts in the Harry Potter films, is a must. Here in the newly redeveloped gardens you will find magnificent water features and even a poison garden!

Tyne & Wear

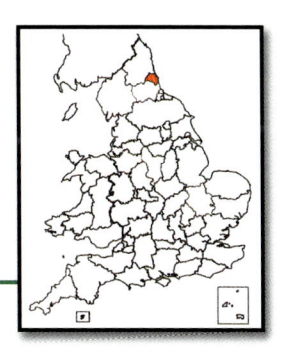

The Gold Medal
Chowdene Bank, Gateshead, Tyne and Wear NE9 6JP • Tel: 0191 4821549
Family pub situated in Gateshead, where drinks and food are served with a smile and both are reasonably priced and generous in quantity. There is regular entertainment, perhaps a quiz, live music, or even live sporting fixtures shown on the big screen.

The Guide Post
Makepeace Terrace, Springwell, Gateshead, Tyne & Wear NE9 7RR
Tel: 0191 4160298 • Fax: 0191 4179841
Situated between Gateshead and Washington, this popular spot attracts a friendly crowd made up of students, regulars and passers by. The food menu is popular, particularly the Sunday Roasts. Attractions include a pool table, dart board, and a big screen TV, plus regular quizzes and live music.

The Beaconsfield
Beaconsfield Road, Low Fell, Gateshead, Tyne and Wear NE9 5EU • Tel: 0191 4820125
Shades of cream, red ochre and sage green, plus suede seats and oak flooring, enhance the elegant decor of this modern venue in Gateshead. Hot and cold snacks are served throughout the day, every day, and live sporting fixtures are shown on large plasma screens.

Looking for holiday accommodation?
for details of hundreds of properties
throughout the UK including
comprehensive coverage of all areas of Scotland try:
www.holidayguides.com

THE LONSDALE
West Jesmond, Newcastle-upon-Tyne, Tyne & Wear NE2 3HQ • Tel: 0191 2810039
Students love this pub venue situated in a popular area just outside West Jesmond. Customers enjoy the live sporting fixtures shown on the big screens, plasma screen or one of the other TVs. Attractions include two pool tables, quiz nights and live bands.

The Corner House
Heaton, Newcastle-upon-Tyne, Tyne & Wear NE6 5RP • Tel: 0191 2659602
Open-plan corner pub with a distinctive long bar, ideal for an after-work drink or meal. The staff are welcoming and add to the relaxed atmosphere. Facilities include a pool table, dart board, quizzes and big screen TVs. Accommodation is in 10 bedrooms (double, twin and family), all with modern facilities.

The Newton Park
Longbenton, Newcastle-upon-Tyne, Tyne & Wear NE7 7EB
Tel: 0191 266 2010 • www.newtonparkheaton.co.uk
Situated next to the Ministry in Benton Park, this U-shaped open-plan bar boasts comfortable sofas and an imaginative food menu. Attractions include a games room, real ale bar, function room and dining area.

The Eye on The Tyne
Broad Chare, Newcastle-upon-Tyne, Tyne & Wear NE1 3DQ • Tel: 0191 2617385
Located in the middle of a prestigious part of the city centre, close to local hotels, and with the Law Courts nearby, this pub attracts a varied clientele. The in-house coffee shop serves coffee and freshly prepared food from 11am.

The Crows Nest
Percy Street, Newcastle-upon-Tyne, Tyne & Wear NE1 7RY • Tel: 0191 2612607
Formerly Bar Oz, the theme is fun, with fantastic food! Convenient for the two universities of Newcastle and Northumbria, the pub is very popular with students. It offers a good choice of draught beers and real ales, with a lively atmosphere during big matches shown on TV.

The Bourgognes
78 Newgate Street, Newcastle upon Tyne, Tyne & Wear NE1 5RQ • Tel: 0191 2326212
Located next to Eldon Square shopping centre and just a short distance from St James' football ground. With leather couches, wooden floors and carpeted recesses, this friendly pub is popular with students who appreciate the reasonably priced fare.

Cheshire

The Pheasant Inn

Tucked in a peaceful corner of rural Cheshire, the 300-year-old Pheasant Inn at Higher Burwardsley stands atop the Peckforton Hills, with the most magnificent panoramic views of the Cheshire plains. Whether you come to drink, dine or unwind for a few days in one of our 12 en suite bedrooms, this atmospheric location will quickly have you under its spell. Freshly cooked wholesome food using local produce is on the menu, rewarded for its quality with a listing in the Michelin Good Pub Guide and Egon Ronay Guide. Delightful old sandstone buildings, open log fires, and the friendly, cosy atmosphere all add to the magic!

The Pheasant Inn
Higher Burwardsley, Tattenhall
Cheshire CH3 9PF
Tel: 01829 770434 • Fax: 01829 771097
e-mail: info@thepheasantinn.co.uk • www.thepheasantinn.co.uk

12 BEDROOMS, ALL WITH PRIVATE BATHROOM. ALL BEDROOMS NON-SMOKING. FREE HOUSE WITH REAL ALE. CHILDREN AND PETS WELCOME. BAR AND RESTAURANT MEALS. CHESTER 9 MILES. S££££, D££.

Pet-Friendly
Pubs, Inns & Hotels
on pages 174-178
Please note that these establishments may not feature in the main section of this book

The Plough
AT EATON

**Macclesfield Road, Eaton,
Near Congleton, Cheshire CW12 2NH
Tel: 01260 280207 • Fax: 01260 298458**

Traditional oak beams and blazing log fires in winter reflect the warm and friendly atmosphere of this half-timbered former coaching inn which dates from the 17th century.

The heart of the 'Plough' is the kitchen where food skilfully prepared is calculated to satisfy the most discerning palate. Luncheons and dinners are served seven days a week with traditional roasts on Sundays.

In peaceful, rolling countryside near the Cheshire/Staffordshire border, this is a tranquil place in which to stay and the hostelry has elegantly colour-co-ordinated guest rooms, all with spacious bathrooms, LCD colour television, direct-dial telephone and tea and coffee-making facilities amongst their impressive appointments. Wireless internet access available.

e-mail: theploughinn@hotmail.co.uk
www.theploughinnateaton.co.uk

The De Trafford
Congleton Road, Alderley Edge, Cheshire SK9 7AA
Tel: 01625 583881 • Fax: 01625 586625

Cobblestone surroundings lead prospective visitors to this elegant inn located in Alderley Edge. Tradition is paramount, with open fires, candlelit tables and cosy nooks for private dining. Accommodation is next door – all bedrooms are en suite, with colour TV and tea/coffee making facilities.

The Shrewsbury Arms
Warrington Road, Mickle Trafford, Chester, Cheshire CH2 4EB • Tel: 01244 300309

The Shrewsbury Arms has everything one could want in a country pub – low oak beams, slate flooring and an impressive stock of cask ales, fine wines and beers. The pub's menu features traditional favourites prepared from fresh fish and locally sourced meat, and a Sunday Roast.

The Oaklands
93 Hoole Road, Chester, Cheshire CH2 3NB • Tel: 01244 345528

A peaceful spot set in an idyllic part of Chester, serving real ales, fine wines and hearty pub meals. There is regular entertainment, and large TV screens mean you can count on the Oaklands for those all-important football matches!

Bromfield Arms
43 Faulkener Street, Chester, Cheshire CH2 3BD • Tel: 01244 345037

Located close to the zoo in Chester is this Cask Marque accredited pub with a pool room and snug. Customers need no encouragement to sample the real ales and delicious meals on offer. There is a weekly quiz, and live sporting fixtures are shown on a large screen TV.

THE WHITE LION
Manley Road, Alvanley, Frodsham, Cheshire WA6 9DD • Tel: 01928 722949

Alvanley is an idyllic location with breathtaking views all around. The White Lion upholds all the traditional pub values, with wooden beams, good food and the warmth of two real fires in winter. There is a good choice of quality wines, real ales and draught beers.

THE PLOUGH AT EATON (on facing page)

17 BEDROOMS, ALL WITH PRIVATE BATHROOM. ALL BEDROOMS NON-SMOKING. FREE HOUSE WITH REAL ALE. CHILDREN WELCOME. BAR AND RESTAURANT MEALS. CONGLETON 2 MILES. S££££, D££££.

Cumbria

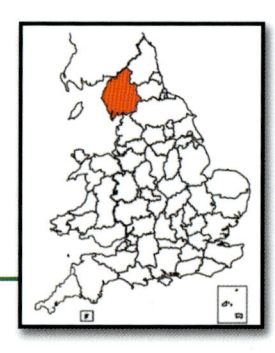

THE EASTERN FELLS, Lake District...where dogs stay for *free!*

the mardale inn @ st. patrick's well
Bampton, Cumbria, CA10 2RQ

Early 18th century Lake District inn. Fresh local food served all day including £5 two-course Farmer's Meal on weekday lunch times (please ring for a table). Hand pulled Cumbrian real ales plus regular guest ale and great wines. Extensive bottled beer list. Fine accommodation. Fantastic walking around nearby Haweswater. Real fires and a warm welcome. Featured in Daily Telegraph '50 Best Pubs' - May '08.

www.mardaleinn.co.uk
info@mardaleinn.co.uk

ETC ★★★★

tel: 01931 713244

Children and dogs welcome *(please note that children must be kept on a short leash at all times!)*

the greyhound @ shap
Main St, Shap, CA10 2PW

The Greyhound @ Shap is a perfect motorway stop-off on the edge of the Lake District. M6 J39 only 5 minutes. Coaching Inn dating from the 15th century. Hand pulled real ales plus regular guest ales. Extensive wine list (also available by the glass). Traditional local food served daily. Great walks from the door onto the Eastern fells. 10 bedrooms with en-suite facilities. Families and walkers welcome. Fantastic Sunday lunch!

tel: 01931 716474

www.greyhoundshap.co.uk
info@greyhoundshap.co.uk

Always open—fresh local produce—open fires—fine cask beers—warm beds

---

MARDALE INN: 4 BEDROOMS, ALL WITH PRIVATE BATHROOM. ALL BEDROOMS NON-SMOKING. FREE HOUSE WITH REAL ALE. CHILDREN AND PETS WELCOME. BAR MEALS, RESTAURANT EVENINGS ONLY. SHAP 3 MILES. S££, D££.

GREYHOUND: 10 BEDROOMS, ALL WITH PRIVATE BATHROOM. ALL BEDROOMS NON-SMOKING. ENTERPRISE INNS HOUSE WITH REAL ALE. CHILDREN AND PETS WELCOME. BAR AND RESTAURANT MEALS. SHAP 3 MILES. S££, D££.

Please mention **FHG's Pubs & Inns of Britain**
when making enquiries about accommodation featured in these pages

The Blacksmith's Arms offers all the hospitality and comforts of a traditional country inn. Enjoy tasty meals served in the bar lounges, or linger over dinner in the well-appointed restaurant. The inn is personally managed by the proprietors, Anne and Donald Jackson, who guarantee the hospitality one would expect from a family concern. Guests are assured of a pleasant and comfortable stay. There are eight lovely bedrooms, all en suite. Peacefully situated in the beautiful village of Talkin, the inn is convenient for the Borders, Hadrian's Wall and the Lake District. There is a good golf course, walking and other country pursuits nearby.

Talkin Village, Brampton, Cumbria
CA8 1LE
Tel: 016977 3452
Fax: 016977 3396

e-mail: blacksmithsarmstalkin@yahoo.co.uk • www.blacksmithstalkin.co.uk

8 BEDROOMS, ALL WITH PRIVATE BATHROOM. ALL BEDROOMS NON-SMOKING. FREE HOUSE WITH REAL ALE. BAR AND RESTAURANT MEALS. CARLISLE 9 MILES. S££, D£.

The Turk's Head

Market Square, Alston, Cumbria CA9 3HS • Tel: 01434 381148

For those in search of an olde world bar with the very best in draught beers and real ales – this is the place. Food is served in the lounge bar at the rear of the pub.

The Sportsman Inn

Compston Road, Ambleside, Cumbria LA22 9DR • Tel: 01539 432535

Set in the lovely village of Ambleside is this welcoming pub and lounge bar. Food is served throughout the day from an extensive menu of pub food favourites. There is an upstairs bar and a basement bar, where discos are regularly held.

The Black Cock Inn

The Black Cock Inn stands at the heart of the attractive little town of Broughton-in-Furness, within easy reach of some of the Lake District's finest scenery. This much-loved village inn is full of history, charm and atmosphere. This 16th century Inn with its low beamed ceiling boasts a suntrap courtyard garden during the summer and a roaring log fire during the winter months, giving it a wonderful traditional ambience.

**Princes Street,
Broughton-in-Furness
Cumbria LA20 6HQ
Tel: 01229 716529
www.blackcockinncumbria.com**

There's always a selection of real ales and lagers on offer in the bar which is open from morning 'til night, every day.

The inn has five comfortable and very well appointed en suite guest bedrooms.

There is excellent walking country in the area, with plenty of history and natural features to discover, and Broughton itself is well worth taking time to explore.

5 BEDROOMS, ALL WITH PRIVATE BATHROOM. FREE HOUSE WITH REAL ALES. CHILDREN AND PETS WELCOME. BAR AND RESTAURANT MEALS. ULVERSTON 8 MILES. S£, D£.

The Drunken Duck Inn
**Barngates, Ambleside, Cumbria LA22 0NG
Tel: 015394 36347 • www.drunkenduckinn.co.uk**

This restaurant inn is very lively in the evenings and is especially popular for its imaginative food menu, which is changed regularly. It has a charming beer garden – perfect during summer months.

The Owl & Pussycat

Hindpool Road, Barrow in Furness, Cumbria LA14 2NA • Tel: 01229 824334

A purpose-built pub with a stylish modern interior and a contemporary carvery offering excellent cuisine. There is an indoor play area where children can escape to, leaving mum and dad in peace!

THE SUN INN (on facing page)

8 BEDROOMS, ALL WITH PRIVATE BATHROOM. ALL BEDROOMS NON-SMOKING. FREE HOUSE WITH REAL ALE. CHILDREN AND PETS WELCOME. RESTAURANT MEALS. NON-SMOKING AREAS. AMBLESIDE 6 MILES. S££, D£££.

Cumbria — NORTH WEST ENGLAND 113

The Sun
CONISTON

bar, restaurant & 4 star inn

The Sun in Coniston has been here for something like 400 years at the start of the mountains and the pack horse trails to the West. Forever associated with Donald Campbell and his world water speed record attempts, the pub remains a classic Lakeland Inn of rare quality.

It offers a unique mix of bar, restaurant & four star inn, with the kind of comfortable informality and atmosphere that many attempt but few achieve.

At its heart is a great bar with 8 real ales on hand-pull, 4 draft lagers, 20+ malts and 30+ wines. The food is freshly prepared using locally sourced ingredients and can be enjoyed in the bar, in the conservatory, outside on the front & on the terrace. The 8 recently refurbished ensuite bedrooms overlook the village with superb panoramic views. Extra thick mattresses & quality comforters help ensure a good nights sleep.

enjoyEngland.com
★★★★ INN

THE SUN CONISTON LA21 8HQ
tel 015394 41248   fax 015394 41219   email info@thesunconiston.com
www.thesunconiston.com

The Sun Inn

www.dentbrewery.co.uk

Main Street, Dent, Sedbergh, Cumbria LA10 5QL
Tel: 01539 625208 • e-mail: thesun@dentbrewery.co.uk

Dent, with its quaint narrow cobbled street lined with stone cottages, some dating from the 15th and 16th centuries, is within the Yorkshire Dales National Park and, completely unspoiled, is a most relaxing holiday venue. So, too, is the Sun's bar, a convivial retreat that will soon cast its spell on all who enter, a happy mood influenced not only by its coin-studded beams, open coal fire and fascinating collection of local photographs, but also by its traditional ales and tempting variety of straightforward meals.

A homely place in which to stay, this friendly hostelry has comfortable rooms with washbasin, colour television and tea and coffee-making facilities.

4 BEDROOMS. DENT BREWERY HOUSE WITH REAL ALE. CHILDREN AND PETS WELCOME. BAR MEALS. NON-SMOKING AREAS. SEDBERGH 4 MILES. S£, D£.

The Langstrath Country Inn

Stonethwaite, Borrowdale, Cumbria CA12 5XG
Tel: 01768 777239 • Fax: 01768 777015 • www.thelangstrath.com

A family-run retreat, ideal for ramblers and countryside enthusiasts, this beautiful inn was originally a miner's cottage but now boasts nine bedrooms with modern facilities. The cuisine is homemade and delicious, and food is served throughout the day. The downstairs lounge is welcoming, with an open fire and well stocked bar.

The Old Captain's House

Springfield Road, Bigrigg, Cumbria CA22 2TN • Tel: 01946 814392

The only pub in the village of Bigrigg, where food is sourced locally and is prepared from the freshest ingredients. Amenities include a dart and dominoes team as well as a pool table and jukebox.

www.holidayguides.com

The Fox & Hounds Inn

Ennerdale Bridge, Lake District CA23 3AR
Tel: 01946 862212 • e-mail: foxandhound@btconnect.com
Accommodation ~ Restaurant ~ Bar

...with an informal and relaxed atmosphere and situated on one of the most attractive stretches of Wainwright's Coast to Coast walk, this splendid inn presents first-rate food and accommodation.

The Inn is situated in the centre of the village opposite the 17th century church and restored cottages, and has a small stream running alongside it.
Several local beers, including real ales, are served alongside the gastro-style menu, using locally sourced quality meat, fish and produce.
In the three letting rooms traditional comforts are much in evidence including central heating, colour televisions and tea/coffee facilities.

Although one of the smaller lakes, Ennerdale can fairly claim to be the most beautiful. From here, valley paths, forest tracks and lake shores offer a variety of rewarding walks suitable for all ages and capabilities.
Other activities in the locality include fishing, canoeing, birdwatching and pony trekking.

3 BEDROOMS. REAL ALE. WHITEHAVEN 8 MILES.

The Beehive

Warwick Road, Carlisle, Cumbria CA1 1LH
Tel: 01228 549731 • Fax: 01228 510152

A John Barras pub located just a short distance from Carlisle city centre and close to Carlisle United Football Ground. The bar is well stocked well with draught beers and real ales, and live sporting fixtures are shown regularly on the big screen.

The Turf Tavern

New Market Road, Carlisle, Cumbria CA1 1JG • Tel: 01228 515367

Families enjoy the atmosphere at this Grade I Listed building, where a selection of delicious and affordable dishes is served throughout the day from a wide-ranging menu. The bar stocks a wide range of lagers, beers, wines and spirits, and there are two pool tables, a jukebox and Sky TV.

The Shepherds Arms Hotel

A gem of a country house hotel and inn, offering first-rate en suite accommodation, an extensive bar menu of home-cooked dishes, and a fine selection of real ales. Ennerdale Bridge is situated on one of the most beautiful stretches of Wainwright's Coast to Coast Walk and very popular with walkers.

The hotel has two twin and two double en suite bedrooms, and one twin/one small double room with private bath and shower. All are non-smoking and have telephone, digital TV, radio alarm, and tea/coffee making facilities. Breakfast is served in the Georgian panelled dining room. Complement your meal with a selection of fine wines and relax afterwards in the comfortable lounge with its open log fire.

The Shepherds Arms bar is open to the public and is included in *The Good Pub Guide* and CAMRA *Good Beer Guide*. Specialities are real ales and home-cooked locally sourced produce from the extensive bar menu. Packed lunches and bikes for hire.

Ennerdale Bridge, Lake District National Park CA23 3AR
Tel: 01946 861249
e-mail: shepherdsarms@btconnect.com
www.shepherdsarmshotel.co.uk

6 BEDROOMS, ALL WITH PRIVATE BATHROOM. ALL BEDROOMS NON-SMOKING. FREE HOUSE WITH REAL ALE. CHILDREN AND PETS WELCOME. BAR MEALS. WHITEHAVEN 8 MILES. S£££, D£££.

The Punch Bowl

Crosthwaite, Near Kendal, Cumbria LA8 8HR
Tel: 01539 568237 • Fax:01539 568875 • www.the-punchbowl.co.uk

Low ceilings and oak beams are an attractive feature here, and log fires are cosy during the colder winter months. The patio overlooks the scenic Lyth Valley, and the comfortable accommodation has all modern facilities.

Family-Friendly
Pubs, Inns & Hotels

See the Supplement on pages 179-182 for establishments which really welcome children

THE BOOT INN (on facing page)

9 BEDROOMS, ALL WITH PRIVATE BATHROOM. REAL ALE. ALL BEDROOMS NON-SMOKING. CHILDREN AND PETS WELCOME. BAR AND RESTAURANT MEALS. RAVENGLASS 6 MILES. S££, D££.

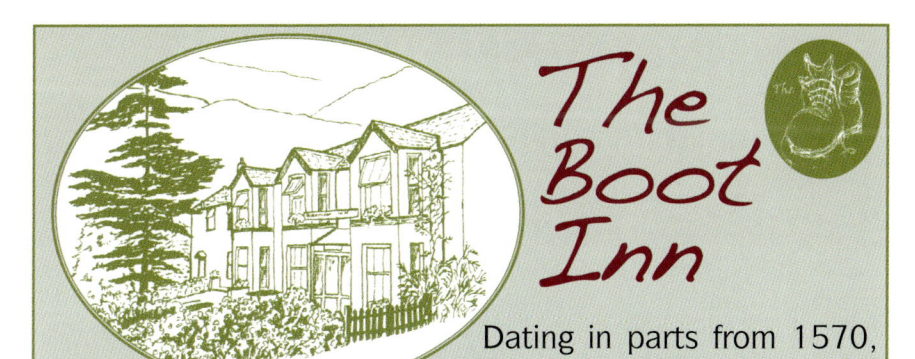

The Boot Inn

Dating in parts from 1570, family-run Boot Inn is in the centre of the tiny village of Boot in Eskdale. This stunning valley offers superb walks for all abilities from a riverside stroll to an assault on Scafell straight from our door.

There are 9 comfortable en suite rooms, a lovely beer garden with separate children's play areas and wonderful fell views.

Pet friendly.

In the restaurant, the bar or the conservatory, we offer a comprehensive menu and a daily Chef's Specials board. All our food is homemade using local produce wherever possible as we are very aware of the impact of 'food miles', including free range eggs from Penny Hill Hens, Bewley's beef and Cumberland Sausages, potatoes from the sandy soil of Gosforth and local cheeses.

We specialise in traditional and hearty home cooking and baking.

The Restaurant

Special Breaks available. Call for a brochure.

The Boot Inn, Boot, Eskdale, Cumbria CA19 1TG
Tel: 019467 23224
e-mail: enquiries@bootinn.co.uk
www.bootinn.co.uk

BROOK HOUSE INN
Boot, Eskdale, Cumbria CA19 1TG
Tel: 019467 23288 • Fax: 019467 23160
e-mail: stay@brookhouseinn.co.uk
www.brookhouseinn.co.uk

An ideal place from which to explore the unspoilt western fells and valleys, the tastefully furnished Brook House is a walker's paradise. It nestles in the heart of Eskdale amidst an enchanted landscape of tinkling streams, forests and waterfalls, all abounding with a vast variety of wildlife. In the bar, a selection of real ales is treated with tender loving care and includes several local brews, whilst delicious home-made dishes are available, complemented by an interesting wine list. The guest rooms all have a bath and shower, central heating, colour television, radio, tea and coffee-making facilities and fine views.

AA ★★★★ INN

7 BEDROOMS, ALL WITH PRIVATE BATHROOM. ALL BEDROOMS NON-SMOKING. FREE HOUSE WITH REAL ALE. CHILDREN WELCOME. BAR AND RESTAURANT MEALS. RAVENGLASS 6 MILES. S£££££, D££.

Queen's Head Hotel • Hawkshead

Surrounded by fells and forests, close to Lake Windermere and centrally positioned to explore the whole of the Lake District, the Queen's Head offers every element of a perfect stay. All bedrooms have en suite or private bathrooms; luxurious 4-posters for romantic breaks. Two charming cottages and a cosy studio apartment, all fully equipped, are available for self-catering.

Tel: 015394 36271 • Freephone: 0800 137263
Main Street, Hawkshead, Cumbria LA22 0NS
e-mail: enquiries@queensheadhotel.co.uk
www.queensheadhotel.co.uk   AA/ETC ★★ AA Rosette

14 BEDROOMS, ALL EN SUITE. ALL BEDROOMS NON-SMOKING. ROBINSONS HOUSE WITH REAL ALE. CHILDREN WELCOME. BAR AND RESTAURANT MEALS. AMBLESIDE 4 MILES. S£££/££££, D££/££££.

www.holidayguides.com

THE KINGS ARMS HOTEL
Hawkshead, Ambleside,
Cumbria LA22 0NZ
Tel: 015394 36372
www.kingsarmshawkshead.co.uk

Join us for a relaxing stay amidst the green hills and dales of Lakeland, and we will be delighted to offer you good food, homely comfort and warm hospitality in historic surroundings.

We hope to see you soon!

- SELF-CATERING COTTAGES ALSO AVAILABLE -

9 BEDROOMS, ALL WITH PRIVATE BATHROOM. ALL BEDROOMS NON-SMOKING. FREE HOUSE WITH REAL ALE. CHILDREN AND PETS WELCOME. BAR AND RESTAURANT MEALS. DESIGNATED COVERED SMOKING AREA. AMBLESIDE 4 MILES. S£££, D££.

Coledale INN
Braithwaite,
Near Keswick CA12 5TN
Tel: 017687 78272
Fax: 017687 78416

A friendly, family-run Victorian Inn in a peaceful hillside position above Braithwaite, and ideally situated for touring and walking, with paths to the mountains immediately outside our gardens. All bedrooms are warm and spacious, with en suite shower room and colour television. Children are welcome, as are pets. Home-cooked meals are served every lunchtime and evening, with a fine selection of inexpensive wines, beers and Jennings, Yates and Theakstons real cask ale. Open all year except midweek lunches in winter. Tariff and menu sent on request.

www.coledale-inn.co.uk
info@coledale-inn.co.uk

20 BEDROOMS, ALL WITH PRIVATE BATHROOM. FREE HOUSE WITH REAL ALE. CHILDREN AND PETS WELCOME. BAR AND RESTAURANT MEALS. NON-SMOKING AREAS. KESWICK 2 MILES. S£, D£.

Please mention FHG Guides when booking

Horse & Farrier Inn
Threlkeld, Keswick CA12 4SQ

The Horse & Farrier has enjoyed an idyllic location in the centre of the picturesque village of Threlkeld, just 4 miles east of Keswick in Cumbria, for over 300 years. Built in 1688 and situated beneath Blencathra, with stunning views looking over towards the Helvellyn Range, this traditional Lakeland Inn offers a warm Cumbrian welcome to all its customers.

Mellow Lakeland stone, traditional architecture and such a peaceful setting make the Horse & Farrier a perfect place to enjoy a quiet pint, delicious food or a short break "away from it all". With superb Lakeland walks on your doorstep including Blencathra and Skiddaw and the Cumbria Way, we're ideally situated for walkers.

Our Restaurant is well known locally for the quality and imagination of its food and our Bar serves some of the best Jennings real ales in the Lake District.

Together with our well appointed en suite bed & breakfast accommodation, this really is a special place to spend some time.

Tel: 017687 79688 • Fax: 017687 79823
info@horseandfarrier.com   www.horseandfarrier.com

9 BEDROOMS, ALL WITH PRIVATE BATHROOM. FREE HOUSE WITH REAL ALE. CHILDREN WELCOME. BAR AND RESTAURANT MEALS. KESWICK 4 MILES.

RATES

Normal Bed & Breakfast rate per person
(single room)

PRICE RANGE	CATEGORY
Under £35	S£
£36-£45	S££
£46-£55	S£££
Over £55	S££££

Normal Bed & Breakfast rate per person
(sharing double/twin room)

PRICE RANGE	CATEGORY
Under £35	D£
£36-£45	D££
£46-£55	D£££
Over £55	D££££

This is meant as an indication only and does not show prices for Special Breaks, Weekends, etc. Guests are therefore advised to verify all prices on enquiring or booking.

Barbon Inn
**Barbon,
Near Kirkby Lonsdale
Cumbria LA6 2LJ
Tel & Fax: 015242 76233**

If you are torn between the scenic delights of the Lake District and the Yorkshire Dales, then you can have the best of both worlds by making your base this friendly 17th century coaching inn nestling in the pretty village of Barbon.

Individually furnished bedrooms provide cosy accommodation, and for that extra touch of luxury enquire about the elegant mini-suite with its mahogany four-poster bed.

Fresh local produce is featured on the good value menus presented in the bar and restaurant, and the Sunday roast lunch with all the trimmings attracts patrons from near and far. A wide range of country pursuits can be enjoyed in the immediate area

Bedrooms, dining room and lounge non-smoking.

www.barbon-inn.co.uk

10 BEDROOMS, ALL WITH PRIVATE BATHROOM. ALL BEDROOMS NON-SMOKING. FREE HOUSE WITH REAL ALE. CHILDREN AND PETS WELCOME. BAR AND RESTAURANT MEALS. KIRKBY LONSDALE 3 MILES. S££££, D££££.

The region now known as **Cumbria**, in England's north west, has been attracting tourists since the end of the 17th century, and the number of visitors has been increasing ever since. The stunning scenery has been extolled by countless travel writers, in fact the poet Wordsworth published his Guide to the Lakes as early as 1810. From the Solway Firth in the north to the coasts of Morecambe Bay in the south, the ports and seaside villages in the west to the Pennines in the east, and including the Lake District National Park, there are outdoor activities.

The area is a walkers' paradise, and whether on foot, in a wheelchair or a pushchair there's a path and trail for everyone. There are magnificent views from the lakesides as well as from the hill and mountain tops, so whether you're following one of the 'Miles without Stiles' on relatively level, well laid tracks around the towns and villages, climbing in the Langdales or tackling Scafell Pike, the highest mountain in England, you won't miss out on all the Lake District has to offer.

The Snooty Fox
Main Street, Kirkby Lonsdale, Cumbria LA6 2AJ

The Snooty Fox is a charming Jacobean Inn, with 9 en suite rooms and a restaurant offering the finest local, seasonal produce. Situated in the heart of the market town of Kirkby Lonsdale and boasting a range of fine cask ales and malt whiskies. The Snooty Fox is the perfect base from which to explore both the Lake District and Yorkshire Dales.

Tel: 01524 271308 • www.thesnootyfoxhotel.co.uk

9 BEDROOMS, ALL WITH PRIVATE BATHROOM. ALL BEDROOMS NON-SMOKING. ENTERPRISE INNS HOUSE WITH REAL ALE. CHILDREN AND PETS WELCOME. RESTAURANT MEALS. DESIGNATED COVERED SMOKING AREA. LANCASTER 14 MILES. S£££, D££.

THE BRITANNIA INN

Book with this advert and claim a FREE bottle of French house wine at dinner

Elterwater, Langdale, Cumbria LA22 9HP
Tel: 015394 37210

A 500 year-old quintessential Lakeland Inn nestled in the centre of the picturesque village of Elterwater amidst the imposing fells of the Langdale Valley. Comfortable, high quality en suite double and twin-bedded rooms. Dogs welcome. Enquire about our Mid-Week Special Offer of three nights B&B for the price of two. Relax in the oak-beamed Bars or Dining Room whilst sampling local real ales and dishes from our extensive menu of fresh, home-cooked food using lots of Cumbrian produce. *Quiz Night most Sundays.*

www.britinn.co.uk • e-mail: info@britinn.co.uk

9 BEDROOMS, ALL WITH PRIVATE BATHROOM. ALL BEDROOMS NON-SMOKING. FREE HOUSE WITH REAL ALE. CHILDREN AND PETS WELCOME. BAR MEALS, RESTAURANT EVENINGS ONLY. AMBLESIDE 3 MILES. S££££, D££.

RATES

S – SINGLE ROOM rate   D – Sharing DOUBLE/TWIN ROOM

S£ D£ =Under £35   S££ D££ =£36-£45   S£££ D£££ =£46-£55   S££££ D££££ =Over £55

This is meant as an indication only and does not show prices for Special Breaks, Weekends, etc. Guests are therefore advised to verify all prices on enquiring or booking.

Cumbria NORTH WEST ENGLAND 123

Tower Bank Arms

Near Sawrey, Ambleside LA22 0LF
Tel: 015394 36334
enquiries@towerbankarms.com

Popular with tourists visiting Beatrix Potter's farmhouse, Hill Top, which adjoins the inn, this appealing cream and green hostelry is particularly recommended as somewhere where one can relax and savour the traditional country atmosphere.

A fine selection of Cumbrian real ales is always available, and food ranges from soup, freshly prepared sandwiches or Cumberland sausage and mash at lunchtimes to more substantial evening menus which feature local produce. Those wishing to indulge in Lakeland pursuits such as fishing (the inn has a licence for two rods a day on selected waters), walking, sailing and birdwatching will find delightful bedrooms, all en suite, with colour television and lovely views of the village.

www.towerbankarms.com

3 BEDROOMS, ALL EN SUITE. ALL BEDROOMS NON-SMOKING. FREE HOUSE WITH REAL ALE.
CHILDREN AND PETS WELCOME. LUNCH AND DINNER AVAILABLE. HAWKSHEAD 2 MILES. S££££, D££££.

The Brackenrigg Inn

Watermillock, Ullswater, Penrith, Cumbria CA11 0LP
Tel: 01768 486206 • Fax: 01768 486945 • www.brackenrigginn.co.uk

The views of Ullswater and the Lakeland fells are a major attraction at this beautiful 18th century inn, which offers a popular food menu and great service. Accommodation is in en suite rooms, which ground floor and dog-friendly rooms, plus one with full disabled facilities.

The Yanwath Gate Inn

Yanwath, Penrith, Cumbria CA10 2LF
Tel: 01768 862386 • www.yanwathgate.com

The 'Yat' as it is fondly referred to, is a fine establishment with a restaurant featuring dishes prepared from locally sourced ingredients whenever possible. There is a carefully selected wine list and a good selection of real ales and draught beers.

124 NORTH WEST ENGLAND — Cumbria

Nestling in the delightful hamlet of Troutbeck, midway between Penrith and Keswick, 10 minutes from Ullswater, and with spectacular views of the surrounding fells, our charming Inn has everything you need for a relaxing break, and to sample everything the Lakes have to offer.

We have seven delightful bedrooms, all en suite, and three self-catering cottages.
Our restaurant is renowned for its excellent food which is sourced locally, and for our fine wines and real ales.

The Troutbeck Inn
Troutbeck, Penrith, Cumbria CA11 0SJ • Tel: 017684 83635
e-mail: info@troutbeckinn.co.uk • www.thetroutbeckinn.co.uk

7 BEDROOMS, ALL WITH PRIVATE BATHROOM. FREE HOUSE WITH REAL ALE. ALL BEDROOMS NON-SMOKING. CHILDREN AND PETS WELCOME. BAR AND RESTAURANT MEALS. KESWICK 8 MILES. S£££, D££££.

The Oddfellows Arms
Caldbeck, Wigton, Cumbria CA7 8EA
Tel: 01697 478227 Fax: 01697 478134

A delightful pub restaurant situated in the rural village of Caldbeck, offering accommodation and a wide range of mouth-watering dishes. Facilities include a jukebox, dart board, TV, and dominoes.
10 bedrooms are en suite, with coffee/tea making facilities.

STORK HOTEL (on facing page)

6 BEDROOMS, ALL WITH PRIVATE BATHROOM. ALL BEDROOMS NON-SMOKING. FREE HOUSE WITH REAL ALE. CHILDREN WELCOME. BAR AND RESTAURANT MEALS. DESIGNATED COVERED SMOKING AREA. ENNERDALE 2 MILES. S£, D£.

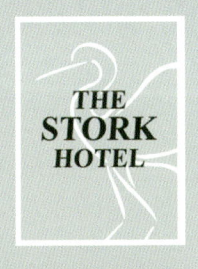

The Stork Hotel

Rowrah Road, Rowrah CA26 3XJ
Tel: 01946 861213
www.storkhotel.co.uk
e-mail: joan@storkhotel.co.uk

- Six newly refurbished rooms, all en suite, with power shower, tea/coffee making and hairdryer.
- Extensive menu of home-made dishes prepared from fresh local produce.
- Local real ales, as well as popular ciders, lagers and beers.
- Situated on the edge of the village, with a wonderful view of the surrounding fells.
- Ideal for Coast to Coast Cycle Way, and two miles from Ennerdale village, first stop for Coast to Coast walkers.
- Free pickup and drop-off service for guests.

THE EAGLE AND CHILD INN

Your No.1 choice for food and accommodation in the Lake District.

- Ideally placed for exploring the Lake District
- Local ales and regular guest beers
- 5 cosy en suite bedrooms, all with great views
- Excellent food from a varied menu
- Beer garden beside the River Kent

INN ★★★
AA ★★★ Inn

Kendal Road,
Staveley,
Cumbria LA8 9LP
01539 821320
info@eaglechildinn.co.uk
www.eaglechildinn.co.uk

5 BEDROOMS, ALL WITH PRIVATE BATHROOM. ALL BEDROOMS NON-SMOKING. FREE HOUSE WITH REAL ALE. CHILDREN WELCOME, PETS IN BAR ONLY. BAR AND RESTAURANT MEALS. DESIGNATED COVERED SMOKING AREA. WINDERMERE 4 MILES. S££, D££.

CUMBRIA has more than 16 lakes, including the deepest and 12 largest in England, and numerous tarns, there's sailing, windsurfing, kayaking and fishing, and long distance swimming events for really keen swimmers. Go for a cruise or hire a boat on Derwentwater near Keswick, Ullswater or Windermere, while fans of Arthur Ransome's Swallows and Amazons will enjoy Coniston, the setting of many of the adventures. See more of the scenery without the car on the Lakeside and Haverthwaite Railway at Newby Bridge and the Ravenglass and Eskdale Railway which runs inland from the coast. Visit nearby haunted Muncaster Castle for a ghostly experience, enjoy the wonderful collection of rhododendrons in spring, watch the wild herons feeding and 'meet the birds' at the World Owl Centre, with more than 200 species of owl to see.

Just along the coast the Edwardian resort of Grange-over-Sands, in a sheltered spot with a mild climate, is a good base from which to explore the South Lakes, with the Lakeland Miniature Village and the award-winning gardens at Holker Hall close by. Children of all ages will want to visit The Beatrix Potter Attraction at Bowness-on-Windermere and Hilltop, the author's home on the other side of the lake. Find out all about the area at Brockhole, the National Park Visitor Centre overlooking Windermere, with an adventure playground and lovely gardens.

Cumbria

NORTH WEST ENGLAND 127

Stan Laurel Inn

We are located close to the town centre and offer six changing cask ales, good quality home-cooked food, and comfortable accommodation.

We are situated on the southern tip of the Lake District, within easy reach of Windermere, Kendal and Coniston. The coast is only two miles away, and the area offers plenty of nice walks.

Good service, good food, good beer...what more could you ask for!

Stan Laurel Inn, 31 The Ellers, Ulverston LA12 0AB
Tel: 01229 582814 • e-mail: thestanlaurel@aol.com

Our website address is www.thestanlaurel.co.uk where further information on menus and pictures can be viewed.

3 BEDROOMS, 2 WITH PRIVATE BATHROOM. ALL BEDROOMS NON-SMOKING. CHILDREN AND PETS WELCOME. FREE HOUSE WITH REAL ALES. BAR MEALS. BARROW-IN-FURNESS 8 MILES. S£, D£.

The Mortal Man Inn
Troutbeck, Windermere, Cumbria LA23 1PL
Tel: 01539 433193 • Fax: 01539 431261 • www.themortalman.co.uk

Poets, authors and painters alike have found inspiration from this delightful spot in the Troutbeck Valley. The alehouse turned inn offers quality real ales, carefully selected wines, and cosy bedrooms with modern facilities, and the cuisine is prepared from fresh, locally sourced ingredients whenever possible.

RATES
S – SINGLE ROOM rate   D – Sharing DOUBLE/TWIN ROOM
S£ D£ =Under £35   S££ D££ =£36-£45   S£££ D£££ =£46-£55   S££££ D££££ =Over £55

This is meant as an indication only and does not show prices for Special Breaks, Weekends, etc. Guests are therefore advised to verify all prices on enquiring or booking.

The Brackenrigg Inn
Watermillock, Ullswater, Penrith CA11 0LP
Tel: 01768 486206 • Fax: 01768 486945
www.brackenrigginn.co.uk

Set on the brow of a hill overlooking Ullswater in the Lake District National Park, the Brackenrigg Inn offers an ideal base from which to explore this beautiful part of the world. This 18th Century coaching inn has been refurbished to modern standards with a relaxed and friendly atmosphere - it's a great place to take a break and unwind. We offer a relaxed and welcoming atmosphere at the Inn, providing quality service, comfortable rooms, delicious food and drink, and excellent value for money. We positively welcome well behaved pets, and families with children of all ages. Our locally sourced food is prepared on the premises by our team of chefs, with real care and attention to detail, and is matched by a well-chosen range of wines and beers.

Only a few minutes from the Motorway (M6 Junction 40), the Brackenrigg Inn also makes a perfect place to stop if you're looking to break your journey on a long drive to or from Scotland.

17 BEDROOMS, ALL WITH PRIVATE BATHROOM. ALL BEDROOMS NON-SMOKING. FREE HOUSE WITH REAL ALE. CHILDREN AND PETS WELCOME. BAR MEALS, RESTAURANT MEALS EVENINGS ONLY. S££, D£££. PENRITH 6 MILES.

Other specialised holiday guides from **FHG**

THE GOLF GUIDE • COUNTRY HOTELS OF BRITAIN
WEEKEND & SHORT BREAK HOLIDAYS IN BRITAIN
The bestselling and original **PETS WELCOME!**
500 GREAT PLACES TO STAY • SELF-CATERING HOLIDAYS IN BRITAIN
BED & BREAKFAST STOPS • CARAVAN & CAMPING HOLIDAYS
FAMILY BREAKS IN BRITAIN

Published annually: available in all good bookshops or direct from the publisher:
FHG Guides, Abbey Mill Business Centre, Seedhill, Paisley PA1 1TJ
Tel: 0141 887 0424 • Fax: 0141 889 7204
e-mail: admin@fhguides.co.uk • www.holidayguides.com

BRIDGE INN (on facing page)

18 BEDROOMS, MOST EN SUITE. ALL BEDROOMS NON-SMOKING. JENNINGS HOUSE WITH REAL ALE. CHILDREN AND PETS WELCOME. BAR AND RESTAURANT MEALS. NON-SMOKING AREAS. GOSFORTH 3 MILES. S££££, D££££.

The Bridge Inn
Santon Bridge

The Bridge Inn, once a coach halt, is now a fine, comfortable, award-winning country inn, offering hospitality to all travellers and visitors.

◆ The Inn has an excellent reputation for good food, with "real" food served in the Dalesman Bar, or in the Eskdale Room.

◆ We serve an excellent selection of Jennings and guest real ales.

◆ 16 bedrooms, most en suite. Bridal Suite.

◆ Weddings and other private and business functions catered for in our large function room with private bar facilities.

◆ Licensed for civil ceremonies, partnerships, naming ceremonies and renewal of vows.

◆ Dogs welcome.

10 minute drive to
"Britain's favourite view – Wastwater"
This unspoiled area of the Lake District offers superb walking and climbing.

Bridge Inn
Santon Bridge, Wasdale
Cumbria CA19 1UX

Tel: 019467 26221 • Fax: 019467 26026
info@santonbridgeinn.com
www.santonbridgeinn.com

WATERMILL INN
& BREWING CO
Ings Village, Near Windermere LA8 9PY
Tel: 01539 821309
e-mail: info@lakelandpub.co.uk • www.lakelandpub.co.uk

CAMRA CUMBRIA PUB OF THE YEAR 2009

Named as one of the Guardian and Observer Best 200 Pubs in the Country 2009

- Up to 16 Real Ales. • Our own on-site Micro Brewery est. 2006.
- Viewing window into the brewery and beer cellar.
- Excellent range of food served 12 noon to 9pm every day.
- Varied menu and constantly changing Chef's Specials Board.
- 8 en suite bedrooms.
- Open all day every day except Christmas Day.
- Children and dogs most welcome.

8 BEDROOMS, ALL WITH PRIVATE BATHROOM. ALL BEDROOMS ARE NON SMOKING. REAL ALE. CHILDREN AND PETS WELCOME. BAR MEALS. KENDAL 7 MILES.

RATES

Normal Bed & Breakfast rate per person
(single room)

PRICE RANGE	CATEGORY
Under £35	S£
£36-£45	S££
£46-£55	S£££
Over £55	S££££

Normal Bed & Breakfast rate per person
(sharing double/twin room)

PRICE RANGE	CATEGORY
Under £35	D£
£36-£45	D££
£46-£55	D£££
Over £55	D££££

This is meant as an indication only and does not show prices for Special Breaks, Weekends, etc. Guests are therefore advised to verify all prices on enquiring or booking.

Lancashire   NORTH WEST ENGLAND 131

Lancashire

The Waterside Inn
Twist Lane, Leigh, Lancashire WN7 4DB • Tel: 01942 605005

This Lancashire pub situated next to the canal was formerly a warehouse, and is an ideal place to come for a business lunch, or to catch up with friends over dinner or evening drinks. There is a beer garden to the side, and at the rear decking overlooks the canal.

Looking for Holiday Accommodation?

FHG
KUPERARD

for details of hundreds of properties throughout the UK, visit our website

www.holidayguides.com

THE FARMERS' ARMS

Situated just two minutes from Jct 27 of the M6, The Farmers Arms is an ideal place to stay in the northwest of England, for visiting family and friends, business or indeed just pleasure.

The same welcome awaits you as it did the weary travellers who used the pub and its stables back in the 1700s. In those days the Farmers Arms was aptly named THE PLEASANT RETREAT and only found its new title of The Farmers in 1902. It has been on the estate of several brewing companies including Matthew Brown, Burtonwood, Duttons, and now is with your hosts, Malcolm and Ann Rothwell.

While still retaining its olde worlde charm, The Farmers continues to provide the very best of traditional cask ales and good hearty fayre. Sit back, enjoy and take in the warmth of this fine country inn.

All of our rooms have been designed to retain the olde worlde charm of The Farmers Arms, yet still meeting the requirements of today's discerning traveller. All rooms are en suite with tea and coffee making facilities and TV.

**Wood Lane, Heskin,
Near Chorley, Lancs PR7 5NP
Tel: 01257 451276
Fax: 01257 453958
www.farmersarms.co.uk**

★★★ INN

Greater Manchester

The Stamford Arms
The Firs, Bowdon, Altrincham, Greater Manchester WA14 2TW • Tel: 0161 9281536
A quintessential English pub standing opposite handsome St Mary's Church, with low-beamed ceilings and a spacious function room. With live sporting fixtures shown on big screens and high quality real ales, there's no reason not to drop in and stay for a while!

The Moss Trooper
Timperley, Altrincham, Greater Manchester WA15 6JU • Tel: 0161 9804610
The Moss Trooper is a CAMRA award-winning pub boasting a heated outdoor seating area, and a stylish interior with comfy sofas and inglenook fires. There is a cosy dining area with candlelit tables, plus an extensive range of wines, ales and beers.

The Old Pelican Inn
Manchester Road, West Timperley, Greater Manchester WA14 5NH
Tel: 0161 9627414 • Fax: 0161 9739144
Spacious 100-year-old inn located in West Timperley, popular with football supporters who enjoy watching live sporting fixtures over a pint of their favourite beer or ale. Food from the John Barras menu is available throughout the day.

The Cotton Kier
Watersmeeting Road, Bolton, Greater Manchester BL1 8TS
Tel: 01204 363010 Fax: 01204 559797
Situated on the outskirts of Bolton, this friendly family pub has a contemporary, light interior. The menu offers a wide choice of dishes, and entertainment comes in the form of a weekly quiz.

FARMERS ARMS (on facing page)

5 BEDROOMS, ALL WITH PRIVATE BATHROOM. ALL BEDROOMS NON SMOKING. ENTERPRISE INNS HOUSE WITH REAL ALE. CHILDREN WELCOME BAR AND RESTAURANT MEALS. NON-SMOKING AREAS. CHORLEY 4 MILES..
SE, DEEL

Scotland • Regions

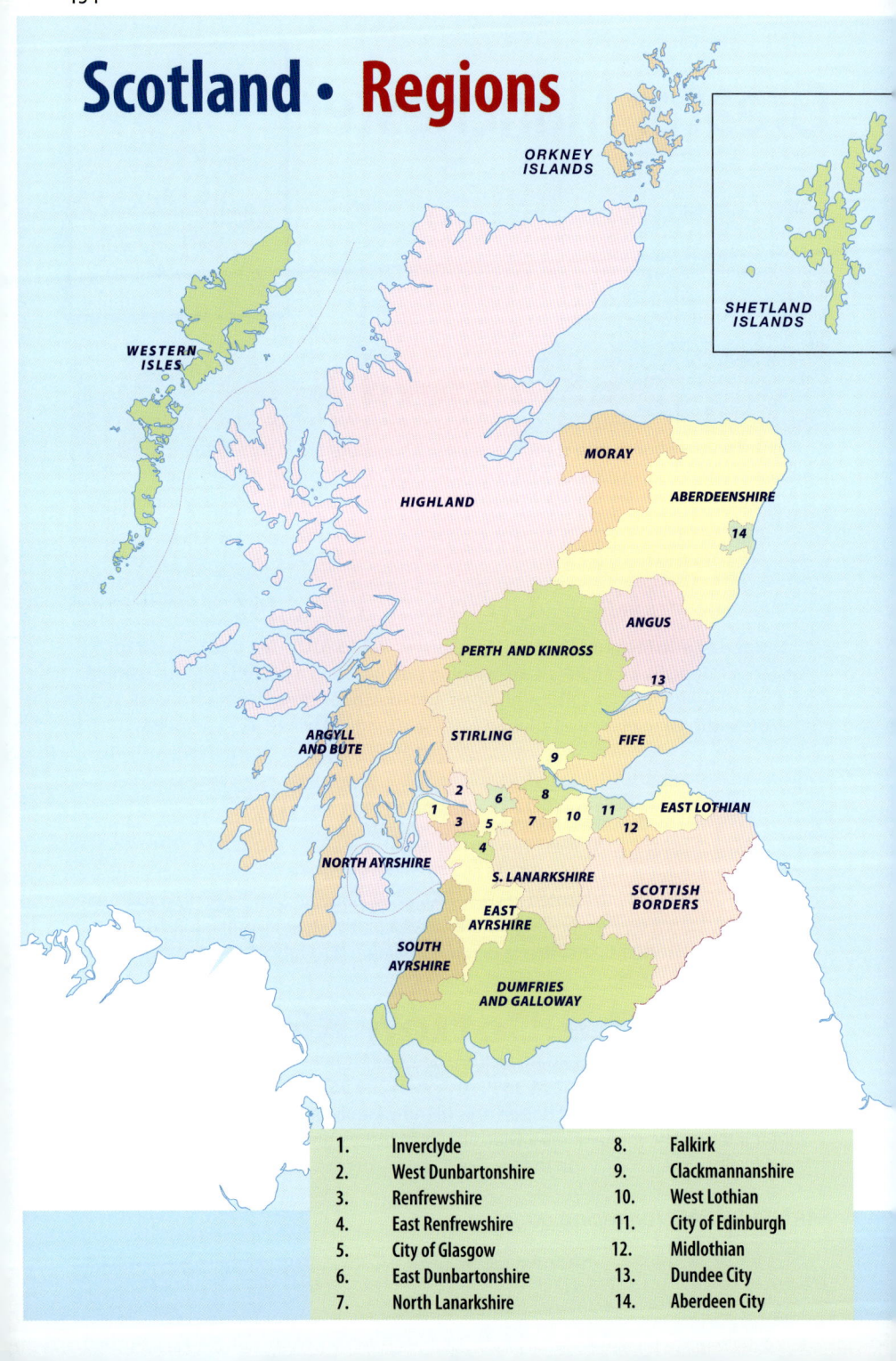

ORKNEY ISLANDS
SHETLAND ISLANDS
WESTERN ISLES
HIGHLAND
MORAY
ABERDEENSHIRE
ANGUS
PERTH AND KINROSS
ARGYLL AND BUTE
STIRLING
FIFE
EAST LOTHIAN
NORTH AYRSHIRE
S. LANARKSHIRE
SCOTTISH BORDERS
EAST AYRSHIRE
SOUTH AYRSHIRE
DUMFRIES AND GALLOWAY

1. Inverclyde
2. West Dunbartonshire
3. Renfrewshire
4. East Renfrewshire
5. City of Glasgow
6. East Dunbartonshire
7. North Lanarkshire
8. Falkirk
9. Clackmannanshire
10. West Lothian
11. City of Edinburgh
12. Midlothian
13. Dundee City
14. Aberdeen City

… SCOTLAND 135

The Coylet Inn, Loch Eck, Argyll, page 141

Scotland

Aberdeen, Banff & Moray

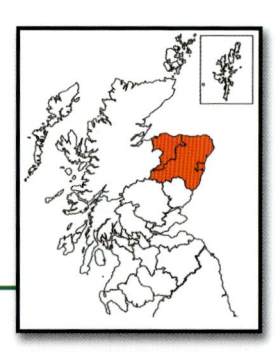

KILDRUMMY INN • Kildrummy, Alford AB33 8QS
enquiries@kildrummyinn.co.uk • www.kildrummyinn.co.uk

- Located in the heart of rural Aberdeenshire, along the main A97, an excellent base for touring.
- All bedrooms are en suite, with tea/coffee making, radio alarm and TV.
- Superior quality cuisine is available in the comfortable Dining Rooms or in the relaxed atmosphere of the Sun Lounge.
- Separate guests' TV lounge.
- Ample parking.

Tel: 01975 571227

Local places of interest & activities include:
- *Kildrummy Castle & Gardens • Huntly Castle • Golf Courses • Pony trekking*
- *Cycling • Hillwalking • Museums • Outdoor pursuits • Sporting Activities*

4 BEDROOMS, ALL WITH PRIVATE BATHROOM. ALL BEDROOMS NON-SMOKING. FREE HOUSE WITH REAL ALE. CHILDREN WELCOME. RESTAURANT MEALS. ALFORD 6½ MILES. S££, D££.

The Grays Inn
Greenfern Road, Aberdeen, Aberdeenshire AB16 5PY • Tel: 01224 690506

Newly furbished inn, with an open-plan kitchen for diners who like to watch their food being prepared. Live sporting fixtures are shown on big screens throughout the pub.

Aberdeen, Banff & Moray   SCOTLAND 137

GRANT ARMS HOTEL
The Square, Monymusk, Inverurie AB51 7HJ
Tel: 01467 651226 • Fax: 01467 651494
e-mail: grantarmshotel@btconnect.com

This splendid former coaching inn of the 18th century has its own exclusive fishing rights on ten miles of the River Don, so it is hardly surprising that fresh salmon and trout are considered specialities of the restaurant, which is open nightly. Bar food is available at lunchtimes and in the evenings, and a pleasing range of fare caters for all tastes.

Double and twin rooms, all with private facilities, accommodate overnight visitors, and some ground floor bedrooms are available, two of which have been specifically designed for wheelchair users.

A traditional Scottish welcome and a real interest in the welfare of guests makes a stay here a particular pleasure.

£75-£80pppn; £85-£90 for 2 persons. Bargain Breaks available.

12 BEDROOMS, ALL EN SUITE. FREE HOUSE WITH REAL ALE. CHILDREN WELCOME. BAR MEALS, RESTAURANT EVENINGS ONLY. INVERURIE 7 MILES. S££££, D££££.

The Shepherd's Rest
Westhill, Aberdeen, Aberdeenshire AB32 6UF
Tel: 01224 740208 • Fax: 01224 745524

This inn is set in countryside surroundings on the way to Braemar, near Aberdeen. Secluded areas, a real fire and soft lighting will enhance your dining experience, and the adjacent Premier Inn provides 60 reasonably priced bedrooms.

THE SHIP INN
5 Shorehead, Stonehaven, Aberdeenshire AB39 2JY
Tel: 01569 762617 • Fax: 01569 767074

Scottish bar serving a wide range of draught beers, real ales and 100 malt whiskies. The Captain's Table restaurant offers a range of home-cooked dishes prepared from fresh, locally sourced ingredients; food is also available in the bar. Accommodation is in six bedrooms, all with en suite shower, hairdryer, colour TV and harbour views!

Angus & Dundee

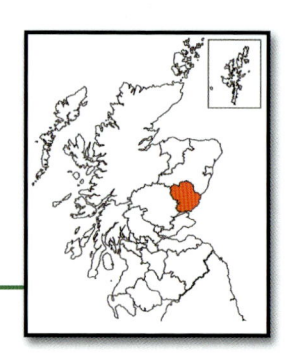

The Bell Tree
Panmurefield Road, Broughty Ferry, Dundee, Angus DD5 3TS
Tel: 01382 738112

A contemporary establishment situated in Broughty Ferry, with a Chef & Brewer-style menu and a traditional interior with real log fires and little nooks. A wide range of whiskies, real ales and beers is available. Accommodation is at the adjacent Premier Inn where 60 en suite bedrooms have all modern facilities.

Looking for Holiday Accommodation?

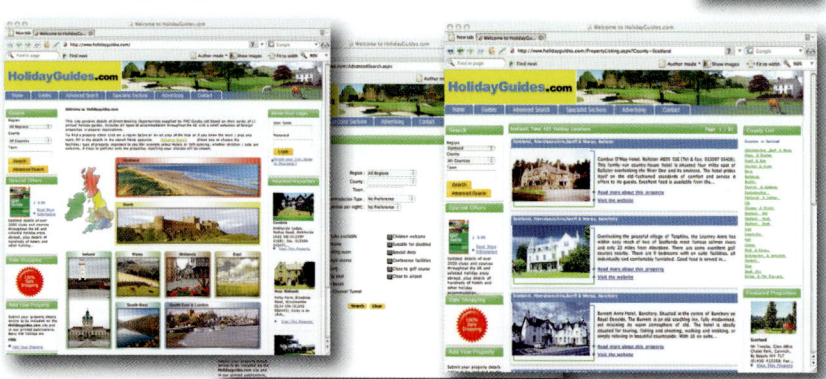

for details of hundreds of properties throughout the UK, visit our website
www.holidayguides.com

Argyll & Bute

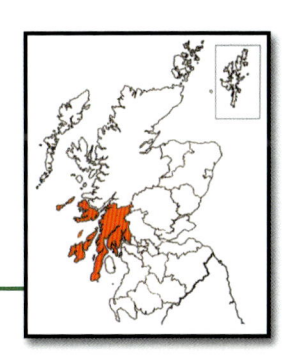

SCOTLAND 139

Cairndow Stagecoach Inn

A Warm Scottish Welcome on the Shores of Loch Fyne

Cairndow, Argyll PA26 8BN
Tel: 01499 600286
Fax: 01499 600220

AA ★★★ HOTEL

Across the Arrochar Alps at the head of Loch Fyne, this historic coaching inn enjoys a perfect position. All bedrooms are en suite with TV, radio, central heating, tea/coffee and direct-dial phone. Seven de luxe bedrooms with king-size beds and five new lochside rooms are available. Dine by candlelight in our Stables Restaurant; bar meals and drinks served all day. Ideal centre for touring Western Highlands and Trossachs.

www.cairndowinn.com

Amenities include a loch-side beer garden, sauna, multi-gym, solarium; tee times are available at Loch Lomond.

SHORT BREAKS AVAILABLE

18 BEDROOMS, ALL WITH PRIVATE BATHROOM. ALL BEDROOMS NON-SMOKING. FREE HOUSE WITH REAL ALE. CHILDREN WELCOME. BAR AND RESTAURANT MEALS. NON-SMOKING AREAS. ARROCHAR 12 MILES. S££, D££.

RATES S – SINGLE ROOM rate   D – Sharing DOUBLE/TWIN ROOM
S£ D£ =Under £35   S££ D££ =£36-£45   S£££ D£££ =£46-£55   S££££ D££££ =Over £55

This is meant as an indication only and does not show prices for Special Breaks, Weekends, etc. Guests are therefore advised to verify all prices on enquiring or booking.

The Argyll Arms Hotel, located on the waterfront of the village of Bunessan, and close to the ferry landing for the famous Isle of Iona, provides accommodation, bar and restaurant facilities on the beautiful Isle of Mull. With spectacular sea and island views, the hotel is the perfect base from which to explore the islands. Island tours available, wildlife watching day tours arranged. The new owners invite you to enjoy their friendly and relaxed Scottish hospitality in comfortable accommodation, value-for-money home cooked style food with many local ingredients, and the unique atmosphere of the Isle of Mull. Single, twin, double and family rooms available, all rooms recently refurbished, all en suite.

Make us your home whilst relaxing on the Isle of Mull.

Check out our website for full up-to-date information.

Open all day 365 days of the year catering for residents and non residents.

From £35.00 single. £60.00 double

Argyll Arms Hotel

Bunessan, Isle of Mull PA67 6DP
Tel: 01681 700240
e-mail: argyllarms@isleofmull.co.uk
www.isleofmull.co.uk

Argyll & Bute

SCOTLAND 141

THE Coylet INN
Loch Eck, Argyll PA23 8SG

The Coylet Inn is one of Scotland's most enchanting 17th century coaching inns, ideally situated on the banks of Loch Eck. Its idyllic location makes it the perfect venue for a short break or romantic weekend away.

The lovingly restored en suite bedrooms offer visitors comfort and a touch of luxury, while the good food, real ales, open log fires and stunning views make The Coylet the perfect country retreat. We now have a civil ceremony licence and tailored wedding packages are available.

www.coyletinn.co.uk
info@coyletinn.co.uk
Tel: 01369 840426

4 BEDROOMS, ALL WITH PRIVATE BATHROOM. FREE HOUSE WITH REAL ALE. CHILDREN WELCOME. BAR AND RESTAURANT MEALS. NON-SMOKING. DUNOON 7 MILES. S££, D££.

Visit the FHG website
www.holidayguides.com
for details of the wide choice of accommodation featured in the full range of FHG titles

---

ARGYLL ARMS HOTEL (on facing page)

6 BEDROOMS, ALL WITH PRIVATE BATHROOM. ALL BEDROOMS NON-SMOKING. FREE HOUSE. CHILDREN WELCOME. BAR AND RESTAURANT MEALS. S££, D££££.

Craignure Inn
Craignure, Isle of Mull, Argyll, PA65 6AY

Craignure Inn is a small characteristic old drovers' inn providing excellent service, food and accommodation whether you're looking for a longer holiday, full of fun outdoor wildlife activities, or simply a relaxing short break for you and your family, partner or friend.

The main attractions of the island, Torosay Castle and its gardens, and Duart Castle with its Clan Maclean history, are at your doorstep. If you are lucky you might just see dolphins in Craignure Bay and otters just across the road by the rocks on the seashore. The Inn is open all year and prides itself on its friendly staff and warm welcome. It is favoured by locals and visitors alike.

There are three letting rooms, all en suite, with colour television and tea/coffee making facilities. The bar has a wide range of malts, fine wines, a large fire for the cooler evenings, outdoor seating and a cosy lounge.

There is an extensive bar menu with many wholesome, home cooked offerings using local produce such as Highland Beef, Hebridean Lamb, Mussels, Mull Cheddar and Smoked Trout.

We have regular live entertainment and welcome well behaved dogs. We provide information on local walks, trips and tours. Bus tours leave from Craignure, making it a great base for those without their own transport.

Craignure Inn
Isle of Mull, Argyll PA65 6AY
Tel: 016808 12305
craignureinn@btconnect.com
www.craignure-inn.co.uk

Argyll & Bute

SCOTLAND 143

The Galley of Lorne Inn
Ardfern, Argyll • Tel: 01852 500 284

Escape to the wilds of Argyll

- 17th Century Drovers Inn
- Loch-side Location in Ardfern, near Oban & Lochgilphead
- Cosy En-suite Bedrooms
- Mouthwatering Menu with Local Seafood, Meats & Game
- Friendly, Welcoming Staff
- Log fires, Real Ales & Malts
- Beach, Forest & Hill Walks
- Golf, Horseriding & Fishing
- Easy Access to Hebridean Islands

www.galleyoflorne.co.uk   Rated Excellent on Tripadvisor!

6 BEDROOMS, ALL WITH PRIVATE BATHROOM. FREE HOUSE WITH REAL ALES. CHILDREN AND DOGS WELCOME. BAR AND RESTAURANT MEALS. NON-SMOKING AREAS. LOCHGILPHEAD 12 MILES. S£££/££££, D£££/££££.

WIDE MOUTHED FROG

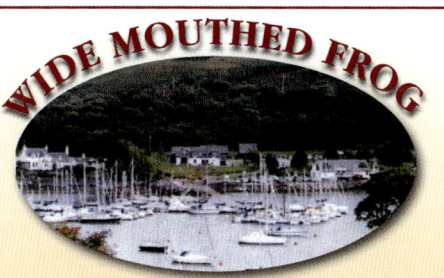

The "Frog" is ideally situated at Dunstaffnage Marina, just three miles north of Oban. The atmosphere is casual and relaxed. Our menus feature the best of local produce and specialise in fresh seafood, and the bars offer a varied selection of refreshments. Accommodation is available in ten en suite bedrooms, all with digital colour television, and tea/coffee making facilities; most bathrooms have bath and power shower. Major credit cards accepted.

Dunstaffnage Bay, Near Oban PA37 1PX • Tel: 01631 567005 • Fax: 01631 571044
e-mail: enquiries@widemouthedfrog.co.uk • www.widemouthedfrog.co.uk

10 BEDROOMS, ALL WITH PRIVATE BATHROOM. FREE HOUSE WITH REAL ALE. CHILDREN WELCOME. BAR AND RESTAURANT MEALS. ALL PUBLIC AREAS NON-SMOKING. CONNEL 2 MILES. S£££, D£££.

CRAIGNURE INN (on facing page)

3 BEDROOMS, ALL WITH PRIVATE BATHROOM. FREE HOUSE. CHILDREN AND PETS WELCOME. BAR MEALS. ALL PUBLIC AREAS NON-SMOKING. TOBERMORY 18 MILES. S£££, D££.

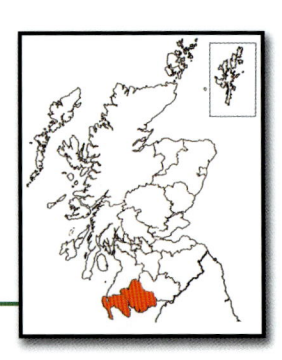

Dumfries & Galloway

The Bladnoch Inn
Bladnoch, Wigtown, Newton Stewart DG8 9AB
Tel: 01988 402200 • www.the-bladnoch-inn.com

A family-run inn in a tranquil setting in an unspoilt area of Dumfries & Galloway. Enjoy relaxing in the friendly bar or dining in the à la carte restaurant which serves the finest traditional food; bar menu also served lunchtime and evenings.
5 bedrooms (3 en suite, 2 with shared bathroom).

Ideal for following country pursuits such as fishing. Just a short distance from Wigtown, Scotland's National Book Town.

5 BEDROOMS, 3 WITH PRIVATE BATHROOM. ALL BEDROOMS NON-SMOKING. FREE HOUSE WITH REAL ALE. CHILDREN AND PETS WELCOME. BAR AND RESTAURANT MEALS. DESIGNATED COVERED SMOKING AREA. WIGTOWN 1 MILE. S££, D££££.

The countryside of **DUMFRIES & GALLOWAY** is a mixture of high moorland and sheltered glens, and presents abundant opportunities for hill walking, rambling, fishing, cycling, bird watching and field sports. There are at least 32 golf courses, including the Stranraer course which has the distinction of being the last course designed by James Braid. The warming influence of the Gulf Stream ensures a mild climate which makes touring a pleasure, and many visitors come here to visit the dozens of interesting castles, gardens, museums and historic sites. In addition, pony trekking and riding plus a never ending succession of ceilidhs, village fairs, country dances, classical music concerts and children's entertainment guarantee plenty of scope for enjoyment.

Discover the many hidden secrets of this lovely and unspoilt landscape such as the many pretty little villages and interesting towns. Stranraer, the principal town and ferry port with its busy shopping streets is the ideal place to break a journey to or from Northern Ireland, or use as a centre for touring the Rhins of Galloway. Those who love 'the written word' must surely visit the book town of Wigtown, and the gourmets amongst us will love the concept of Castle Douglas, the designated 'Food Town'.

Edinburgh & Lothians

Jusinlees Inn
Esbank Toll, Dalkeith, Midlothian EH22 3AT • Tel: 0131 6632166

Prominently positioned on the roundabout in Dalkeith is this colossal white building with a beautifully traditional interior. With a circular centre bar and open plan layout, patrons may drink or dine where they choose. Amenities include free wifi, plasma screens, a large TV screen, pool table, dart board, and a beer garden.

IGLU (Bar & Ethical Eaterie)
2b Jamaica Street, Edinburgh, Midlothian EH3 6HH
Tel: 0131 476 5333 • www.theiglu.com/

Try food and drink from a different direction! Edinburgh is home to many fine establishments but none as special as this. Since the addition of a food service in 2005, its popularity has gone from strength to strength, offering all your favourite alcoholic beverages including cocktails.

THE MALT SHOVEL
11-15 Cockburn Street, Edinburgh, Lothians EH1 1BP • Tel: 01312 256 843

This charming public house is located between the Royal Mile and the railway station. The interior is furnished in old dark wood, from the picture frames and fireplaces to the beams and flooring, with original stained glass on the doors. The pub boasts the biggest selection (105!) of malt whiskies in the area, plus well kept real ales. With haggis on the menu and live entertainment, this is definitely worth a visit!

The Shakespeare
65 Lothian Road, Edinburgh, Lothians EH1 2DJ • Tel: 0131 2288400

The Shakespeare is one of Edinburgh's best-known and oldest pubs, and its location in the centre of the city means that it attracts a remarkably cosmopolitan crowd. Food is served throughout the day and live sporting fixtures are shown on an extra-large screen. Entertainment includes a weekly quiz and fortnightly karaoke.

The Rose Street Brewery
55 Rose Street, Edinburgh, Lothians EH2 2NH • Tel: 0131 2201227

The Rose was once a brewery, but is now a lively social centre on famous cobbled Rose Street in Edinburgh. Having undergone a recent refurbishment, the colour scheme is now an elegant blend of creams, browns and burgundy. Attractions include a great wine list and a range of dishes cooked to order – steaks are very popular here!

Hopetoun Inn
8 McDonald Road, Edinburgh, Lothians EH7 4LU
Tel: 0131 5583523 • Fax: 0131 5587338 • www.hopetouninn.co.uk

Regulars enjoy live sporting fixtures shown on a large screen, but that's not the only reason for coming to the Hopetoun. The facilities are great, with a pool table and dart boards, plus weekly entertainment such as a quiz, karaoke and live bands.

The Lady Nairne
228 Willowbrae Road, Edinburgh, Lothians EH8 7NG • Tel: 0131 6613396

The perfect venue for a stag or hen weekend, The Lady Nairne is located just three miles from Edinburgh city centre. There is an extensive à la carte menu, with a good choice of wines as the perfect accompaniment. Accommodation is in 39 en suite bedrooms, all with modern facilities.

THE BALMWELL
39/41 Howden Hall Road, Edinburgh, Lothians EH16 6PG
Tel: 0131 6721408 • Fax: 0131 6661271

Lovers of wildlife can expect to see squirrels and foxes running about in the extensive gardens of this former convent. With a Two For One meal deals on delicious food and a wide range of wines from around the world, there's something for everyone.

The Cuddie Brae
Newcraighall, Edinburgh, Lothians EH21 8SG • Tel: 01316 571212

This Chef & Brewer pub venue is situated opposite the railway station, just five miles from the city centre. The interior is contemporary in style and the menu features mouth-watering dishes prepared from fresh ingredients. Accommodation is in 42 rooms, all en suite, with modern facilities.

The Granary
Almondvale Boulevard, Livingston, West Lothian EH54 6QT
Tel: 01506 410661 • Fax: 01506 415027

Purpose-built building located next to the Arndale Centre, offering great value for money and a comfortable environment in which to relax, dine and enjoy a glass of your favourite wine. The regulars are a friendly bunch who enjoy the weekly entertainment.

Fife

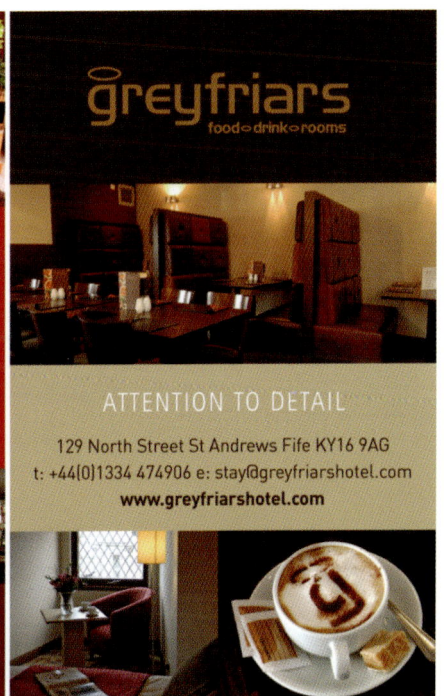

SCOTLAND 147

DEAN PARK HOTEL

the best place to dine, relax and enjoy excellent food and amazing service

weddings | functions | conferences | rooms | dining
The Dean Park Hotel, Chapel Level, Kirkcaldy, KY2 6QW
www.deanparkhotel.co.uk

greyfriars
food • drink • rooms

ATTENTION TO DETAIL

129 North Street St Andrews Fife KY16 9AG
t: +44(0)1334 474906 e: stay@greyfriarshotel.com
www.greyfriarshotel.com

DEAN PARK. 33 BEDROOMS, ALL WITH PRIVATE BATHROOM. RESTAURANT MEALS. ST ANDREWS 17 MILES.

GREYFRIARS. 20 BEDROOMS, ALL WITH PRIVATE BATHROOM. BAR AND RESTAURANT MEALS. DUNDEE 11 MILES.

Pet-Friendly
Pubs, Inns & Hotels
on pages 174-178
Please note that these establishments may not feature in the main section of this book

148 **SCOTLAND** Fife

THE PEAT INN
RESTAURANT WITH ROOMS

Beautiful 5 Star restaurant with rooms situated just 6 miles from St Andrews in the village named after the Inn.

The restaurant has earned an international reputation over 30 years offering fresh Scottish produce, creativity and value, and is consistently voted one of the best restaurants in Scotland. A few steps away is 'The Residence', with 8 individual luxury suites, offering peace and comfort of the best of small country house hotels, but with a convivial and unpretentious atmosphere.

Peat Inn, by St Andrews, Fife KY15 5LH
Tel: 01334 840206 • Fax: 01334 840530
e-mail: stay@thepeatinn.co.uk
www.thepeatinn.co.uk

8 SUITES, ALL WITH PRIVATE BATHROOM. ALL BEDROOMS NON-SMOKING. RESTAURANT MEALS. ST ANDREWS 6 MILES. S££££, D££££.

RATES

Normal Bed & Breakfast rate per person
(single room)

PRICE RANGE	CATEGORY
Under £35	S£
£36-£45	S££
£46-£55	S£££
Over £55	S££££

Normal Bed & Breakfast rate per person
(sharing double/twin room)

PRICE RANGE	CATEGORY
Under £35	D£
£36-£45	D££
£46-£55	D£££
Over £55	D££££

This is meant as an indication only and does not show prices for Special Breaks, Weekends, etc. Guests are therefore advised to verify all prices on enquiring or booking.

Highlands

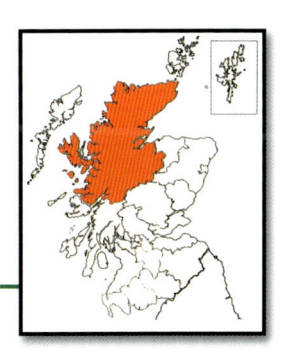

Inn at Dalwhinnie
Dalwhinnie, Inverness-shire PH19 1AG
Tel: 01528 522257 • room@theinndalwhinnie.com • www.theinndalwhinnie.com

The Dalwhinnie provides guests with maximum comfort and offers lots of information on things to do and see. With live music and an abundance of traditional and modern fish dishes on the menu, it's an ideal spot to leave your troubles behind. All rooms are en suite and spacious with beautiful window views. Great selection of malt whiskies.

THE BEN NEVIS BAR
103 High Street, Fort William, Inverness-shire PH33 6DG • Tel: 01397 702295

Formerly this was the inn for the castle drovers; today, having undergone a contemporary makeover, the establishment exudes style and panache. The bar is split across two levels, with a restaurant upstairs affording stunning views. Enjoy a glass of fine wine on the new decking area overlooking the loch.

The Fluke
Culcabock Road, Inverness, Inverness-shire IV2 3XQ • Tel: 01463 220957

The Fluke is an ideal spot in which to dine, drink and celebrate the victory of your favourite football team, with live fixtures shown regularly on big screens. Facilities include a pool table, dart board and two large alcoves for private functions.

The Old Inn
Flowerdale, Gairloch, Ross-shire IV21 2BD
Tel: 01445 712006 • Fax: 01445 712445

Perfectly positioned by the harbour in Gairloch, and popular with local fishermen who appreciate the wholesome food that is served. A good selection of draught beers and real ales is offered behind the bar, and accommodation is available in well equipped bedrooms.

Lairg Highland Hotel

Lying in the centre of the village, Lairg Highland Hotel is an ideal base from which to tour the North of Scotland. Superb, home-cooked food, using the best local ingredients, is served in the elegant restaurant and in the attractive setting of the lounge bar. All meals can be complemented by a bottle of wine from a comprehensive list.

All bedrooms are individual in character, and furnished to a high standard, with en suite facilities, colour TV and tea/coffee hospitality tray.

The popular lounge bar, boasting some fine malt whiskies and good draught beers, is just the place to unwind and relax.

Main Street, Lairg, Sutherland IV27 4DB
Tel: 01549 402243 • Fax: 01549 402593
www.highland-hotel.co.uk • info@highland-hotel.co.uk

Among the many attractions of this scenic area are fishing, boating, sailing and golf, including Royal Dornoch nearby. Local places of interest include the Falls of Shin, Dunrobin Castle and Clynelish Distillery.

Highlands
SCOTLAND

This former 19th century coaching inn on the John O'Groats peninsula is set in six acres of parkland, close to the Queen Mother's former Highland home, the Castle of Mey. Fully modernised, the hotel has eight centrally heated en suite bedrooms with colour television and tea making facilities; the spacious Pentland Suite offers a double and family room with en suite bathroom. Locally caught salmon, crab and other fine Highland produce feature on the varied table d'hôte and grill menus available in the Garden Room, while lighter meals and snacks can be enjoyed in the cosy Pentland Lounge. A warm Highland welcome awaits you.

www.castlearms.co.uk

THE CASTLE ARMS HOTEL Mey, By Thurso, Caithness KW14 8XH
Tel & Fax: 01847 851244 • e-mail: info@castlearms.co.uk

8 BEDROOMS, ALL WITH PRIVATE BATHROOM. ALL BEDROOMS NON-SMOKING. FREE HOUSE.
CHILDREN AND PETS WELCOME. BAR AND RESTAURANT MEALS. JOHN O'GROATS 6 MILES. S££, D£.

RATES

Normal Bed & Breakfast rate per person
(single room)

PRICE RANGE	CATEGORY
Under £35	S£
£36-£45	S££
£46-£55	S£££
Over £55	S££££

Normal Bed & Breakfast rate per person
(sharing double/twin room)

PRICE RANGE	CATEGORY
Under £35	D£
£36-£45	D££
£46-£55	D£££
Over £55	D££££

This is meant as an indication only and does not show prices for Special Breaks, Weekends, etc. Guests are therefore advised to verify all prices on enquiring or booking.

Family-Friendly
Pubs, Inns & Hotels
See the Supplement on pages 179-182 for establishments which really welcome children

LAIRG HIGHLAND HOTEL *(on facing page)*

ALL BEDROOMS WITH PRIVATE BATHROOM. CHILDREN WELCOME, PETS BY ARRANGEMENT.
BAR AND RESTAURANT MEALS. GOLSPIE 17 MILES.

THE FERRY BOAT INN & THE FRIGATE

We welcome you to The Ferry Boat Inn on the shorefront in Ullapool. All of our 9 bedrooms are en suite and we offer Bar Meals or fine dining in our beautiful Restaurant.

**Ferry Boat Inn
Shore Street
Ullapool IV26 2UJ
Tel: 01854 612 366
www.ferryboat-inn.com**

THE FRIGATE CAFÉ & BISTRO

High quality licensed Bistro, Café, Outside Caterers, Deli, Bakery and Take Away

Frigate Café, Shore Street, Ullapool, IV26 2UJ
Tel: 01854 612 969
www.ullapoolcatering.co.uk

Perth & Kinross

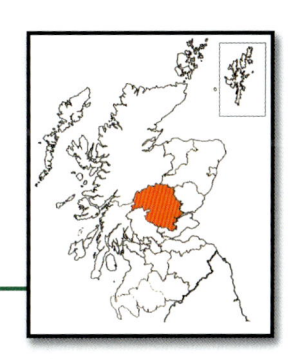

Yann's at Glenearn House is a busy restaurant with rooms in Crieff, the gateway to the Highlands. The ambience is relaxed while the bistro has a real convivial atmosphere. The emphasis is on good food, kept simple and traditional, and featuring many bistro classics and a few Savoyard specialities. We have five spacious bedrooms, all with en suite shower room or adjoining bathroom, and a large lounge where you can relax.

Glenearn House, Perth Road, Crieff PH7 3EQ
Tel: 01764 650111
info@yannsatglenearnhouse.com
www.yannsatglenearnhouse.com

5 BEDROOMS, ALL WITH PRIVATE BATHROOM. ALL BEDROOMS NON-SMOKING. FREE HOUSE. CHILDREN AND PETS WELCOME. RESTAURANT MEALS WED-SUN. PERTH 16 MILES. S£££, D££££.

The Auld Bond
198 Dunkeld Road, Perth, Perthshire PH1 3GD • Tel: 01738 446079

This well-known public house is located on the western border of Perth, offering high quality food and ale. The Hungry Horse menu is simply bursting with choice and all the pub favourites are prepared from fresh ingredients. Facilities include an outdoor patio area, a children's play area, and a giant screen on which to watch the live sporting fixtures.

RATES
S – SINGLE ROOM rate   D – Sharing DOUBLE/TWIN ROOM
S£ D£ =Under £35   S££ D££ =£36-£45   S£££ D£££ =£46-£55   S££££ D££££ =Over £55

This is meant as an indication only and does not show prices for Special Breaks, Weekends, etc. Guests are therefore advised to verify all prices on enquiring or booking.

FERRY BOAT INN (on facing page)

9 BEDROOMS, ALL WITH PRIVATE BATHROOM. REAL ALE. CHILDREN WELCOME. BAR AND RESTAURANT MEALS. INVERNESS 55 MILES.

The Old Mill Inn

rooms • food • drink

The Old Mill Inn, Mill Lane, Pitlochry,
Perthshire PH16 5BH
Phone: 01796 474020
Email: admin@theoldmillpitlochry.co.uk
www.theoldmillinnpitlochry.co.uk

"Enjoy a friendly welcome in the heart of Pitlochry..."

ALL ROOMS EN SUITE. CHILDREN WELCOME. RESTAURANT MEALS.
DUNKELD 11 MILES. D££.

Other specialised holiday guides from FHG

THE GOLF GUIDE • **COUNTRY HOTELS** OF BRITAIN

WEEKEND & SHORT BREAK HOLIDAYS IN BRITAIN

The bestselling and original **PETS WELCOME!**

500 GREAT PLACES TO STAY • **SELF-CATERING HOLIDAYS** IN BRITAIN

BED & BREAKFAST STOPS • **CARAVAN & CAMPING HOLIDAYS**

FAMILY BREAKS IN BRITAIN

Published annually: available in all good bookshops or direct from the publisher:
FHG Guides, Abbey Mill Business Centre, Seedhill, Paisley PA1 1TJ
Tel: 0141 887 0428 • Fax: 0141 889 7204
e-mail: admin@fhguides.co.uk • www.holidayguides.com

THE MUNRO INN (on facing page)

ALL ROOMS EN SUITE. CHILDREN AND PETS WELCOME. RESTAURANT MEALS.
CALLANDER 8 MILES.

The Munro Inn

Tel: 01877 384333
enquiries@munro-inn.com • www.munro-inn.com

The Munro Inn
Strathyre, Perthshire FK18 8NA

Just an hour from the sights of Loch Lomond, Glasgow and Edinburgh we're just far enough away from it all to still guarantee you either a restful Highlands retreat, or a fantastic base camp for an array of exciting outdoor activities and challenging hillwalking.

- Based in Queen Elizabeth Forest Park in the beautiful Trossachs •
- Home cooked food served all day every day •
- Public and lounge bars with over 30 malt whiskies •
- Child-friendly with well fitted games room •

Whether you're looking for relaxing rambles, a fun family holiday, challenging hill walking or simply a retreat to get some peace and quiet you'll find everything you need at the Inn or the surrounding area.

We are also 100% dog friendly - why leave your dog at home when they'll love the Highlands so much? At the Munro they're guests like any other and stay in your room with you!

Why stay at the Munro Inn?
Traditional Scottish inn hospitality
Great dining and drinking
Perfectly located to enjoy the Trossachs or the cities
Child and dog friendly
Endless outdoor activities nearby
Perfect stopoff on the Rob Roy Way
Exceptional quality standards
Welcoming to all ages and groups
Wifi throughout

Stirling & The Trossachs

Behind The Wall
14 Melville Street, Falkirk, Stirlingshire FK1 1HZ
Tel: 01324633338 • www.behindthewall.co.uk

The radical way to live! Anything goes here at Behind The Wall, who proclaim that they 'make their own rules and then bend them'. This bar, eatery and entertainment venue is open all day and is ideal for the whole family, including young children. Facilities include an outdoor area and conservatory; wifi throughout.

The Rosebank
Main Street, Camelon, Falkirk, Stirlingshire FK1 4DS
Tel: 01324 611842 • Fax: 01324 617154

This prestigious Listed building is located in the small village of Camelon, beside the Forth and Clyde Canal between Edinburgh and Glasgow, and stands on the site of a former whisky distillery. Now a bar and 200-cover restaurant, it is ideal for a relaxing meal with friends or family.

The Outside Inn
Bellsdyke Road, Larbert, Stirlingshire FK5 4EG • Tel: 01324 579411

A newly refurbished inn, particularly popular with business people, shoppers and family diners. Original features include waterfalls and paths running through the indoor space; in summer, take advantage of the attractive beer garden. Facilities include wifi throughout and a smoking shelter.

RATES   S – SINGLE ROOM rate   D – Sharing DOUBLE/TWIN ROOM

S£ D£ =Under £35   S££ D££ =£36-£45   S£££ D£££ =£46-£55   S££££ D££££ =Over £55

This is meant as an indication only and does not show prices for Special Breaks, Weekends, etc. Guests are therefore advised to verify all prices on enquiring or booking.

Scottish Islands   **SCOTLAND** 157

Scottish Islands

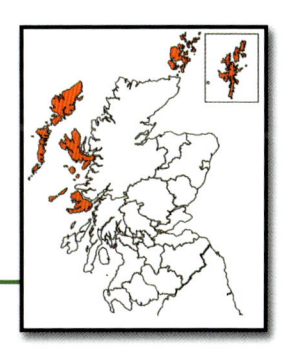

Orkney Isles

The Taversoe, Rousay, Orkney KW17 2PT • 01856 821325
www.taversoehotel.co.uk • careymaguire@taversoehotel.co.uk

Rousay, just 20 minutes' ferry crossing from the Orkney mainland, is a small friendly island graced with archaeological treasures, spectacular views and abundant wildlife. The Taversoe lies between the historic Tomb Trail and the renowned Westness Walk. Be as energetic as you like: walk, cycle or laze, unwind in a 'get away from it all' atmosphere.

- Rural location with panoramic sea views
- Accommodation available year round
- Friendly bar with games room • Private guest lounge
- A selection of local produce meals served daily
- Special diets catered for

3 BEDROOMS, 1 WITH PRIVATE BATHROOM. RESTAURANT MEALS. CAITHNESS 10 MILES.

RATES

Normal Bed & Breakfast rate per person
(single room)

PRICE RANGE	CATEGORY
Under £35	S£
£36-£45	S££
£46-£55	S£££
Over £55	S££££

Normal Bed & Breakfast rate per person
(sharing double/twin room)

PRICE RANGE	CATEGORY
Under £35	D£
£36-£45	D££
£46-£55	D£££
Over £55	D££££

This is meant as an indication only and does not show prices for Special Breaks, Weekends, etc. Guests are therefore advised to verify all prices on enquiring or booking.

SCOTLAND — Scottish Islands

Isle of Skye

Since the 1700s this solid white-washed hotel has gazed over the Sound of Sleat to the Knoydart Mountains and the beautiful Sands of Morar, and as well as being one of the oldest coaching inns on the west coast, it is surely one of the most idyllically situated.

Not surprisingly, seafood features extensively on the menu here, together with local venison and other fine Scottish produce, and tasty bar lunches and suppers are offered as an alternative to the more formal cuisine served in the restaurant.

A private residents' lounge is furnished to the same high standard of comfort as the cosy guest rooms, all of which have private facilities.

ARDVASAR HOTEL
Ardvasar, Sleat, Isle of Skye IV45 8RS
Tel: 01471 844223 • Fax: 01471 844495
www.ardvasarhotel.com
e-mail: richard@ardvasar-hotel.demon.co.uk

10 BEDROOMS, ALL WITH PRIVATE BATHROOM. ALL BEDROOMS NON-SMOKING. FREE HOUSE WITH REAL ALE. CHILDREN AND PETS WELCOME. BAR MEALS AND RESTAURANT MEALS. BROADFORD 16 MILES. S££££, D££££.

Other specialised holiday guides from FHG

THE GOLF GUIDE • COUNTRY HOTELS OF BRITAIN
WEEKEND & SHORT BREAK HOLIDAYS IN BRITAIN
The bestselling and original **PETS WELCOME!**
500 GREAT PLACES TO STAY • SELF-CATERING HOLIDAYS IN BRITAIN
BED & BREAKFAST STOPS • CARAVAN & CAMPING HOLIDAYS
FAMILY BREAKS IN BRITAIN

Published annually: available in all good bookshops or direct from the publisher:
FHG Guides, Abbey Mill Business Centre, Seedhill, Paisley PA1 1TJ
Tel: 0141 887 0428 • Fax: 0141 889 7204
e-mail: admin@fhguides.co.uk • www.holidayguides.com

WALES 159

Trewern Arms Hotel, Nevern, Newport, Pembrokeshire, page 169

Wales

Anglesey & Gwynedd

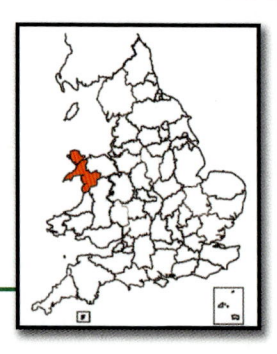

The Antelope Inn
Holyhead Road, Bangor, Gwynedd LL57 2HZ
Tel: 01248 362162 • Fax: 01248 363710

This country inn offers stunning views of the Menai Straits. The interior has an open plan layout, with oak-beamed ceilings and comfortable seating. The restaurant has built up a reputation for serving fresh fish dishes from an adventurous specials board, plus a range of pub favourites. Attractions include a large beer garden and weekly quizzes.

RATES

Normal Bed & Breakfast rate per person **(single room)**

PRICE RANGE	CATEGORY
Under £35	S£
£36-£45	S££
£46-£55	S£££
Over £55	S££££

Normal Bed & Breakfast rate per person **(sharing double/twin room)**

PRICE RANGE	CATEGORY
Under £35	D£
£36-£45	D££
£46-£55	D£££
Over £55	D££££

This is meant as an indication only and does not show prices for Special Breaks, Weekends, etc. Guests are therefore advised to verify all prices on enquiring or booking.

Family-Friendly
Pubs, Inns & Hotels
See the Supplement on pages 179-182 for establishments which really welcome children

TYN-Y-GROES HOTEL (on facing page)

ALL BEDROOMS WITH PRIVATE BATHROOM. CHILDREN WELCOME, DOGS BY ARRANGEMENT. BAR SNACKS AND RESTAURANT MEALS. NON-SMOKING AREAS. DOLGELLAU 4 MILES. S££, D££.

Anglesey & Gwynedd WALES 161

TYN-Y-GROES HOTEL
Accommodation in Snowdonia National Park

Wales Cymru ★★★

16th century coaching inn on the A470 near the village of Ganllwyd overlooking the Mawddach river. Close to Coed-y-Brenin mountain bike centre. Nature trails, walks, fishing (permits issued).

- En suite bedrooms with central heating and TV
- Cot/high chair available • Restaurant and dining room. Bar snacks
- Beer garden • Dogs by arrangement • Open all year

Ganllwyd, Dolgellau LL40 2HN • Tel: 01341 440275
www.tynygroes.com
e-mail: nephi@tynyg.wanadoo.co.uk

North Wales

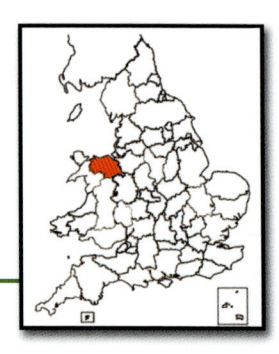

The Halfway House
Church Street, Golftyn, Connahs Quay, North Wales CH5 4AS • Tel: 01244 819013

The Halfway House has recently undergone a major refurbishment and is now a stylish venue for the enjoyment of delicious food and well-kept beers and ales. The interior remains traditional and homely and facilities include a beer garden and a children's play area.

RATES

Normal Bed & Breakfast rate per person (single room)

PRICE RANGE	CATEGORY
Under £35	S£
£36-£45	S££
£46-£55	S£££
Over £55	S££££

Normal Bed & Breakfast rate per person (sharing double/twin room)

PRICE RANGE	CATEGORY
Under £35	D£
£36-£45	D££
£46-£55	D£££
Over £55	D££££

This is meant as an indication only and does not show prices for Special Breaks, Weekends, etc. Guests are therefore advised to verify all prices on enquiring or booking.

THE HAWK & BUCKLE INN (on facing page)

10 BEDROOMS, ALL WITH PRIVATE BATHROOM. FREE HOUSE WITH REAL ALE.
CHILDREN WELCOME, PETS BY ARRANGEMENT. BAR AND RESTAURANT MEALS. DENBIGH 5 MILES.

The Hawk & Buckle Inn

Llannefydd, Denbigh, Denbighshire LL16 5ED
Tel: 01745 540249

This 17th century coaching inn, recently under new management and with extensive renovation throughout, is located on the old stagecoach route to Holyhead between Denbigh and Abergele. Llannefydd is a peaceful, unspoilt village sitting high in the hills. This spot 200m above sea level looks out to beautiful views of the sea - on a clear day it is possible to see as far as Blackpool and the Cumbrian mountains.

The inn's black beamed lounge bar has undergone a complete renovation and transformation while retaining its character and charm, ideal if you want to take it easy after an invigorating countryside walk, while enjoying a wide range of fine wines, ales and spirits.

There is an extensive menu and where possible food is prepared from fresh, local ingredients; in addition to our usual evening menu we offer special Early Bird and Sunday lunch menus, and unique menus during the many special functions and themed nights the Inn holds.

The Hawk and Buckle also offers fine overnight accommodation in individually decorated and furnished en suite rooms, each of which has had complete renovation to reflect our desire for a cleaner, more elegant setting to complement the renovation in the rest of the building. Each bathroom includes a jacuzzi bath, shower and complimentary toiletries; one room has a double jacuzzi bath and complimentary bathrobes provided. TV and Internet access (via wireless) is available in each room.

Guests may travel in any direction and be assured of interesting, scenic and charming places to visit. Whilst off the beaten track, the Inn is not far from the A55 which allows access to Snowdonia National Park, Llandudno, Betws-y-Coed, Bodnant Gardens and Chester, to name but a few. A member of staff will be happy to help you with suggestions for places to see during your stay as well as any events of interest during the tourist season, so please do not hesitate to ask.

e-mail: enquiries@hawkandbuckleinn.com
www.hawkandbuckleinn.com

The White Horse Inn
The Square, Cilcain, Mold, North Wales CH7 5NN • Tel: 01352 740142

Located on the slope of Moel Fammau in North wales, an area of outstanding natural beauty. Homemade bar meals are prepared fresh to order, and the bar is stocked with a choice of real ales, draught beers, lagers and wines. The pub is especially popular with walkers, cyclists and horse riders. Children over 14 years welcome.

THE HARBOUR
Foryd Road, Rhyl, North Wales LL18 5BA • Tel: 01745 360644

The Harbour can be found just over the bridge in the little town of Rhyl. The building is attractively decorated inside and out, with comfortable fittings and furnishings, and the bar is well stocked with draught beers, spirits, ales and wines. Sample one of the pub's hearty meals which are available at most reasonable prices.

The Grapes Inn
Francis Road, Moss, Wrexham, North Wales LL11 6EB • Tel: 01978 720585

A free house with a homely interior made up of wooden furnishings, an open log fire and family artefacts including a collection of 250 jugs on beamed shelving. Beers, real ales, wines, spirits and whiskies are available - and don;t forget to try the delicious grills with chips and vegetables. Facilities include a beer garden, pool table and jukebox.

The Black Horse
Hall Street, Penycae, Wrexham, North Wales LL14 2RU • Tel: 01978 840796

A pint at the Black Horse comes with the guarantee of exeptional views over Llangollen and Castle Dinas Brian. It is situated on the edge of Penycae, just a short walk to the lakes and resevoirs, and popular with hikers, walkers and cyclists. Food is served throughout the day. Regular entertainment includes live music, karaoke, discos and djs.

THE HAND AT LLANARMON (on facing page)

13 BEDROOMS, ALL WITH PRIVATE BATHROOM. ALL BEDROOMS NON-SMOKING. FREE HOUSE WITH REAL ALE. CHILDREN AND PETS WELCOME. BAR AND RESTAURANT MEALS. LLANGOLLEN 10 MILES. S£££, D££.

The Hand at Llanarmon

Standing in the glorious and hidden Ceiriog Valley, The Hand at Llanarmon radiates charm and character. With 13 comfortable en suite bedrooms, roaring log fires, and fabulous food served with flair and generosity, this is a wonderful base for most country pursuits, or just relaxing in good company.

Tel: 01691 600666
e-mail: reception@thehandhotel.co.uk
www.TheHandHotel.co.uk

Llanarmon DC
Ceiriog Valley
Near Llangollen
North Wales
LL20 7LD

Carmarthenshire

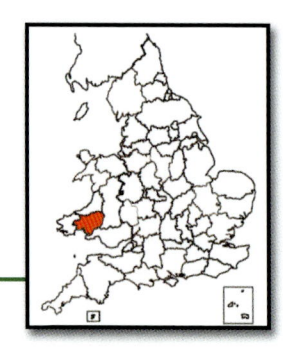

The Prince of Wales Inn
Mynyddygarreg, Kidwelly, Carmarthenshire SA17 4RP • Tel: 01554 890522
This free house boasts six of its own real ales as well as several other Welsh ones and one real cider - all on tap! The size of the pub helps create a cosy, intimate ambience, with a log fire and interesting artefacts and memorabilia throughout.

The Phoenix
Penygroes Road, Gorslas, Llanelli, Carmarthenshire SA14 7LA • Tel: 01269 844438
The Phoenix is set in the rural village of Gorslas, a regular ramblers' haunt. The bar is stocked with a wide range of lagers, beers and wines and is the only public house in the village where food is served. The menu is imaginative and all dishes are prepared from fresh ingredients. Regular entertainment includes 60/70s nights, quiz nights and themed food evenings.

The Thomas Arms Hotel
Thomas Street, Llanelli, Carmarthenshire SA15 3JF • Tel: 01554 772043
Having undergone a major refurbishment, the pub now boasts a unique atmosphere, with a neutral colour scheme and homely fixtures and furnishings. This is the ideal spot for a relaxing drink after a hard day at work or for a family lunch or dinner. Accommodation is in ten en suite bedrooms with all modern facilities.

THE STRADLEY ARMS
1 Stradley Road, Furnace, Llanelli, Carmarthenshire SA15 4ET
Tel: 01554 757968
For a quiet drink or meal, pop in to the Stradley Arms, located in the heart of the village of Furnace. Regular attractions include a weekly quiz, a large beer garden, a plasma screen and free wi-fi throughout.

www.holidayguides.com

Ceredigion

The Ship Inn
Tresaith, Cardigan, Ceredigion SA43 2JL • Tel: 01239 811816

Tresaith is a quaint little coastal village with popular beaches and one pub - the Ship Inn. Patrons can relax and enjoy the stunning views of the sea, and food is served throughout the day at reasonable prices. Accommodation is in four en suite rooms with colour TV.

The Black Lion Hotel
Ponyrhydfendigaid, Ystrad Meurig, Ceredigion SY25 6BE
Tel: 01974 831624 • Fax: 01974 831052 • www.blacklionhotel.co.uk

Located only 20 minutes from Aberystwyth is this cosy, comfortable pub hotel, ideal for a walking holiday, with many walkways, cycle paths and nature trails to explore. There is a stylish bar and restuarant, plus five en suite bedrooms, each with modern facilities.

THE THREE HORSESHOES INN
Llangeitho, Tregaron, Ceredigion SY25 6TW • Tel: 01974 821244

Set in the rural heart of West Wales is this family-run pub with a large beer garden, a games room and a takeaway food service. All dishes are home-made and prepared from fresh ingredients. The bar offers a good selection of ales, draught beers and fine wines.

The Lord Beechings
Alexardra Road, Aberystwyth, Ceredigion ST23 1LE • Tel: 01970 625069

Aberystwyth is a university town and this large pub venue is a student favourite. Order food at the contemporary bar and relax with a pint of guest ale in a comfy chair while it is cooked to your liking. Facilities include free wi-fi.

Pembrokeshire

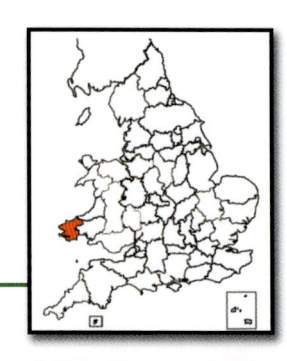

The Dial Inn is situated in Lamphey village, two miles east of Pembroke, and only a stone's throw from the Bishop's Palace.

THE DIAL INN
Ridgeway Road, Lamphey, Pembroke, Pembrokeshire SA71 5NU
Tel: 01646 672426
e-mail: dialinn@btconnect.com

This elegant, interesting and deceptively large village pub has excellent bar food, a daily blackboard menu, and an imaginative dining room menu.

All food is freshly prepared and cooked.

Also available are fine wines and cask-conditioned ales, and the inn is open for coffee, lunch, dinner and bar meals.

It is listed in all the best food and beer guides including 'Which?' and the AA. CAMRA.

5 BEDROOMS, ALL WITH PRIVATE BATHROOM. FREE HOUSE WITH REAL ALE. CHILDREN WELCOME. BAR AND RESTAURANT MEALS. NON-SMOKING AREAS. PEMBROKE 2 MILES. S£££served, D££££.

TREWERN ARMS HOTEL (on facing page)

10 BEDROOMS, ALL WITH PRIVATE BATHROOM. ALL BEDROOMS NON-SMOKING. FREE HOUSE WITH REAL ALE. CHILDREN WELCOME. BAR MEALS, RESTAURANT EVENINGS ONLY. NON-SMOKING AREAS. NEWPORT 2 MILES. S£££, D££££.

TREWERN ARMS HOTEL

Nevern, Newport, Pembrokeshire SA42 0NB
Tel: 01239 820395 • Fax: 01239 820173

Wales Cymru
★★★★
Inn

AA
★★★★
INN

www.trewernarms.com
e-mail: info@trewern-arms-pembrokeshire.co.uk

Set deep in a forested and secluded valley on the banks of the River Nevern, this picturesque, 16th century hostelry has a warmth of welcome that is immediately apparent in the interestingly-shaped Brew House Bar with its original flagstone floors, stone walls, old settles and beams decorated with an accumulated collection of bric-a-brac. Bar meals are served here from a popular grill area. By contrast, the Lounge Bar is furnished on cottage lines and the fine restaurant has received many accolades from far and wide for its culinary delights.

The tranquil village of Nevern is ideally placed for Pembrokeshire's historic sites and uncrowded, sandy beaches and the accommodation offered at this recommended retreat is in the multi-starred class.

Powys

The Castle of Brecon Hotel
The Castle Square, Brecon, Powys LD3 9DB
Tel: 01874 624611 • www.breconcastle.co.uk

The hotel has recently undergone refurbishment yet retains original features such as an open log fire and a medieval room with leaded windows. Food plays an important role in the day-to-day running of this establishment, dishes being prepared from local produce and home-grown herbs and vegetables. 30 en suite rooms have all modern facilities.

The Farmer's Arms
Cwmdu, Near Crickhowell, Powys NP8 1RU • Tel: 01874 730464

A Welsh country inn serving good Welsh ales, guest ales and affordable wines, as well as exceptional food prepared from local produce. Those who enjoy fishing, pony trekking and walking will appreciate the pub"s ideal location as a base for such activities. Bed and breakfast accommodation is also available in two single and two twin/double/family bedrooms with modern facilities.

RATES

Normal Bed & Breakfast rate per person
(single room)

PRICE RANGE	CATEGORY
Under £35	S£
£36-£45	S££
£46-£55	S£££
Over £55	S££££

Normal Bed & Breakfast rate per person
(sharing double/twin room)

PRICE RANGE	CATEGORY
Under £35	D£
£36-£45	D££
£46-£55	D£££
Over £55	D££££

This is meant as an indication only and does not show prices for Special Breaks, Weekends, etc. Guests are therefore advised to verify all prices on enquiring or booking.

BASKERVILLE ARMS HOTEL (on facing page)

13 BEDROOMS, ALL WITH PRIVATE BATHROOM. ALL BEDROOMS NON-SMOKING. FREE HOUSE WITH REAL ALE. CHILDREN AND PETS WELCOME. BAR AND RESTAURANT MEALS. BRECON 17 MILES. S££, D££.

BASKERVILLE ARMS HOTEL

Delightfully placed in the upper reaches of the Wye Valley with the Black Mountains and Brecon Beacons on the doorstep, this comfortable retreat could not be better placed for lovers of both lush and wild unspoilt scenery. Hay-on-Wye, the 'town of books' is only 1.2 miles away with its narrow streets, antique shops and over 30 bookshops.

Run by resident proprietors, June and David, the hotel provides tasty, home-cooked food in bar and restaurant, using the best local produce.

With so many pursuits to enjoy in the area, this little hotel is a fine holiday base and well-appointed en suite bedrooms serve the purpose excellently. Totally non-smoking.

Single from £45, Double/Twin from £42.
See website for Special Rate Breaks.

Clyro, Near Hay-on-Wye, Herefordshire HR3 5RZ
Tel: 01497 820670
e-mail: info@baskervillearms.co.uk
www.baskervillearms.co.uk

Red Lion Inn

Llanfihangel-nant-Melan
New Radnor • Powys LD8 2TN

Wales Cymru ★★★

A cosy, 16th century Drovers Inn with a log-burning fire in the beamed lounge bar. Renowned for acclaimed hospitality, traditional and modern cookery, wines and ales.

Guests can relax in front of the log burning fires in our beamed lounge bars or go through to our dining room or terrace conservatory for a meal. Or stroll in the lovely gardens with wonderful views.

Seven warm, comfortable, en suite rooms, all with colour TV, radio alarm clock, and complimentary tea/coffee tray. Three double, one twin, and three motel-style rooms, whose freedom and privacy makes them much favoured with walkers, riders and bikers.

The Inn has a large private car park
- Sun trap pub garden • Residents' private garden
- Facilities for washing off mud from bicycles
- Locked storage room for bicycles

The wild and ancient landscape of Mid Wales is one of Britain's best-kept secrets, and nestling in the Cwm Neigl, three miles west of New Radnor on the A44, is The Red Lion Inn – the perfect base for exploring the rolling Radnorshire Hills, the glorious Elan Valley and the spectacular lakes and mountains of Mid Wales. It is in an area of breathtaking natural beauty which has inspired Welsh Poets over the centuries.

Well behaved pets welcome. Short Breaks available.

New for 2010 Bunk Room – £12 pppn

Tel: 01544 350220 • Mobile: 07766 296145
e-mail: john@redlionmidwales.co.uk • www.redlionmidwales

South Wales

THE LION INN

An award-winning 16th century coaching inn with luxury B&B or Self-catering cottage.

Situated in the heart of the beautiful Wye Valley, bordered by the Welsh Mountains and the Royal Forest of Dean.

The Inn serves a large selection of bar snacks, as well as cask ales, with a variety of specialist dishes to tempt the more adventurous diner.

The Lion Inn Cottage is tastefully decorated in traditional style and sleeps four. Colour TV with Sky, central heating, fully equipped kitchen, walled patio.

The Lion Inn, Trelleck, Monmouthshire NP25 4PA
Tel: 01600 860322 • Fax: 01600 860060
e-mail: Debs@LionInn.co.uk • www.lioninn.co.uk

FREE HOUSE WITH REAL ALE. CHILDREN WELCOME. BAR AND RESTAURANT MEALS. NON-SMOKING AREAS. MONMOUTH 5 MILES. S£££, D££££.

RED LION INN (on facing page)

7 BEDROOMS, ALL WITH PRIVATE BATHROOM. REAL ALES. BAR MEALS. KINGTON 6 MILES.

174 PET FRIENDLY PUBS

Pet-Friendly Pubs

A selection of Pubs and Inns where pets are especially welcome!

The Bell Inn, Adderbury, Oxfordshire

The Hood Arms, Kilve, Somerset

The Springer Spaniel
Treburley, near Launceston, Cornwall PL15 9NS
Tel: 01579 370424 • e-mail: enquiries@thespringerspaniel.org.uk
www.thespringerspaniel.org.uk
Country pub providing a warm welcome and specialising in home cooked, fresh, locally sourced food. Emphasis upon game, with beef and lamb from the owner's organic farm. Dogs can snooze by the fire or lounge in the beer garden - water provided
Pet Regulars: some very regular customers and their accompanying owners.

the mardale inn @ st patrick's well
Bampton, Cumbria CA10 2RQ Tel: 01931 713244
www.mardaleinn.co.uk info@mardaleinn.co.uk
Always open • fresh local produce • open fires
fine cask beers • warm beds • Haweswater location.
Daily Telegraph '50 Best Pubs' - May 2008.
Children and dogs welcome
(children must be kept on a short leash at all times!)

The Coledale Inn
Braithwaite, Near Keswick, Cumbria CA12 5TN
Tel: 017687 78272
e-mail: info@coledale-inn.co.uk • www.coledale-inn.co.uk
Friendly, family-run Victorian inn in peaceful location. Ideally situated for touring and walking direct from the hotel grounds. Fine selection of wines and local real ales. Families and pets welcome.

the greyhound @ shap
Shap, Cumbria CA10 3PW • Tel: 01931 716474
www.thegreyhoundshap.co.uk info@greyhoundshap.co.uk
15thC coaching inn • handpulled real ales plus extensive wine list • traditional local food served daily • bedrooms with en suite facilities • families, walkers and dogs welcome
• fantastic Sunday lunch • M6 J39 only 5 minutes.

PET FRIENDLY PUBS 175

Tower Bank Arms
Near Sawrey, Ambleside, Cumbria LA22 0LF • Tel: 015394 36334
enquiries@towerbankarms.com • www.towerbankarms.co.uk

17thC Inn situated in the village of Near Sawrey, next to Hilltop, Beatrix Potter's former home. With many original features, and offering fresh local food and traditional local ales.

Water and treats provided • Dogs allowed in bar and accommodation

PORT LIGHT Hotel, Restaurant & Inn
Bolberry Down, Malborough, Near Salcombe, Devon TQ7 3DY
Tel: (01548) 561384 or (07970) 859992 • Sean & Hazel Hassall
e-mail: info@portlight.co.uk • www.portlight.co.uk

Luxury en suite rooms, easy access onto the gardens. Close to secluded sandy cove (dogs permitted). No charge for pets which are most welcome throughout the hotel. Outstanding food and service. Winner 2004 "Dogs Trust" Best Pet Hotel in England. Self-catering cottages also available.

Pets may dine in bar area • Pet food fridge available

The Trout & Tipple

Julie and Shaun invite you to The Trout & Tipple, a quiet pub just a mile outside Tavistock, with a keen following for its real ale, (locally brewed Jail Ale and Teignworthy), real food and real welcome. It is a family-friendly pub – children are welcome – with a games room, patio area, dining room and a large car park. Traditional pub fare is served, with trout from the Tavistock Trout Fishery featuring on the menu; Sunday roasts are very popular.

Dogs welcome, bowls of water and treats available on request.

Parkwood Road, Tavistock Devon PL19 0JS
Tel: 01822 618886
www.troutandtipple.co.uk

The Gaggle of Geese
Buckland Newton, Dorchester, Dorset DT2 7BS
01300 345249 • www.thegaggle.co.uk

Large pub with skittle alley, five acres of land including an orchard. Everything on our menu we make ourselves and as much of it is as locally sourced and seasonal as possible. Sister pub to The European Inn at Piddletrenthide.

Pets welcome throughout • Water/food; fire in winter

The Fisherman's Haunt
Salisbury Road, Winkton, Christchurch, Dorset BH23 7AS
Tel: 01202 477283

Traditional coaching inn with 12 stylishly refurbished bedrooms, some adapted for disabled access. Good food, wine and Fuller's cask ales. Close to Bournemouth Airport and many places of interest. Pets welcome.
Pets allowed in main bar and lounge for dining.
Two pet-friendly rooms in accommodation block.

www.fullershotels.com

Please mention **Pubs & Inns**
when making enquiries about accommodation featured in these pages

PET FRIENDLY PUBS

The European Inn
www.european-inn.co.uk
Piddletrenthide, Dorchester, Dorset DT2 7QT
Tel: 01300 348308 • info@european-inn.co.uk

Small country pub with two sumptuous bedrooms.
Taste of the West South West Dining Pub of the Year 2007.
Sister pub to The Gaggle of Geese at Buckland Newton.
Pets welcome throughout • Water/food; fire in winter • Good local walks.
Pet Residents: Summer and her daughters Minnie and Maude (Cocker Spaniels)

Three Horseshoes
Powerstock, Bridport, Dorset DT6 3TF • 01308 485328
info@threehorseshoesinn.com
www.threehorseshoesinn.com

'The Shoes' is a Victorian inn tucked away in a peaceful part of West Dorset. The Inn boasts a great reputation for excellent cuisine. An à la carte menu with specials board is served daily, plus lunchtime snacks. Dogs and children welcome.
Pets welcome in bar, garden and accommodation.
Pet Residents: JJ and Piglet. Pet Regular: Guinness

The White Swan
The Square, 31 High Street, Swanage, Dorset BH19 2LJ • 01929 423804
e-mail: info@whiteswansanage.co.uk • www.whiteswansanage.co.uk

A pub with a warm and friendly atmosphere, three minutes from the beach. Traditional pub food, Sunday roasts. Large beer garden. En suite accommodation with parking. Free wifi and internet access. TV and pool table. Children and dogs welcome.
Water, treats • Dogs allowed in beer garden, bar area and accommodation.
Pet resident: Bagsy (Sharpei). Regulars: Liddy and Em (Black Labradors), Sally and Sophie (Jack Russells), Patch (Jack Russell), Prince (King Charles Spaniel).

The Whalebone Freehouse
www.thewhaleboneinn.co.uk
Chapel Road, Fingringhoe, Colchester, Essex CO5 7BG
Tel/Fax: 01206 729307 • vicki@thewhaleboneinn.co.uk

Only minutes from Colchester, the Whalebone offers a wide range of excellent food and real ales. Pets are most welcome inside the pub and in the beer garden. Excellent dog-walking trails in and around Fingringhoe. Water bowls provided on request.
Pet Residents: Rosie and Poppy (Basset Hounds)

The Tunnel House Inn
Coates, Cirencester, Gloucestershire GL7 6PW • 01285 770280
e-mail: bookings@tunnelhouse.com • www.tunnelhouse.com

A traditional Cotswold pub set on the edge of a wood. The perfect haven for pets, families, in fact everyone. Home-cooked pub food, traditional ales and ciders. Endless walks lead off from the pub in all directions.
Pets are welcome in all areas inside and out
Plenty of space; water and occasional treats provided.
Pet Regular: Madge, very friendly Patterdale terrier - loves other dogs too!

The White Buck
www.fullershotels.com • **01425 402264**
Bisterne Close, Burley, Ringwood, Hampshire BH24 4AZ

Victorian Inn blending tradition with modern comfort, located in the heart of the New Forest, with 7 stylish bedrooms, excellent restaurant and bar. Play area and log trail available for children. Pets welcome.
Dogs are permitted in the bar area and bedrooms 1, 3 and 8 only.

PET FRIENDLY PUBS 177

BLACK HORSE INN
Pilgrims Way, Thurnham, Kent ME14 3LD
Tel: 01622 737185 • info@wellieboot.net • www.wellieboot.net

A homely and welcoming inn with its origins in the 18thC, The Black Horse is adorned with hops and beams, and has an open log fireplace to welcome you in winter. A separate annexe has 30 beautiful en suite bedrooms.

Pets can stay in B&B rooms • Welcome in bar on lead
Dog bin and poop bags provided • Maps of local walks available.

The Assheton Arms, Downham, Near Clitheroe BB7 4BJ

A delightful traditional country pub in a picturesque village in the beautiful Ribble Valley. Hosts, David and Wendy Busby offer a range of food to suit all tastes, specialising in seafood. There is a variety of modern and traditional beers; ample parking; patio for summer months. Children and dogs welcome.

Tel: 01200 441227 • www.assheton-arms.co.uk

The Inn at Whitewell • Forest of Bowland
Near Clitheroe, Lancs BB7 3AT • Tel: 01200 448222
reception@innatwhitewell.com • www.innatwhitewell.com

14thC inn in the beautiful Forest of Bowland.
7 miles fishing from our doorstep - trout, sea trout and salmon.
23 glamorous bedrooms, award-winning kitchen.
Voted by *The Independent* "One of the 50 Best UK Hotels"
Pets welcome in all areas except the kitchen!

Stiffkey Red Lion Tel: 01328 830552
44 Wells Road, Stiffkey, Norfolk NR23 1AJ
e-mail: redlion@stiffkey.com • www.stiffkey.com

5 ground floor en suite bedrooms, 5 on first floor;
all with their own external door.
Pets warmly welcomed

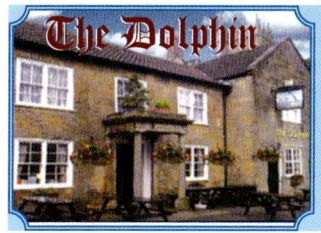

The Dolphin
22 Silver Street, Ilminster, Somerset TA19 0DR • 01460 57904

Cosy, friendly atmosphere. Fully stocked bar, serving a good selection of real ales, lagers, spirits, and fine wines. Excellent home-cooked food served daily. Families welcome. Pool table. Parking nearby. Good walks close by.

Clean water • Dog treats • Pets allowed inside and outside

www.holidayguides.com

178 PET FRIENDLY PUBS

Old Ship Inn
Uckfield Road, Ringmer, East Sussex BN8 5RP • 01273 814223
e-mail: info@oldshippub.co.uk • www.oldshippub.co.uk

On the A26 between Lewes and Uckfield, this family-run 17thC inn is the perfect place to relax, with food served from 12 to 9.30pm daily. The charming oak-beamed bar and restaurant is set in one acre of well tended, enclosed gardens. Well behaved dogs welcome inside.
Pet Resident: Marley (Bernese Mountain Dog)

The Lamb Inn
High Street, Hindon, Wiltshire SP3 6DP
Tel: 01747 820573 • Fax: 01747 820605
www.lambathindon.co.uk

12th Century historic inn with bedrooms full of character. Outstanding food and great wine selection.
Pets welcome in the bar and bedrooms. ETC/AA ★★★★

The Castle Inn
7 Wistowgate, Cawood
Selby, North Yorkshire YO8 3SH
Tel: 01757 268324
info@castleinncawood.co.uk • www.castleinncawood.co.uk

18thC village pub with a 60-seat restaurant and an 18-pitch caravan site. All food is local and fresh.
Water bowls outside.
Pet Resident: Elvis (10-year old Springer Spaniel)

Simonstone Hall
Hawes, North Yorkshire DL8 3LY
Tel: 01969 667255 • www.simonstonehall.com

Welcoming bar with great atmosphere.
Wide range of bar meals from snacks to Sunday Lunch.
Comfortable accommodation.
Dogs of all shapes sizes and breeds welcome.

THE MUNRO INN
Strathyre, Perthshire FK18 8NA • Tel: 01877 384333
www.munro-inn.com

Chilled out Robbie warmly welcomes doggy friends to the Munro Inn in beautiful highland Perthshire. Perfect base for walking, cycling, climbing, water sports, fishing or relaxing! Great home cooking, lively bar, luxurious en suite bedrooms, drying room, broadband internet.

Four Seasons Hotel
St Fillans, Perthshire • Tel: 01764 685333

Hotel in picturesque setting offering comfortable bedrooms, chalets and apartment. Fine dining restaurant and bar.
Dogs allowed in all non-food areas.

# Family-Friendly Pubs & Inns

This is a selection of establishments which make an extra effort to cater for parents and children. The majority provide a separate children's menu or they may be willing to serve small portions of main course dishes on request; there are often separate outdoor or indoor play areas where the junior members of the family can let off steam while Mum and Dad unwind over a drink.

NB: Not all of the establishments featured here have a listing in the main section of this book.

- half portions
- children's menu
- garden or play area
- baby-changing facilities
- high chairs
- family room

THE WELLINGTON ARMS
203 Yorktown Road, Sandhurst,
Berkshire GU47 9BN
Tel: 01252 872408
www.thewellingtonarms.co.uk

CHURCH HOUSE HOTEL
50 Rowsham Dell, Giffard Park
Milton Keynes MK14 5SJ
Tel: 01908 216030
www.churchhousehotel.co.uk

CROOKED INN
Stoketon Cross, Trematon,
Saltash, Cornwall PL12 4RZ
Tel: 01752 848177
www.crooked-inn.co.uk

KINGS ARMS HOTEL
Hawkshead, Ambleside,
Cumbria LA22 0NZ
Tel: 015394 36372
www.kingsarmshawkshead.co.uk

EAGLE & CHILD INN
Kendal Road, Staveley,
Cumbria LA8 9LP
Tel: 01539 821320
www.eaglechildinn.co.uk

FAMILY-FRIENDLY PUBS & INNS

MARDALE INN
St Patrick's Well, Bampton,
Cumbria CA19 2RQ
Tel: 01931 713244
www.mardaleinn.co.uk

BRACKENRIGG INN
Watermillock, Ullswater,
Cumbria CA11 0LP
Tel: 01768 486206
www.brackenrigginn.co.uk

GREYHOUND HOTEL
Main Street, Shap, Penrith,
Cumbria CA10 3PW
Tel: 01931 716474
www.greyhoundshap.co.uk

QUEEN'S HEAD
Main Street, Hawkshead,
Cumbria LA22 0NS
Tel: 015394 36271
www.queensheadhotel.co.uk

DOG & PARTRIDGE
Swinscoe, Ashbourne,
Derbyshire DE6 2HS
Tel: 01335 343183
www.dogandpartridge.co.uk

MALTSTERS ARMS
Bow Creek, Tuckenhay,
Near Totnes, Devon TQ9 7EQ
Tel: 01803 732350
www.tuckenhay.com

THE CRICKETERS
Clavering, Near Saffron Walden,
Essex CB11 4QT
Tel: 01799 550442
www.thecricketers.co.uk

RHYDSPENCE INN
Whitney-on-Wye, Near Hay-on-Wye,
Herefordshire HR3 6EU
Tel: 01497 831262
www.rhydspence-inn.co.uk

FAMILY-FRIENDLY PUBS & INNS 181

WHIPPER-IN HOTEL
Market Place, Oakham,
Leicestershire & Rutland LE15 6DT
Tel: 01572 756971
www.brook-hotels.co.uk

- half portions
- children's menu
- garden or play area
- baby-changing facilities
- high chairs
- family room

MYTTON AND MERMAID
Atcham, Shrewsbury,
Shropshire SY5 6QG
Tel: 01743 761220
www.myttonandmermaid.co.uk

THE REST AND BE THANKFUL
Wheddon Cross, Minehead,
Somerset TA24 7DR
Tel: 01643 841222
www.restandbethankful.co.uk

YANN'S AT GLENEARN HOUSE
Perth Road, Crieff,
Perth & Kinross PH7 3EQ
Tel: 01764 650111
www.yannsatglenearnhouse.com

ABERDOUR HOTEL
38 High Street, Aberdour,
Fife KY3 0SW
Tel: 01383 860325
www.aberdourhotel.co.uk

THE AULD BOND
198 Dunkeld Road, Perth,
Perthshire PH1 3GD
Tel: 01738 446079

THE HALFWAY HOUSE
Church Street, Golftyn,
Connahs Quay, North Wales CH5 4AS
Tel: 01244 819013

Visit the Winalot website today!

Winalot knows how important giving your dog a balanced diet and plenty of exercise is for their wellbeing. Our website showcases our great balanced range of foods, and the best walks that Britain can offer for you and your furry friend.

www.winalot-dog.co.uk

Trademark owned by Société des Produits Nestlé S.A., Vevey, Switzerland

PURINA
Your Pet, Our Passion.®

FHG READERS' OFFER 2010

LEIGHTON BUZZARD RAILWAY
Page's Park Station, Billington Road,
Leighton Buzzard, Bedfordshire LU7 4TN
Tel: 01525 373888
e-mail: station@lbngrs.org.uk
www.buzzrail.co.uk

One FREE adult/child with full-fare adult ticket
Valid 14/3/2010 - 31/10/2010

NOT TO BE USED IN CONJUNCTION WITH ANY OTHER OFFER

FHG READERS' OFFER 2010

BEKONSCOT MODEL VILLAGE & RAILWAY
Warwick Road, Beaconsfield,
Buckinghamshire HP9 2PL
Tel: 01494 672919
e-mail: info@bekonscot.co.uk
www.bekonscot.co.uk

One child FREE when accompanied by full-paying adult
Valid February to October 2010

NOT TO BE USED IN CONJUNCTION WITH ANY OTHER OFFER

FHG READERS' OFFER 2010

BUCKINGHAMSHIRE RAILWAY CENTRE
Quainton Road Station, Quainton,
Aylesbury HP22 4BY
Tel: 01296 655720
e-mail: office@bucksrailcentre.org
www.bucksrailcentre.org

One child FREE with each full-paying adult
Not valid for Special Events or Day Out with Thomas

NOT TO BE USED IN CONJUNCTION WITH ANY OTHER OFFER

FHG READERS' OFFER 2010

THE RAPTOR FOUNDATION
The Heath, St Ives Road,
Woodhurst, Huntingdon, Cambs PE28 3BT
Tel: 01487 741140 • Fax: 01487 841140
e-mail: heleowl@aol.com
www.raptorfoundation.org.uk

TWO for the price of ONE
Valid until end 2010 (not Bank Holidays)

NOT TO BE USED IN CONJUNCTION WITH ANY OTHER OFFER

A 70-minute journey into the lost world of the English narrow gauge light railway. Features historic steam locomotives from many countries.

PETS MUST BE KEPT UNDER CONTROL AND NOT ALLOWED ON TRACKS

Open: Sundays and Bank Holiday weekends 14 March to 31 October. Additional days in summer, and school holidays.

Directions: on south side of Leighton Buzzard. Follow brown signs from town centre or A505/A4146 bypass.

FHG GUIDES, ABBEY MILL BUSINESS CENTRE, PAISLEY PA1 1TJ • www.holidayguides.com

---

Be a giant in a magical miniature world of make-believe depicting rural England in the 1930s. "A little piece of history that is forever England."

Open: 10am-5pm daily mid February to end October.

Directions: Junction 16 M25, Junction 2 M40.

FHG GUIDES, ABBEY MILL BUSINESS CENTRE, PAISLEY PA1 1TJ • www.holidayguides.com

---

A working steam railway centre. Steam train rides, miniature railway rides, large collection of historic preserved steam locomotives, carriages and wagons.

Open: daily April to October 10.30am to 4.30pm. Variable programme - check website or call.

Directions: off A41 Aylesbury to Bicester Road, 6 miles north west of Aylesbury.

FHG GUIDES, ABBEY MILL BUSINESS CENTRE, PAISLEY PA1 1TJ • www.holidayguides.com

---

Birds of Prey Centre offering audience participation in flying displays which are held 3 times daily. Tours, picnic area, gift shop, tearoom, craft shop.

Open: 10am-5pm all year except Christmas and New Year.

Directions: follow brown tourist signs from B1040.

FHG GUIDES, ABBEY MILL BUSINESS CENTRE, PAISLEY PA1 1TJ • www.holidayguides.com

FHG READERS' OFFER 2010
K·U·P·E·R·A·R·D

NENE VALLEY RAILWAY
Wansford Station, Stibbington,
Peterborough, Cambs PE8 6LR
Tel: 01780 784444
e-mail: nvrorg@nvr.org.uk
www.nvr.org.uk

One child FREE with each full paying adult.
Valid Jan. to end Oct. 2010 (excludes galas and pre-ticketed events)

NOT TO BE USED IN CONJUNCTION WITH ANY OTHER OFFER

FHG READERS' OFFER 2010
K·U·P·E·R·A·R·D

ANSON ENGINE MUSEUM
Anson Road, Poynton,
Cheshire SK12 1TD
Tel: 01625 874426
e-mail: enquiry@enginemuseum.org
www.enginemuseum.org

Saturdays - 2 for 1 entry (when one of equal or greater value is purchased). Valid 12 April-30 Sept 2010

NOT TO BE USED IN CONJUNCTION WITH ANY OTHER OFFER

FHG READERS' OFFER 2010
K·U·P·E·R·A·R·D

NATIONAL SEAL SANCTUARY
Gweek, Helston,
Cornwall TR12 6UG
Tel: 01326 221361
e-mail: seals@sealsanctuary.co.uk
www.sealsanctuary.co.uk

TWO for ONE - on purchase of another ticket of equal or greater value. Valid until December 2010.

NOT TO BE USED IN CONJUNCTION WITH ANY OTHER OFFER

FHG READERS' OFFER 2010
K·U·P·E·R·A·R·D

LAPPA VALLEY RAILWAY
Benny Halt, St Newlyn East,
Newquay, Cornwall TR8 5LX
Tel: 01872 510317
e-mail: info@lappavalley.co.uk
www.lappavalley.co.uk

*75p per person OFF up to a maximum of £3
Valid Easter to end October 2010.*

NOT TO BE USED IN CONJUNCTION WITH ANY OTHER OFFER

Take a trip back in time on the delightful Nene Valley Railway with its heritage steam and diesel locomotives, There is a 7½ mile ride from Wansford to Peterborough via Yarwell, with shop, museum and excellent cafe at Wansford Station (free parking).	**Open:** please phone or see website for details. **Directions:** situated 4 miles north of Peterborough on the A1

FHG GUIDES, ABBEY MILL BUSINESS CENTRE, PAISLEY PA1 1TJ • www.holidayguides.com

As seen on TV, this multi award-winning attraction has a great deal to offer visitors. It houses the largest collection of engines in Europe, local history area, craft centre (bodging and smithy work), with changing exhibitions throughout the season.	**Open:** Easter Sunday until end October, Friday to Sunday and Bank Holidays, 10am to 5pm. **Directions:** approx 7 miles from J1 M60 and 9 miles J3 M60. Follow brown tourist signs from Poynton traffic lights.

FHG GUIDES, ABBEY MILL BUSINESS CENTRE, PAISLEY PA1 1TJ • www.holidayguides.com

Set on the beautiful Helford Estuary, the National Seal Sanctuary is Europe's busiest seal rescue centre. Every year the Sanctuary rescues and releases over 30 injured or abandoned seal pups and provides a refuge for those seals/sea lions unable to be returned to the wild.	**Open:** daily (except Christmas Day) from 10am. **Directions:** from A30 follow signs to Helston, then brown tourist signs to Seal Sanctuary.

FHG GUIDES, ABBEY MILL BUSINESS CENTRE, PAISLEY PA1 1TJ • www.holidayguides.com

Three miniature railways, plus leisure park with canoes, crazy golf, large children's play area with fort, brickpath maze, wooded walks (all inclusive). Dogs welcome (50p).	**Open:** Easter to end October **Directions:** follow brown tourist signs from A30 and A3075

FHG GUIDES, ABBEY MILL BUSINESS CENTRE, PAISLEY PA1 1TJ • www.holidayguides.com

THE BOND MUSEUM
Southey Hill, Keswick,
Cumbria CA12 5NR
Tel: 017687 74044
e-mail: thebondmuseum@aol.com
www.thebondmuseum.com

FHG READERS' OFFER 2010

One FREE child with two paying adults.
Valid February to October 2010.

NOT TO BE USED IN CONJUNCTION WITH ANY OTHER OFFER

THE BEACON
West Strand, Whitehaven,
Cumbria CA28 7LY
Tel: 01946 592302 • Fax: 01946 598150
e-mail: thebeacon@copelandbc.gov.uk
www.thebeacon-whitehaven.co.uk

FHG READERS' OFFER 2010

One FREE adult/concesssion when accompanied by one full paying adult/concession. Under 16s free. Valid from Oct 2009 to end 2010. Not valid for special events. Day tickets only.

NOT TO BE USED IN CONJUNCTION WITH ANY OTHER OFFER

CRICH TRAMWAY VILLAGE
Crich, Matlock
Derbyshire DE4 5DP
Tel: 01773 854321 • Fax: 01773 854320
e-mail: enquiry@tramway.co.uk
www.tramway.co.uk

FHG READERS' OFFER 2010

One child FREE with every full-paying adult
Valid during 2010

NOT TO BE USED IN CONJUNCTION WITH ANY OTHER OFFER

THE MILKY WAY ADVENTURE PARK
The Milky Way, Clovelly,
Bideford, Devon EX39 5RY
Tel: 01237 431255
e-mail: info@themilkyway.co.uk
www.themilkyway.co.uk

FHG READERS' OFFER 2010

10% discount on entrance charge.
Valid Easter to end October (not August).

NOT TO BE USED IN CONJUNCTION WITH ANY OTHER OFFER

For all "Bond" or car fans this is a must! Aston Martins, Lotus, even a T55 Russsian tank from the film "Goldeneye". Also cinema and shop.	**Open:** 10am to 5pm February to end October; weekends November and December. **Directions:** from Penrith (M6) take A66 to Keswick. Free parking.

FHG GUIDES, ABBEY MILL BUSINESS CENTRE, PAISLEY PA1 1TJ • www.holidayguides.com

The Beacon is the Copeland area's interactive museum, tracing the area's rich history, from as far back as prehistoric times to the modern day. Enjoy panoramic views of the Georgian town and harbour from the 4th floor viewing gallery. Art gallery, gift shop, restaurant. Fully accessible.	**Open:** open all year (excl. 24-26 Dec) Tuesday to Sunday, plus Monday Bank Holidays. **Directions:** enter Whitehaven from north or south on A595. Follow the town centre and brown museum signs; located on harbourside.

FHG GUIDES, ABBEY MILL BUSINESS CENTRE, PAISLEY PA1 1TJ • www.holidayguides.com

A superb family day out in the atmosphere of a bygone era. Explore the recreated period street and fascinating exhibitions. Unlimited tram rides are free with entry. Play areas, woodland walk and sculpture trail, shops, tea rooms, pub, restaurant and lots more.	**Open:** daily April to end October 10am to 5.30pm. **Directions:** eight miles from M1 Junction 28, follow brown and white signs for "Tramway Museum".

FHG GUIDES, ABBEY MILL BUSINESS CENTRE, PAISLEY PA1 1TJ • www.holidayguides.com

The day in the country that's out of this world! With 5 major rides and loads of great live shows. See Merlin from 'Britain's Got Talent' 5 days a week. All rides and shows included in entrance fee.	**Open:** 10.30am - 6pm. Check for winter opening hours. **Directions:** on the main A39 one mile from Clovelly.

FHG GUIDES, ABBEY MILL BUSINESS CENTRE, PAISLEY PA1 1TJ • www.holidayguides.com

FHG KUPERARD READERS' OFFER 2010

THE BIG SHEEP
Abbotsham, Bideford,
North Devon EX39 5AP
Tel: 01237 472366 • Fax: 01237 477916
e-mail: info@thebigsheep.co.uk
www.thebigsheep.co.uk

2 for 1 admission. Valid all year

NOT TO BE USED IN CONJUNCTION WITH ANY OTHER OFFER

FHG KUPERARD READERS' OFFER 2010

DEVONSHIRE COLLECTION OF PERIOD COSTUME
Totnes Costume Museum,
Bogan House, 43 High Street,
Totnes,
Devon TQ9 5NP

FREE child with a paying adult with voucher
Valid from Spring Bank Holiday to end of Sept 2010

NOT TO BE USED IN CONJUNCTION WITH ANY OTHER OFFER

FHG KUPERARD READERS' OFFER 2010

WOODLANDS FAMILY THEME PARK
Blackawton, Dartmouth,
Devon TQ9 7DQ
Tel: 01803 712598 • Fax: 01803 712680
e-mail: fun@woodlandspark.com
www.woodlandspark.com

12% discount off individual admission price.
No photocopies. Valid 26 March to 7 November 2010.

NOT TO BE USED IN CONJUNCTION WITH ANY OTHER OFFER

FHG KUPERARD READERS' OFFER 2010

COMBE MARTIN WILDLIFE & DINOSAUR PARK
Higher Leigh, Combe Martin,
North Devon EX34 0NG
Tel: 01271 882486
e-mail: info@dinosaur-park.com
www.dinosaur-park.com

One child FREE with two paying adults.
Valid February to November 2010

NOT TO BE USED IN CONJUNCTION WITH ANY OTHER OFFER

The best day of your holiday baa none! Sheep racing, dog and duck trialling, huge indoor playground, animal barn with pets' corner and lamb bottle feeding, train and tractor rides, and much more.	**Open:** 10am-6pm daily April to October. From Nov-March weekends and school holidays only. Please check opening times before visiting. **Directions:** two miles west of Bideford, on the A39 Atlantic Highway. Look for the big flag.

FHG GUIDES, ABBEY MILL BUSINESS CENTRE, PAISLEY PA1 1TJ • www.holidayguides.com

Themed exhibition, changed annually, based in a Tudor house. Collection contains items of dress for women, men and children from 17th century to 1990s, from high fashion to everyday wear.	**Open:** Open from Spring Bank Holiday to end September. 11am to 5pm Tuesday to Friday. **Directions:** centre of town, opposite Market Square. Mini bus up High Street stops outside.

FHG GUIDES, ABBEY MILL BUSINESS CENTRE, PAISLEY PA1 1TJ • www.holidayguides.com

A wide variety of rides, plus zoo and farm, makes a fantastic day out for all ages. Awesome indoor adventure centres, ball blasting arenas, mirror maze and soft play ensures wet days are fun. 16 family rides including white knuckle Swing Ship, electrifying Watercoasters, terrifying Toboggan Run, Superb Falconry Centre, Big Fun Farm, animals, tractor ride, weird and wonderful zoo creatures. An all-weather attraction.	**Open:** 26 March to 7 November 2010 open daily 9.30am. In winter open weekends and local school holidays. **Directions:** 5 miles from Dartmouth on A3122. Follow brown tourist signs from A38.

FHG GUIDES, ABBEY MILL BUSINESS CENTRE, PAISLEY PA1 1TJ • www.holidayguides.com

The home of the only full size animatronic T-Rex. Explore 26 acres of stunning gardens with cascading waterfalls, exotic birds and animals. Daily sea lion shows, falconry displays, lemur encounters, 3 magnificent lions, brass rubbing centre. A great day out for all the family.	**Open:** 10am to 5pm (last entry 3pm). February half term to 8th Nov. **Directions:** take M5 to Junction 27. Go west along the A361 towards Barnstaple, turn right on to the A399, and then follow signs for Combe Martin and Ilfracombe.

FHG GUIDES, ABBEY MILL BUSINESS CENTRE, PAISLEY PA1 1TJ • www.holidayguides.com

FHG READERS' OFFER 2010
K·U·P·E·R·A·R·D

TWEDDLE CHILDREN'S ANIMAL FARM
Fillpoke Lane, Blackhall Colliery,
Co. Durham TS27 4BT
Tel: 0191 586 3311
e-mail: info@tweddlefarm.co.uk
www.tweddlefarm.co.uk

FREE bag of animal food to every paying customer.
Valid until end 2010

NOT TO BE USED IN CONJUNCTION WITH ANY OTHER OFFER

FHG READERS' OFFER 2010
K·U·P·E·R·A·R·D

BARLEYLANDS FARM & CRAFT VILLAGE
Barleylands Road, Billericay,
Essex CM11 2UD
Tel: 01268 290223 • Fax: 01268 290222
e-mail: info@barleylands.co.uk
www.barleylands.co.uk

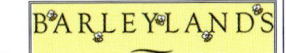

FREE entry for one child with each full paying adult
Valid during 2010

NOT TO BE USED IN CONJUNCTION WITH ANY OTHER OFFER

FHG READERS' OFFER 2010
K·U·P·E·R·A·R·D

AVON VALLEY RAILWAY
Bitton Station, Bath Road, Bitton,
Bristol BS30 6HD
Tel: 0117 932 5538
e-mail: info@avonvalleyrailway.org
www.avonvalleyrailway.org

One FREE child with every fare-paying adult
Valid April-Oct 2010 (not 'Day Out with Thomas' events)

NOT TO BE USED IN CONJUNCTION WITH ANY OTHER OFFER

FHG READERS' OFFER 2010
K·U·P·E·R·A·R·D

CIDER MUSEUM & KING OFFA DISTILLERY
21 Ryelands Street, Hereford,
Herefordshire HR4 0LW
Tel: 01432 354207
e-mail: enquiries@cidermuseum.co.uk
www.cidermuseum.co.uk

TWO for the price of ONE admission
Valid to end December 2010

NOT TO BE USED IN CONJUNCTION WITH ANY OTHER OFFER

Children's farm and petting centre with lots of farm animals and exotic animals too, including camels, otters, monkeys, meerkats and lots more. Lots of hands-on, with bottle feeding, reptile handling and bunny cuddling happening daily.	**Open:** March to Oct: 10am-5pm daily; Nov to Feb 10am to 4pm daily. Closed Christmas, Boxing Day and New Year's Day. **Directions:** A181 from A19, head towards coast; signposted from there.

FHG GUIDES, ABBEY MILL BUSINESS CENTRE, PAISLEY PA1 1TJ • www.holidayguides.com

Set in over 700 acres of unspoilt Essex countryside, this former working farm is one of the county's most popular tourist attractions. The spectacular craft village and educational farm provide the perfect setting for a great day out.	**Open:** 7 days a week. March to October 10am-5pm; November to February 10am-4pm. **Directions:** follow brown tourist signs from A127 and A12.

FHG GUIDES, ABBEY MILL BUSINESS CENTRE, PAISLEY PA1 1TJ • www.holidayguides.com

The Avon Valley Railway offers a whole new experience for some, and a nostalgic memory for others. **PETS MUST BE KEPT ON LEADS AND OFF TRAIN SEATS**	**Open:** Steam trains operate every Sunday, Easter to October, plus Bank Holidays and Christmas. **Directions:** on the A431 midway between Bristol and Bath at Bitton.

FHG GUIDES, ABBEY MILL BUSINESS CENTRE, PAISLEY PA1 1TJ • www.holidayguides.com

Learn how traditional cider and perry was made, how the fruit was harvested, milled, pressed and bottled. Walk through original champagne cider cellars, and view 18th century lead crystal cider glasses.	**Open:** April to October: 10am-5pm Tues-Sat. November to March 11am-3pm Tues-Sat. **Directions:** off A438 Hereford to Brecon road, near Sainsbury's supermarket.

FHG GUIDES, ABBEY MILL BUSINESS CENTRE, PAISLEY PA1 1TJ • www.holidayguides.com

193

FHG K·U·P·E·R·A·R·D
READERS' OFFER 2010

DINOSAUR ISLE
Culver Parade, Sandown,
Isle of Wight PO36 8QA
Tel: 01983 404344 • Fax: 01983 407502
e-mail: dinosaur@iow.gov.uk
www.dinosaurisle.com

*One child FREE when accompanied by full paying adult.
Valid from February to December 24th 2010.*

NOT TO BE USED IN CONJUNCTION WITH ANY OTHER OFFER

FHG K·U·P·E·R·A·R·D
READERS' OFFER 2010

ROMNEY, HYTHE & DYMCHURCH RAILWAY
New Romney Station,
New Romney,
Kent TN28 8PL
Tel: 01797 362353
www.rhdr.org.uk

*One child FREE with every two full paying adults.
Valid until end 2010 except on special event days.*

NOT TO BE USED IN CONJUNCTION WITH ANY OTHER OFFER

FHG K·U·P·E·R·A·R·D
READERS' OFFER 2010

CHISLEHURST CAVES
Old Hill, Chislehurst,
Kent BR7 5NL
Tel: 020 8467 3264 • Fax: 020 8295 0407
e-mail: info@chislehurstcaves.co.uk
www.chislehurstcaves.co.uk

*FREE child entry with full paying adult.
Valid until end 2010 (not Bank Holiday weekends)*

NOT TO BE USED IN CONJUNCTION WITH ANY OTHER OFFER

FHG K·U·P·E·R·A·R·D
READERS' OFFER 2010

NATURELAND SEAL SANCTUARY
North Parade, Skegness
Lincolnshire PE25 1DB
Tel: 01754 764345
e-mail: info@skegnessnatureland.co.uk
www.skegnessnatureland.co.uk

*One child admitted FREE when accompanied by full
paying adult on production of voucher. Valid to end 2010.*

NOT TO BE USED IN CONJUNCTION WITH ANY OTHER OFFER

In a spectacular pterosaur-shaped building, watching over Sandown's Blue Flag beach, is Britain's first purpose-built dinosaur museum. Walk back through fossilised time and meet life-size model dinosaurs including an animated Neovenator.	**Open:** open all year except 24-26th December and 1st January (call for opening hours Jan/Feb). Daily 10am-5pm (March-Oct), 10am-4pm (Nov-Feb). **Directions:** on B3395 coastal road.

Heritage steam miniature railway and model exhibition. 27 miles round trip following the Kent coastline. The railway runs from Hythe, Dymchurch, New Romney, Romney Sands and Dungeness.	**Open:** 9.45am to 6pm. Check website for details.

Miles of mystery and history beneath your feet! Grab a lantern and get ready for an amazing underground adventure. Your whole family can travel back in time as you explore this labyrinth of dark mysterious passageways. See the caves, church, Druid altar and more.	**Open:** Wed to Sun from 10am; last tour 4pm. Open daily during local school and Bank holidays (except Christmas). Entrance by guided tour only. **Directions:** A222 between A20 and A21; at Chislehurst Station turn into Station Approach; turn right at end, then right again into Caveside Close.

A specialised collection of animals including seals, penguins, tropical birds and butterflies (April to October), reptiles, aquarium, pets' corner etc. Known worldwide for rescuing orphaned and injured seal pups and returning almost 600 back to the wild.	**Open:** daily except Christmas Day, Boxing Day and New Year's Day. **Directions:** north end of Skegness seafront.

FHG READERS' OFFER 2010
K·U·P·E·R·A·R·D

EXMOOR FALCONRY & ANIMAL FARM
Allerford, Near Porlock, Minehead,
Somerset TA24 8HJ
Tel: 01643 862816
e-mail: exmoor.falcon@virgin.net
www.exmoorfalconry.co.uk

10% off entry to Falconry Centre
Valid during 2010

NOT TO BE USED IN CONJUNCTION WITH ANY OTHER OFFER

FHG READERS' OFFER 2010
K·U·P·E·R·A·R·D

THE NATIONAL HORSERACING MUSEUM
99 High Street,
Newmarket,
Suffolk CB8 8JH
Tel: 01638 667333
www.nhrm.co.uk

One FREE adult or concession with on paying full price.
Valid Easter to end October 2010. Museum admission only.

NOT TO BE USED IN CONJUNCTION WITH ANY OTHER OFFER

FHG READERS' OFFER 2010
K·U·P·E·R·A·R·D

EASTON FARM PARK
Pound Corner, Easton, Woodbridge,
Suffolk IP13 0EQ
Tel: 01728 746475
e-mail: info@eastonfarmpark.co.uk
www.eastonfarmpark.co.uk

One FREE child entry with a full paying adult
Only one voucher per group. Valid during 2010.

NOT TO BE USED IN CONJUNCTION WITH ANY OTHER OFFER

FHG READERS' OFFER 2010
K·U·P·E·R·A·R·D

PARADISE PARK
Avis Road, Newhaven,
East Sussex BN9 0DH
Tel: 01273 512123 • Fax: Fax: 01273 616005
e-mail: enquiries@paradisepark.co.uk
www.paradisepark.co.uk

One child FREE with one full paying adult.
Valid January - end October 2010.

NOT TO BE USED IN CONJUNCTION WITH ANY OTHER OFFER

Falconry centre with animals - flying displays, animal handling, feeding and bottle feeding - in 15th century NT farmyard setting on Exmoor. Also falconry and outdoor activities, hawk walks and riding.	**Open:** 10.30am to 5pm daily **Directions:** A39 west of Minehead, turn right at Allerford, half a mile along lane on left.

FHG GUIDES, ABBEY MILL BUSINESS CENTRE, PAISLEY PA1 1TJ • www.holidayguides.com

Stories of racing, ride the horse simulator, or take a 'behind the scenes' tour of the training grounds and yards.	**Open:** Easter to end October, 7 days a week 11am to 5pm. Last admission 4pm. **Directions:** on the High Street in the centre of Newmarket.

FHG GUIDES, ABBEY MILL BUSINESS CENTRE, PAISLEY PA1 1TJ • www.holidayguides.com

Family day out down on the farm, with activities for children every half hour (included in entry price). Indoor and outdoor play areas. Riverside cafe, gift shop. For more details visit the website.	**Open:** 10.30am-6pm daily March to September. **Directions:** signposted from A12 in the direction of Framlingham.

FHG GUIDES, ABBEY MILL BUSINESS CENTRE, PAISLEY PA1 1TJ • www.holidayguides.com

Discover 'Planet Earth' for an unforgettable experience. A unique Museum of Life, Dinosaur Safari, beautiful Water Gardens with fish and wildfowl, plant houses, themed gardens, Heritage Trail, miniature railway. Playzone includes crazy golf and adventure play areas. Garden Centre and Terrace Cafe.	**Open:** 9am - 6pm daily except Christmas/Boxing Days. **Directions:** signposted from A26 and A259.

FHG GUIDES, ABBEY MILL BUSINESS CENTRE, PAISLEY PA1 1TJ • www.holidayguides.com

FHG KUPERARD READERS' OFFER 2010

EARNLEY BUTTERFLIES & GARDENS
133 Almodington Lane, Earnley, Chichester,
West Sussex PO20 7JR
Tel: 01243 512637
e-mail: earnleygardens@msn.com
www.earnleybutterfliesandgardens.co.uk

*£1 per person off normal entry prices.
Valid late March to end October 2010.*

NOT TO BE USED IN CONJUNCTION WITH ANY OTHER OFFER

FHG KUPERARD READERS' OFFER 2010

HATTON FARM VILLAGE AT HATTON COUNTRY WORLD
Dark Lane, Hatton, Near Warwick,
Warwickshire CV35 8XA
Tel: 01926 843411
e-mail: hatton@hattonworld.com
www.hattonworld.com

*Admit one child FREE with one full-paying adult day ticket. Valid during
2010 except Bank Holidays or for entrance to Santa's Grotto promotion.*

NOT TO BE USED IN CONJUNCTION WITH ANY OTHER OFFER

FHG KUPERARD READERS' OFFER 2010

CHOLDERTON CHARLIE'S FARM & YOUTH HOSTEL
Amesbury Road, Cholderton, Salisbury,
Wiltshire SP4 0EW
Tel: 01980 629438 • Fax: 01980 629594
e-mail: choldertonrbf@aol.com
www.choldertoncharliesfarm.com

*One child FREE with full paying adult.
Valid September 2009 - end March 2010.*

NOT TO BE USED IN CONJUNCTION WITH ANY OTHER OFFER

FHG KUPERARD READERS' OFFER 2010

FALCONRY UK BIRDS OF PREY CENTRE
Sion Hill Hall, Kirby Wiske
Near Thirsk, North Yorkshire YO7 4GU
Tel: 01845 587522
e-mail: mail@falconrycentre.co.uk
www.falconrycentre.co.uk

*TWO for ONE on admission to Centre. Cheapest ticket
free with voucher. Valid 1st March to 31st October.*

NOT TO BE USED IN CONJUNCTION WITH ANY OTHER OFFER

*3 attractions in 1.
Tropical butterflies, exotic animals of many types in our Noah's Ark Rescue Centre. Theme gardens with a free competition for kids.
Rejectamenta - the nostalgia museum.*

Open: 10am - 6pm daily late March to end October.

Directions: signposted from A27/A286 junction at Chichester.

FHG GUIDES, ABBEY MILL BUSINESS CENTRE, PAISLEY PA1 1TJ • www.holidayguides.com

---

Hatton Farm Village offers a wonderful mix of farmyard animals, adventure play, shows, demonstrations, and events, all set in the stunning Warwickshire countryside.

Open: daily 10am-5pm (4pm during winter). Closed Christmas Day and Boxing Day.

Directions: 5 minutes from M40 (J15), A46 towards Coventry, then just off A4177 (follow brown tourist signs).

FHG GUIDES, ABBEY MILL BUSINESS CENTRE, PAISLEY PA1 1TJ • www.holidayguides.com

---

A farm park that rears and keeps rare breed animals. Animal handling, indoor play equipment etc. Cafe serving delicious home-made food. Plus a newly opened 70-bed youth hostel.

Open: April to October 10am-6pm November-March 10am-4pm

Directions: just off the A303 and the A338 near Stonehenge.

FHG GUIDES, ABBEY MILL BUSINESS CENTRE, PAISLEY PA1 1TJ • www.holidayguides.com

---

*Birds of prey centre with over 60 birds including owls, hawks, falcons, kites, vultures and eagles. 3 flying displays daily.
When possible public welcome to handle birds after each display.
No dogs allowed.*

Open: 1st March to 31st October 10.30am to 5pm. Flying displays 11.30am, 1.30pm and 3.30pm daily.

Directions: on the A167 between Northallerton and the Ripon turn off. Follow brown tourist signs.

FHG GUIDES, ABBEY MILL BUSINESS CENTRE, PAISLEY PA1 1TJ • www.holidayguides.com

FHG READERS' OFFER 2010

WORLD OF JAMES HERRIOT
23 Kirkgate, Thirsk,
North Yorkshire YO7 1PL
Tel: 01845 524234
Fax: 01845 525333
www.worldofjamesherriot.org

Admit TWO for the price of ONE (one voucher per transaction only). Valid until October 2010

NOT TO BE USED IN CONJUNCTION WITH ANY OTHER OFFER

FHG READERS' OFFER 2010

MUSEUM OF RAIL TRAVEL
Ingrow Railway Centre, Near Keighley,
West Yorkshire BD21 5AX
Tel: 01535 680425
e-mail: admin@vintagecarriagestrust.org
www.vintagecarriagestrust.org

*"ONE for ONE" free admission
Valid during 2010 except during special events (ring to check)*

NOT TO BE USED IN CONJUNCTION WITH ANY OTHER OFFER

FHG READERS' OFFER 2010

EUREKA! THE NATIONAL CHILDREN'S MUSEUM
Discovery Road, Halifax,
West Yorkshire HX1 2NE
Tel: 01422 330069 • Fax: 01422 398490
e-mail: info@eureka.org.uk
www.eureka.org.uk

*One FREE child on purchase of full price adult ticket
Valid from 1/10/09 to 31/12/10. Excludes groups. Promo Code 243*

NOT TO BE USED IN CONJUNCTION WITH ANY OTHER OFFER

FHG READERS' OFFER 2010

THE GRASSIC GIBBON CENTRE
Arbuthnott, Laurencekirk,
Aberdeenshire AB30 1PB
Tel: 01561 361668
e-mail: lgginfo@grassicgibbon.com
www.grassicgibbon.com

TWO for the price of ONE entry to exhibition (based on full adult rate only). Valid during 2010 (not groups)

NOT TO BE USED IN CONJUNCTION WITH ANY OTHER OFFER

Visit James Herriot's original house recreated as it was in the 1940s. Television sets used in the series 'All Creatures Great and Small'. There is a children's interactive gallery with life-size model farm animals and three rooms dedicated to the history of veterinary medicine.	**Open:** daily. Easter-Oct 10am-5pm; Nov-Easter 11am to 4pm **Directions:** follow signs off A1 or A19 to Thirsk, then A168, off Thirsk market place

A fascinating display of railway carriages and a wide range of railway items telling the story of rail travel over the years. **ALL PETS MUST BE KEPT ON LEADS**	**Open:** daily 11am to 4.30pm **Directions:** approximately one mile from Keighley on A629 Halifax road. Follow brown tourist signs

As the UK's National Children's Museum, Eureka! is a place where children play to learn and grown-ups learn to play.	**Open:** daily except 24-26 December, 10am to 5pm **Directions:** leave M62 at J24 for Halifax. Take A629 to town centre, following brown tourist signs.

Visitor Centre dedicated to the much-loved Scottish writer Lewis Grassic Gibbon. Exhibition, cafe, gift shop. Outdoor children's play area. Disabled access throughout.	**Open:** daily March to October 10am to 4.30pm. Groups by appointment including evenings. **Directions:** on the B967, accessible and signposted from both A90 and A92.

201

FHG KUPERARD READERS' OFFER 2010

SCOTTISH MARITIME MUSEUM
Harbourside, Irvine,
Ayrshire KA12 8QE
Tel: 01294 278283
Fax: 01294 313211
www.scottishmaritimemuseum.org

TWO for the price of ONE
Valid from April to October 2010

NOT TO BE USED IN CONJUNCTION WITH ANY OTHER OFFER

FHG KUPERARD READERS' OFFER 2010

GALLOWAY WILDLIFE CONSERVATION PARK
Lochfergus Plantation, Kirkcudbright,
Dumfries & Galloway DG6 4XX
Tel & Fax: 01557 331645
e-mail: info@gallowaywildlife.co.uk
www.gallowaywildlife.co.uk

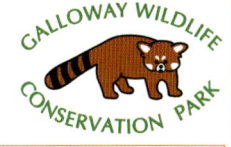

One FREE child or Senior Citizen with two full paying adults.
Valid Feb - Nov 2010 (not Easter weekend and Bank Holidays)

NOT TO BE USED IN CONJUNCTION WITH ANY OTHER OFFER

FHG KUPERARD READERS' OFFER 2010

BO'NESS & KINNEIL RAILWAY
Bo'ness Station, Union Street,
Bo'ness, West Lothian EH51 9AQ
Tel: 01506 822298
e-mail: enquiries.railway@srps.org.uk
www.srps.org.uk

FREE child train fare with one paying adult/concession. Valid
March-Oct 2010. Not Days Out with Thomas or Santa Steam trains

NOT TO BE USED IN CONJUNCTION WITH ANY OTHER OFFER

FHG KUPERARD READERS' OFFER 2010

MYRETON MOTOR MUSEUM
Aberlady,
East Lothian EH32 0PZ
Tel: 01875 870288
www.myretonmotormuseum.co.uk

One child FREE with each paying adult
Valid during 2010

NOT TO BE USED IN CONJUNCTION WITH ANY OTHER OFFER

Scotland's seafaring heritage is among the world's richest and you can relive the heyday of Scottish shipping at the Maritime Museum.	**Open:** 1st April to 31st October - 10am-5pm. **Directions:** situated on Irvine harbourside and only a 10 minute walk from Irvine train station.

The wild animal conservation centre of Southern Scotland. A varied collection of over 150 animals from all over the world can be seen within natural woodland settings. Picnic areas, cafe/gift shop, outdoor play area, woodland walks, close animal encounters.	**Open:** 10am to dusk 1st February to 30 November. **Directions:** follow brown tourist signs from A75; one mile from Kirkcudbright on the B727.

Steam and heritage diesel passenger trains from Bo'ness to Birkhill for guided tours of Birkhill fireclay mines. Explore the history of Scotland's railways in the Scottish Railway Exhibition. Coffee shop and souvenir shop.	**Open:** weekends Easter to October, daily July and August. See website for dates and timetables. **Directions:** in the town of Bo'ness. Leave M9 at Junction 3 or 5, then follow brown tourist signs.

On show is a large collection, from 1899, of cars, bicycles, motor cycles and commercials. There is also a large collection of period advertising, posters and enamel signs.	**Open:** March-Oct: open daily 10.30am to 4.30pm. Nov-Feb: weekends 11am to 3pm or by special appointment. **Directions:** off A198 near Aberlady. Two miles from A1.

FHG
·K·U·P·E·R·A·R·D·
**READERS'
OFFER
2010**

BRITISH GOLF MUSEUM
Bruce Embankment, St Andrews,
Fife KY16 9AB
Tel: 01334 460046 • Fax: 01334 460064
e-mail: judychance@randa.org
www.britishgolfmuseum.co.uk

*10% off price of admission (one per customer).
Valid during 2010.*

NOT TO BE USED IN CONJUNCTION WITH ANY OTHER OFFER

FHG
·K·U·P·E·R·A·R·D·
**READERS'
OFFER
2010**

SCOTTISH DEER CENTRE
Cupar,
Fife KY15 4NQ
Tel: 01337 810391
e-mail: info@tsdc.co.uk
www.tsdc.co.uk

*One child FREE with one full paying adult on
production of voucher. Not valid during December.*

NOT TO BE USED IN CONJUNCTION WITH ANY OTHER OFFER

FHG
·K·U·P·E·R·A·R·D·
**READERS'
OFFER
2010**

LOCH NESS CENTRE
& EXHIBITION EXPERIENCE
Drumnadrochit, Loch Ness,
Inverness-shire IV63 6TU
Tel: 01456 450573 • 01456 450770
www.lochness.com

*'2 for the price of 1' entry to the world famous
Exhibition Centre. Valid during 2010.*

NOT TO BE USED IN CONJUNCTION WITH ANY OTHER OFFER

FHG
·K·U·P·E·R·A·R·D·
**READERS'
OFFER
2010**

NATIONAL CYCLE COLLECTION
Automobile Palace, Temple Street,
Llandrindod Wells, Powys LD1 5DL
Tel: 01597 825531
e-mail: cycle.museum@powys.org.uk
www.cyclemuseum.org.uk

*TWO for the price of ONE
Valid during 2010 except Special Event days*

NOT TO BE USED IN CONJUNCTION WITH ANY OTHER OFFER

The 5-Star British Golf Museum explores 500 years of golfing history using exciting interactives and diverse displays. A visit here makes the perfect break from playing golf.	**Open:** Mon-Sat 9.30am-5pm, Sun 10am-4pm. Closed Christmas and New Year periods. **Directions:** opposite the Old Course in St Andrews.

FHG GUIDES, ABBEY MILL BUSINESS CENTRE, PAISLEY PA1 1TJ • www.holidayguides.com

55-acre park with 10 species of deer from around the world. Guided tours, trailer rides, treetop walkway, children's adventure playground and picnic area. Other animals include wolves, foxes, otters and a bird of prey centre.	**Open:** 10am to 5pm daily except Christmas Day and New Year's Day. **Directions:** A91 south of Cupar. Take J9 M90 from the north, J8 from the south.

FHG GUIDES, ABBEY MILL BUSINESS CENTRE, PAISLEY PA1 1TJ • www.holidayguides.com

VisitScotland 5-Star Visitor Attraction, described by Scottish Natural Heritage as "a portal to the unique natural phenomenon that is Loch Ness'. Cafe and restaurant on site with large shopping complex and cruises on Loch Ness.	**Open:** all year except Christmas Day. **Directions:** directly on A82 trunk road, 12 miles south of Inverness.

FHG GUIDES, ABBEY MILL BUSINESS CENTRE, PAISLEY PA1 1TJ • www.holidayguides.com

Journey through the lanes of cycle history and see bicycles from Boneshakers and Penny Farthings up to modern Raleigh cycles. Over 250 machines on display **PETS MUST BE KEPT ON LEADS**	**Open:** 1st March to 1st November daily 10am onwards. **Directions:** brown signs to car park. Town centre attraction.

FHG GUIDES, ABBEY MILL BUSINESS CENTRE, PAISLEY PA1 1TJ • www.holidayguides.com

Index of Towns and Counties

Alford, Aberdeen & Moray	SCOTLAND
Ashbourne, Derbyshire	MIDLANDS
Aylesbury, Buckinghamshire	LONDON & SOUTH EAST
Bamford, Derbyshire	MIDLANDS
Bedale, North Yorkshire	YORKSHIRE
Bedford, Bedfordshire	EAST
Berwick-upon-Tweed, Northumberland	NORTH EAST
Blandford, Dorset	SOUTH WEST
Boxford, Berkshire	LONDON & SOUTH EAST
Brampton, Cumbria	NORTH WEST
Bridgwater, Somerset	SOUTH WEST
Broughton-in-Furness, Cumbria	NORTH WEST
Bude, Cornwall	SOUTH WEST
Bunessan, Argyll & Bute	SCOTLAND
Burford, Oxfordshire	LONDON & SOUTH EAST
Burley, Hampshire	LONDON & SOUTH EAST
Bury St Edmunds, Suffolk	EAST
Buxton, Derbyshire	MIDLANDS
Cairndow, Argyll & Bute	SCOTLAND
Carperby, North Yorkshire	YORKSHIRE
Chester, Cheshire	NORTH WEST
Chorley, Lancashire	NORTH WEST
Christchurch, Dorset	SOUTH WEST
Clapham, North Yorkshire	YORKSHIRE
Clovelly, Devon	SOUTH WEST
Coniston, Cumbria	NORTH WEST
Craignure, Argyll & Bute	SCOTLAND
Craster, Northumberland	NORTH EAST
Craven Arms, Shropshire	MIDLANDS
Crieff, Perth & Kinross	SCOTLAND
Dalwood, Devon	SOUTH WEST
Danby, North Yorkshire	YORKSHIRE
Denbigh, North Wales	WALES
Dent, Cumbria	NORTH WEST
Dersingham, Norfolk	EAST
Dittisham, Devon	SOUTH WEST
Dolgellau, Anglesey & Gwynedd	WALES
Dunsford, Devon	SOUTH WEST
Eaton, Cheshire	NORTH WEST
Ennerdale Bridge, Cumbria	NORTH WEST
Eskdale, Cumbria	NORTH WEST
Exmoor, Devon	SOUTH WEST
Fording Bridge, Hampshire	LONDON & SOUTH EAST
Fowey, Cornwall	SOUTH WEST
Gomshall, Surrey	LONDON & SOUTH EAST
Grassington, North Yorkshire	YORKSHIRE
Great Ayton, North Yorkshire	YORKSHIRE
Happisburgh, Norfolk	EAST
Harrogate, North Yorkshire	YORKSHIRE
Hawkshead, Cumbria	NORTH WEST
Hay-on-Wye, Herefordshire	MIDLANDS
Hay-on-Wye, Powys	WALES
Hexham, Northumberland	NORTH EAST
Hindon, Wiltshire	SOUTH WEST
Hope Valley, Derbyshire	MIDLANDS
Hubberholme, North Yorkshire	YORKSHIRE
Huggate, East Yorkshire	YORKSHIRE
Ilfracombe, Devon	SOUTH WEST
Inkpen, Berkshire	LONDON & SOUTH EAST
Inverurie, Aberdeen & Moray	SCOTLAND
Keswick, Cumbria	NORTH WEST
Kilburn, North Yorkshire	YORKSHIRE
Kirkby Lonsdale, Cumbria	NORTH WEST
Kirkcaldy, Fife	SCOTLAND
Lairg, Highlands	SCOTLAND
Lamphey, Pembrokeshire	WALES
Langdale, Cumbria	NORTH WEST
Leighton Buzzard, Bedfordshire	EAST
Liskeard, Cornwall	SOUTH WEST
Llangollen, North Wales	WALES
Loch Eck, Argyll & Bute	SCOTLAND
Lochgilphead, Argyll & Bute	SCOTLAND

INDEX OF TOWNS AND COUNTIES

Longframlington, Northumberland	NORTH EAST
Lostwithiel, Cornwall	SOUTH WEST
Lynmouth, Devon	SOUTH WEST
Market Drayton, Shropshire	MIDLANDS
Mells, Somerset	SOUTH WEST
Milton Keynes, Buckinghamshire	LONDON & SOUTH EAST
Minehead, Somerset	SOUTH WEST
Moreton-in-Marsh, Gloucestershire	SOUTH WEST
Mortehoe, Devon	SOUTH WEST
Near Sawrey, Cumbria	NORTH WEST
New Radnor, Powys	WALES
Newport, Pembrokeshire	WALES
Oban, Argyll	SCOTLAND
Parkend, Gloucestershire	SOUTH WEST
Pennard, Somerset	SOUTH WEST
Penrith, Cumbria	NORTH WEST
Penzance, Cornwall	SOUTH WEST
Petworth, West Sussex	LONDON & SOUTH EAST
Pitlochry, Perth & Kinross	SCOTLAND
Port Isaac, Cornwall	SOUTH WEST
Rousay, Isle of Orkney	SCOTLAND
Rowrah, Cumbria	NORTH WEST
Sandhurst, Berkshire	LONDON & SOUTH EAST
Sea Palling, Norfolk	EAST
Seahouses, Northumberland	NORTH EAST
Sleat, Isle of Skye	SCOTLAND
St Andrews, Fie	SCOTLAND
St Austell, Cornwall	SOUTH WEST
Staveley, Cumbria	NORTH WEST
Strathyre, Perth & Kinross	SCOTLAND
Tavistock, Devon	SOUTH WEST
Thornham, Norfolk	EAST
Thurso, Highlands	SCOTLAND
Topsham, Devon	SOUTH WEST
Trelleck, South Wales	WALES
Ullapool, Highlands	SCOTLAND
Ulverston, Cumbria	NORTH WEST
Wareham, Dorset	SOUTH WEST
Wasdale, Cumbria	NORTH WEST
Watermillock Cumbria	NORTH WEST
Wigtown, Dumfries & Galloway	SCOTLAND
Windermere, Cumbria	NORTH WEST
Winterton-on-Sea, Norfolk	EAST
Yelverton, Devon	SOUTH WEST
York, North Yorkshire	YORKSHIRE

Other specialised holiday guides from FHG

THE GOLF GUIDE • COUNTRY HOTELS OF BRITAIN
WEEKEND & SHORT BREAK HOLIDAYS IN BRITAIN
The bestselling and original **PETS WELCOME!**
500 GREAT PLACES TO STAY • SELF-CATERING HOLIDAYS IN BRITAIN
BED & BREAKFAST STOPS • CARAVAN & CAMPING HOLIDAYS
FAMILY BREAKS IN BRITAIN

Published annually: available in all good bookshops or direct from the publisher:
FHG Guides, Abbey Mill Business Centre, Seedhill, Paisley PA1 1TJ
Tel: 0141 887 0428 • Fax: 0141 889 7204
e-mail: admin@fhguides.co.uk • www.holidayguides.com